Stettinius, Sr.
Portrait of a Morgan Partner

Publications of the Graduate School of Business Administration of the University of Virginia

Bank Expansion in Virginia, 1962–1966: The Holding Company and the Direct Merger. By Paul Foster.

Basic Research in Finance: Needs and Prospects. By Charles C. Abbott.

A Financial Planning Model for Private Colleges: A Research Report. By William J. Arthur.

Forty Years of Public Utility Finance. By Harold H. Young.

Management of Small Enterprises: Cases and Readings. By William Rotch.

A Selected Bibliography of Applied Ethics in the Professions, 1950–1970: A Working Sourcebook with Annotations and Indexes. By Daniel L. Gothie.

STETTINIUS, SR.

PORTRAIT OF A MORGAN PARTNER

John Douglas Forbes

University Press of Virginia

Charlottesville

The publication of this study has been
assisted by the Graduate School of
Business Administration, University of Virginia.

THE UNIVERSITY PRESS OF VIRGINIA
Copyright © 1974 by the Rector and Visitors
of the University of Virginia

First published 1974

ISBN: 0-8139-0517-6
Library of Congress Catalog Card Number: 73-89906
Printed in the United States of America

For Margaret

Contents

Preface

FROM January 7 to February 5, 1936, J. P. Morgan and two of his partners, Thomas W. Lamont and George Whitney, were called upon to be interrogated by the United States Senate Committee Investigating the Munitions Industry.

The Munitions Committee (or "Nye Committee," from its chairman, Senator Gerald P. Nye, Republican, South Dakota) was trying to determine whether the munitions manufacturers and the bankers who had extended credits and floated loans to enable the Western Allies to buy the munitions were responsible for American involvement in World War I.

The Committee questioned the Morgan partners in the course of an inquiry carried on during the years 1934 to 1936. This was a period when it was fashionable to blame World War I and the United States participation in it on the selfishness and greed readily attributed to businessmen and bankers. Books with the titles *Merchants of Death*,[1] *Iron, Blood and Profits*,[2] and *Private Manufacture of Armaments* [3] were popular.

The economic depression had caused the business community to be out of favor; it seemed a good time for antibusiness interests to blame businessmen for the last war and to plan measures to prevent them from starting the next one in their alleged avarice, and politicians found it expedient to climb aboard this bandwagon.

In the words of one writer on the investigation, "The committee acted on the hypothesis that manufacturers and salesmen of armaments had committed crimes against humanity." He elsewhere poses the central question: "Had economic intercourse with the Allied belligerents led the United States to war? The Munitions Committee majority in 1936 was sure it had." [4] This latter statement is

---

[1] Helmuth C. Engelbrecht and Frank C. Hanighen (New York, 1934).

[2] George Seldes (New York and London, 1934).

[3] Philip Noel-Barker (London, 1937).

[4] John E. Wiltz, *In Search of Peace: The Senate Munitions Inquiry, 1934–36* (Baton Rouge, La., 1963), pp. 48, 199. Colin Simpson's article *"Lusitania,"* *Life*, Oct. 13, 1972, pp. 59–80, gives support to this belief. The article, an excerpt from the book of that title subsequently published by Little, Brown and

somewhat modified by the subsequent observation that "the committee did not proceed on the hypothesis that Wall Street had
taken America to war (although some members suspected the financiers might have, and were alert for evidence of pressure by
bankers on the government)." [5] But the picture that emerges is the
familiar one of a congressional committee interrogating prominent
individuals at length in the hope of securing some damaging admission to support a preconceived position. No specific and therefore
refutable charges were made, but the Morgan partners were clearly
suspected of wrongdoing, and the hearings were a series of great
public spectacles at which the firm was put in an undefined
prejudicial role.

The Morgan phase of the investigation produced large headlines
but turned up little. "Nye and other committee members said they
had proved nothing to the discredit of Morgan and his banking
house in more than two weeks of investigation of the company's
wartime operations." [6] In the middle of the proceedings the em-
phasis shifted from blaming businessmen to blaming Woodrow
Wilson for his unneutral "neutrality." This so antagonized the
Wilson admirers in the Senate that they shut off the hearings, and
the whole inquiry collapsed. One constructive result of the hearings was to discredit completely the villain theory of the cause of
war. Presumably the committee members learned at the taxpayers'
expense that there are no tidy, simple causes of world events.

The irony of this widely publicized attempt to label J. P. Morgan & Co. as "merchants of death" is that twenty years earlier the
firm had been just as widely acclaimed for their part in helping
to save the Western world from the German war machine. Edward
Reilly Stettinius was the man who directed the vast mechanism
set up by the Morgan firm to buy munitions of war for Britain and
France and in the process built up a productive capacity in this
country that made it possible for the United States to meet its commitments when it entered the war on the Allied side in 1917. This

Company (Boston, 1973), presents evidence indicating that the *Lusitania* carried munitions, specifically 1,248 cases of three-inch shells manufactured by
the Bethlehem Steel Company and 6,000,000 rounds of rifle ammunition manufactured by the Remington Arms Company. The sinking of this supposedly
innocent merchantman by a German submarine off the coast of Ireland on
May 7, 1915, has often been mentioned as a factor in the entry of the United
States into the war on the Allied side. But the fear for national survival in a
German-dominated world was a greater cause of U.S. concern than any
ship sinking or Allied propaganda campaign.
[5] Wiltz, *In Search of Peace*, p. 227.
[6] *Ibid.*, p. 208.

wartime undertaking marked the first of two high points in Stettinius's career and led directly to the second. As chief buyer for the Allies he became an international personage almost overnight. His effectiveness in the job had enormous significance for the course and outcome of the war. That same forcefulness caused his colleagues to elect him to partnership in J. P. Morgan & Co., where he became one of the most powerful figures of the postwar financial community.

This is the man whose life and business career we are about to examine.

As the poet said, no man is an island, and this is especially true in the writing of a book. I am most appreciative of the help and encouragement of a great many people. I wish particularly to thank the following:

Wallace Stettinius, grandson of Edward Reilly Stettinius, Sr., and my former student at the University of Virginia Graduate School of Business Administration, who has given moral support from the beginning and together with his twin brother Joseph Stettinius made available the Stettinius Papers at the University of Virginia.

Mr. Stettinius's two daughters, Mrs. John B. Marsh (Isabel Stettinius Marsh) and Mrs. Juan T. Trippe (Elizabeth Stettinius Trippe), who overcame their very natural misgivings about the idea of anything so personal as a biography of their father to provide illuminating insights into his nature and information about his life.

The staff of the Alderman Library of the University of Virginia, especially Miss Anne Freudenberg, former head of the Manuscript Division, who first suggested this whole undertaking; the late John Cook Wyllie, who as Librarian encouraged the project and helped to make the Stettinius Papers available; Edmund Berkeley, Jr., head of the Manuscript Division; William G. Ray, formerly of the Manuscript Division; and William D. Barnard, sometime Stettinius Fellow, who catalogued the Stettinius Papers and put them in usable order.

Members of the J. P. Morgan & Co. "family," especially Henry Sturgis Morgan of Morgan Stanley & Company, a son of John Pierpont Morgan, Jr., who made available highly confidential material about the firm's World War I munitions purchasing arrangement with the British and French governments and then generously undertook to read the completed manuscript of the book; Mrs. F. Carrington Weems, whose late husband assembled the data on munitions purchasing and other biographical material about Stettinius and the war; Guido F. Verbeck, Jr., formerly a senior vice-president of the Morgan Guaranty Trust Company; the late Nelson Dean Jay, long a partner of Morgan, Harjes & Co., the Paris house of J. P. Morgan & Co.; Mrs. F. Trubee Davison, daughter-in-law of Mr. Stettinius's partner and contemporary Henry P. Davison.

Members of Davis Polk & Wardwell, especially Frederick A. O. Schwarz and Andrew Y. Rogers. This firm and its predecessor firms were lawyers for J. P. Morgan & Co.

Anthony J. Davey, former head of the legal department of Diamond National Corporation; Lt. Col. Guillaume M. du Chesne, Service historique de l'armée, Château de Vincennes; Robert W. Lovett, head of the Manuscript Division, Baker Library, Harvard Business School; Miss Ethel M. Ritchie, formerly secretary to W. A. Fairburn, late president of the Diamond Match Company; Leon N. Brown and Homan F. Hallock, both for many years with the Diamond Match Company; and Mrs. Joseph C. Fennelly and Thomas Carr Howe of San Francisco.

In the academic community I wish to thank for their encouragement Charles Stewart Sheppard, Dean, Charles C. Abbott, former Dean, and William Rotch, Chairman of the Research Committee, of the University of Virginia Graduate School of Business Administration; and Miss Barbara J. Wilcox, who typed and retyped the manuscript.

My gratitude to Margaret F. Forbes is reflected in the dedication.

Stettinius, Sr.
Portrait of a Morgan Partner

I. St. Louis (1865–1892) and Chicago (1892–1905)

THIS biography of Edward Reilly Stettinius is concerned primarily with his business career and his work for the Allied cause in World War I. In the course of the study we are inevitably concerned with a number of related matters important on their own account. We look behind the scenes at J. P. Morgan & Co. and see the workings of the firm's munitions-purchasing program for Great Britain and France in 1915–1917, the unsuccessful attempt to engage in international trade in the confused postwar world, and the Morgan company's contributions to national and international financial stability in the economic depression of 1920–1921 with their rescue of business concerns threatened with collapse. We also observe certain aspects of the management and operations of a number of leading American corporations during the first quarter of the twentieth century, especially Stettinius's own Babcock & Wilcox Company and Diamond Match Company. From his correspondence, the letters of others, and the accounts of those who knew him or his work, we are able to see Stettinius as a major figure in the business and financial community of his time and catch glimpses of him as a person. Finally, from these same sources we get views of the way of life of a man of property in the World War I period.

The only reason for examining the early life of a man who later becomes preeminent in a given field is to determine whether or not we can identify influences or find evidence anticipating the subsequent greatness. Sometimes we get an incidental insight into the life of a period or place. In general, however, this search is unrewarding. History has produced few individuals like Mozart or John Stuart Mill, whose genius was apparent in their childhood.

The youth and early manhood of Edward R. Stettinius were not exceptional. His experiences were those of most boys and young men of his social and economic background in St. Louis in the 1870's and 80's. To readers of a century later, this story has only a limited antiquarian interest. But these years do reveal one noteworthy characteristic of the later executive and financier: the fire that burned within him. He was prodigal with his energies, throwing himself into everything he undertook. He was rash by nature and disciplined only by a conscious application of will.[1]

On September 19, 1855, a wedding took place in the church of St. Francis Xavier in St. Louis, Missouri. On that day Father A. Damen, S. J., married Joseph Stettinius to Isabel Reilly Gorman. The groom was aged 47, the bride 35. Both were widowed. The groom had three children by an earlier marriage. He was a member of Stettinius & January, grocers and commission and forwarding merchants with premises at 60 North Front Street, facing the Mississippi River. It seems to have been a large wedding. The church records show a number of prominent people among the witnesses: the bankers G. G. Presburg and Jas. M. Franciscus, the doctor S[imon] Gratz Moses (of the distinguished Sephardic Gratz clan),[2] Captain Joseph Throckmorton of the river steamboat *Genoa*, and the well-known merchants W. D. W. Barnard, J. B. Wilcox, and James H. P. Blackwood.

Following their marriage, the Joseph Stettiniuses lived in a house on the south side of Washington Avenue between Sixth and Seventh Streets. Here they began their new family. They had three sons: Derick, born November 26, 1856; Joseph, born on October 28, 1859; and Edward Reilly Stettinius, born February 15, 1865. The two older boys were born in St. Louis and their baptisms are recorded at St. Francis Xavier, where their parents were married. It was just before the outbreak of the Civil War. Young Joseph was born less than ten days after John Brown's attack on the federal arsenal at Harper's Ferry. A year later the Civil War began, and for the next four years the Stettinius family lived under the strain of war.

Derick Stettinius, the eldest son, had suffered a spinal injury in infancy when dropped by his nursemaid. The worried parents

[1] The chief source of material on Stettinius's life is the Stettinius Papers in the Alderman Library of the University of Virginia, Charlottesville, which include among other documents incomplete files of the elder Stettinius's business correspondence (classified into four categories, Pre-Morgan, Regular Series, Personal Series, and War Years, cited below as PM, RS, PS, and WY) and a series of scrapbooks identified as "Research Material on the Life of Edward R. Stettinius, Sr., 1865–1925." Material in this chapter, unless otherwise identified, is based on research on Stettinius's early life carried out in 1932 by Miss Nancy Ring, found in Scrapbook I (pages unnumbered). (For further details about the Ring research and other Stettinius materials see the Bibliographical Note, below.)

[2] Information provided by Helen Gratz Rockefeller (Mrs. Godfrey S. Rockefeller) of Greenwich, Connecticut, in a letter of April 7, 1972, to the author.

hoped to find better medical treatment for him in Chicago. So early in 1865 the Stettiniuses made the journey northward, with another child due at any time. Meanwhile the country awaited the end of the long war; victory was in sight for the Union forces. Almost by chance, the third son, Edward Reilly Stettinius, was born in Chicago. We find his baptism in the records of the Holy Family Church in Chicago, which give the date of his birth as February 15, 1865.[3]

The family returned to St. Louis and continued to live at 1918 Morgan Street (when the streets were subsequently renumbered this became 1818), and here they lived until shortly after Edward's fourth birthday. It was here that Joseph, the father of the family, died in 1868.

On the national scene the Reconstruction controversy was raging. Meanwhile, the Stettinius boys were growing up. All three were sent to St. Louis University, starting in as children in the preparatory department. There was a family tradition both of education and of attending St. Louis University. The names of the boys' uncles Robert and Edward Reilly appear in the 1830 student register of the earlier St. Louis College. Edward entered the preparatory department of St. Louis University on September 8, 1874, when he was nine years old. He did very well in school. His academic record for the next seven years, still preserved at the university, was excellent, and so were his "deportment and diligence." While a student he was active in oratory and drama. These interests were combined on the evening of June 27, 1877, at the university's commencement exercises when Edward, cast as "a pert pupil," declaimed "The death of Napoleon" with what the *St. Louis Republican* described as "telling effect." But his longest-remembered appearance was in the title role of *Elma, or the Druid Martyr*, a melodrama in three acts presented on September 25, 1878, to benefit victims of the yellow fever epidemic of that year.[4]

To the tragedy of his elder brother's crippled state was added his second brother's death by drowning, and these combined with

[3] There is something of a puzzle about Stettinius's birthplace. He always indicated that he was born in St. Louis except on one occasion: in response to a routine inquiry from M. T. Murray, Jr., secretary of the Guaranty Trust Company, upon his election to the board, he gave Chicago as his birthplace (RS 679, ERS to Murray, October 17, 1921). Researches initiated by E. R. Stettinius, Jr., and aided by William E. Hall, a prominent Catholic layman, revealed the baptismal record in Chicago in 1938 (Scrapbook I).

[4] William B. Faherty, S.J., *Better the Dream: Saint Louis University and Community, 1818–1968* (St. Louis, 1968), p. 156.

the family's worsening finances to mature young Edward at an early age. He soon realized that he was responsible for his mother and brother and left St. Louis University on May 24, 1881, at the age of 16. But something influenced him to want more education. In the fall of 1882 he enrolled briefly at Mount Saint Mary's College in Emmitsburg, Maryland.[5]

On his return from Mount Saint Mary's Edward Stettinius went to work in St. Louis. His early business activities are not well documented, and the recollections of the friends of his youth became confused in later years. According to one account, he was bookkeeper in 1882 for the wholesale grocery firm of Jarratt, Gilliland, and Roberts.[6] Another writer says he was billing clerk for the Greely Burnham Reynolds Grocery Company.[7] It makes little difference. He tried a succession of jobs. The detailed records of St. Louis University note that in the academic year 1879–1880 he finished "Distinguished in Bookkeeping" (as well as "Distinguished in Christian Doctrine"), so it is not surprising to find him working as a bookkeeper. During one period he is said to have kept books for Mayberry and Rothschild, wholesale dealers in hats and furs.[8] There is some agreement that he went into partnership with Ruffin S. Winter in a cigar store, but was it on the corner of Fifth and Chestnut or at Third and Olive? [9]

We do know that in the 1880's he became a passionate bicycle rider, a devotee of the large-wheel-in-front variety of bicycle. During his cycling phase, he bought an interest in the bicycle magazine, *The American Wheelman*.[10] The cycling recollections of Louis J. Berger (later Bergère), quoted by Chris Sinsabaugh, show Stettinius as "A brilliant but systematic chap, bubbling with good-humored energy – somewhat like Teddy Roosevelt-type. Our Saturday night runs out the Manchester Road sometimes were made more pleasurable (if somewhat less ridable) by his ousting the rube kid from behind the bar at Barthold's Valley roadhouse, on the way to Manchester, and getting behind the bar himself and mixing the finest whisky punches imaginable. He had a good singing voice, with a pleasing huskiness in it." [11]

---

[5] Joseph W. Shoemaker, Librarian of Mount Saint Mary's College, to the author, April 17, 1971, and May 4, 1971.

[6] Scrapbook I, Ring research.

[7] *Ibid.*, Thomas J. Reynolds to ERS, Jr., April 6, 1938.

[8] *Ibid.*, Ring research.

[9] *Ibid.*, Reynolds to ERS, Jr., April 6, 1938; Lindell Gordon to ERS, Jr., April 7, 1938.

[10] *Ibid.*, Ring research.   [11] *Ibid.*, Sinsabaugh to ERS, Jr., April 27, 1938.

Another bicycling friend, later a business associate at the Diamond Match Company, Thomas J. Reynolds, recalls that, "As a boy and young man his hair was coal black, and his eyes were black and piercing, the same as they were in later years. He had a wonderful personality and was generous to a fault. In his youth he was impulsive and quick tempered, which he later overcame." [12] Actually, he never did overcome these traits completely. Reynolds also speaks of his fondness for poker. An interest in cards was something else that he did not outgrow.

A third cycling acquaintance, Lindell Gordon, describes him as "a man always resourceful and fertile in imagination, when one scheme failed he always had another to fall back upon. One scheme I can remember was an attempt to extract silver from black mud which was found in great abundance near Hot Springs, Arkansas. We raised a small amount of money quite large for us in those days I expecting to become rich over night. We found plenty of the peculiar black mud, but no silver." [13]

The national economy in the 1880's was stimulated by the mechanization of agriculture and the rise of large-scale manufacture. These movements led to a rise in the demand for capital and an increase in the importance of securities and commodity exchanges. The national economic trends are reflected in the business career of Stettinius during these years. After drifting from one job to another he found that his interest lay in finance. His last ventures in St. Louis were in the securities and commodity brokerage business. William H. Danforth of the Ralston Purina Company confirms that Stettinius was a member of the St. Louis Merchants Exchange from February 14, 1887, to June 6, 1893.[14] Arthur P. McDonald, long connected with the St. Louis Merchants Exchange, remembers having worked with Stettinius at L. G. McNair's office, "where he came to learn the bond and stock brokerage business." McDonald says that while he himself was with D. R. Francis and Brothers, who had a leased wire to Kenneth, Hopkins, and Company of Chicago, he suggested to the Chicago firm that they have a representative in the St. Louis wheat pit, and he recommended young Stettinius.[15] In 1888 and 1889 Stettinius is reported to have been a broker with Page McPherson and Company. We are on more solid ground when we find in the St. Louis city directory for 1890 the Stettinius-Rogers Commission Company Brokers, Stocks and Bonds, doing

[12] *Ibid.*, Reynolds to ERS, Jr., April 6, 1938.
[13] *Ibid.*, Gordon to ERS, Jr., April 7, 1938.
[14] *Ibid.*, Danforth to ERS, Jr., Feb. 16, 1938.
[15] *Ibid.*, McDonald to ERS, Jr., Nov. 30, 1933.

business at 202 North Third Street, across the street from the Merchants Exchange.

In the fall of 1890 Stettinius was in serious financial difficulties as the result of rash speculation. His brokerage business failed. Stettinius's money troubles from this period were to pursue him off and on for the next twenty-five years. Many years later he was to write James Van S. Barrett of his trials at this time, "I was not only staggering under a heavy load of indebtedness, but was compelled to bear all the expenses of my mother and brother owing to reverses that had overtaken my mother on account of unfortunate investments." [16]

These circumstances are illustrated in an exchange with one of his creditors. A letter dated November 11, 1890, from Arthur B. Barrett, commission merchant of St. Louis, asks what has become of three hundred shares of mining stock he sent him on September 10 to dispose of. [17] On April 23, 1893, Stettinius wrote Barrett, "I owe you about $300 which I intend and want to pay. You have placed the thing in a lawyer's hands and are simply heaping up costs without doing any good." He went on to suggest a compromise of $75 down and a note for $75 due in six months with the assurance that "if you accept this proposition, you shall lose no money if I ever get on my feet and have anything." He concluded, "I don't want to be considered a dead beat, and am anxious to do all I can to pay my debts, and I will pay them if I am let alone." [18]

Isabel Reilly Stettinius, Edward's mother, died in 1891, and Stettinius left St. Louis for Chicago the following year. [19] He returned to St. Louis only briefly in September 1892 for the funeral of his brother Derick.

Speculation in Chicago turned out just as disastrously as had earlier ventures in St. Louis. So, as he assured Arthur Barrett from his office at Room 606, Pullman Building, Chicago, he was finished with this business:

I owe $8,800 to firms and individuals on the Chicago and St. Louis board of trade and outside about $4,800 more, not including $5,000 I owe the estate of Mrs. W. Patterson. As long as I was in speculation I lost money and whatever amount of money I could raise from time to time was not taken by me with a view of beating my creditors but with a view of making a plunge, making enough to pay my debts and enabling me to start afresh. I have failed in every attempt and have simply increased my indebtedness each time. I have quit the Board of Trade and am

[16] RS 294, ERS to James Barrett, Aug. 22, 1917.
[17] RS 294, Arthur Barrett to ERS, Nov. 11, 1890.
[18] RS 294, ERS to Arthur Barrett, April 23, 1893.
[19] *Who's Who in America*, XIII (1924–25), 3035–36.

going to try something else, and in doing so am anxious to square up as many of my debts as possible.[20]

This decision to stop speculating must have taken a considerable exercise of will, because gambling can become a strong addiction. But Stettinius seems to have had only a single lapse, which occurred in the autumn of 1907. In a letter of April 1908 to Griff G. Glover he declines Glover's invitation to put money into an invention, "After the pleasurable sensation that I experienced last fall, I registered a mighty oath that in the future my conduct financially would be as blameless as my behavior morally. . . . The experience that I had last fall, however, was not altogether a pleasant one and I have been working along pretty religiously during the last three or four months in an effort to reduce my obligations and keep more stuff in my box and less pinned to my promissory notes." [21]

In 1892 Stettinius went to work for the Stirling Company, manufacturers of heavy machinery.[22] There is no evidence to suggest that this choice was anything other than purely accidental. He needed a job and given his training and experience probably started out as a bookkeeper. His progress in the company was rapid. On April 17, 1893, the minutes of the Stirling Company mentioned him for the first time: "On motion of O. C. Barber seconded by J. K. Robinson that E. R. Stettinius be and is hereby appointed Treasurer of the Company for the balance of the fiscal year. Carried." [23]

Two things are important here: First, this was the real beginning of Stettinius's business career. Second, he became the protégé of O. C. Barber.

Ohio Columbus Barber had recently survived an internal power struggle to emerge as the dominant figure at Stirling. He was one of the self-made magnates of the post-Civil War American business scene. Born in what is now Akron, Ohio, in 1841, Barber left school at fifteen to peddle the matches that his father made in the barn. In 1862, at twenty-one, he took over the family match business and in 1864 established the Barber Match Company, a corporation. In 1880 Barber's company combined with other similar small concerns to form the Diamond Match Company, which became a giant in the field.[24]

[20] RS 294, ERS to Barrett, April 23, 1893.
[21] PM 5, bound letters, No. 88, ERS to Glover, April 14, 1908.
[22] *Who's Who in America, loc. cit.*
[23] Scrapbook I. See Chapter II, note 1, below.
[24] *Dictionary of American Biography*, s.v. "Barber, Ohio Columbus." See also Herbert Manchester, *The Diamond Match Company: A Century of Service, of Progress, and of Growth, 1835–1935* (New York, 1935), p. 59.

Stettinius's appointment as treasurer of the Stirling Company turned out to be an honor as empty as the company treasury itself. Two and a half months after he received this promotion the bottom dropped out of the national economy. The panic of 1893 had come.[25]

The year 1893 was a good time to be in Chicago, despite the depression. The World's Columbian Exposition opened that year. This vast exposition had been conceived to celebrate the four hundredth anniversary of Columbus's first voyage to the New World. While he was battling the 1893 depression for the Stirling Company, Stettinius met Miss Judith Carrington of Richmond, Virginia. Could she have come out to Chicago for the Fair?

They were married at her family's house at 521 West Grace Street in Richmond on October 18, 1894. Following the wedding, the bridal pair went by train to Covington, Virginia, for several days and then on to Hot Springs, where they occupied Cottage B at The Homestead for a fortnight. Following the honeymoon they returned to Chicago and lived there until they moved to New York in 1905.[26] Their four children were born in Chicago, William Carrington in 1895, Isabel in 1897, Edward Reilly, Jr., in 1900, and Elizabeth in 1904.

[25] For discussions of the 1893 economic depression see Arthur C. Bining and Thomas C. Cochran, *The Rise of American Economic Life*, 4th ed. (New York, 1964), pp. 412ff. and Ernest Ludlow Bogart, *Economic History of the American People* (New York, 1931), pp. 725ff.

[26] PM 3, ERS to Arthur Man, Dec. 19, 1905.

II. *The Boiler Industry* (*1892–1915*)

The Stirling Company

IN 1892, when Stettinius joined the company, the Stirling Company was a small concern with its head office in Chicago and its manufacturing plant in Barberton, Ohio. O. C. Barber was the chief figure in the company, which accounts for the location of the plant in the town he had laid out in 1891 on the outskirts of Akron.

The Stirling Company was incorporated in Illinois on August 13, 1890, with an authorized capital of $500,000. The incorporators were Allan Stirling, O. C. Barber, Charles Baird, Thomas Deegan, John Jardine, and Robert C. Alexander. The preliminary certificate states that "The object for which the corporation is to be formed is the manufacture and sale of Steam boilers, machinery and apparatus, the carrying on of the mining and manufacturing operations essential thereto, and the transaction of such other business as may be necessarily incident to such manufacture and sale, including the licensing of other persons or corporations." [1]

The first meeting of the board of directors was held in Chicago on August 20, 1890. O. C. Barber was elected president and Allan Stirling was elected secretary and treasurer. At that meeting the board voted to buy the International Boiler Company for $510,000.

Apparently all was not harmonious, as indicated by the fact that at the directors' meeting of November 2, 1891, attended by Messrs. Stirling, Jardine, and Alexander, the following resolution was passed:

Whereas, the interests of the company seem to this board to require the dismissal of Mr. O. C. Barber as President,
Resolved that the said O. C. Barber be and hereby is dismissed and removed as President of this Company.

But the Barber forces rallied the stockholders to their cause, and at the shareholders' meeting of February 9, 1892, the three rebel-

---

[1] Unless otherwise noted, material in this chapter is drawn from excerpts from the minutes of directors' and stockholders' meetings of the Stirling Company and successor companies prepared by the office of A. G. Pratt, when Pratt was president of Babcock & Wilcox, at the request of ERS, Jr. These excerpts are preserved in Scrapbook I (see Pratt to ERS, Jr., Aug. 18, 1932).

lious directors were ousted and a new group, including Barber, was
elected to office. At the directors' meeting of the same day Barber
was made president of the company. The earlier action of the
board was rescinded, Allan Stirling fired, and new bylaws adopted.

The Stirling Company manufactured water-tube boilers for steam
engines. In the water-tube boiler the fire surrounds water-filled
tubes, an improvement over earlier fire-tube boilers, in which the
flame and hot gases are forced through pipes surrounded by water.
The principal product of the company was the Stirling boiler for
use with stationary engines. The particular virtue of this boiler was
its bent-tube construction. "This design had particular value in
installations in low headroom conditions. The continuous and eco-
nomical production of clean, dry steam, even when using poor feed-
water, and the ability to meet sudden load swings also characterize
the Stirling type boilers. By 1906, Stirling boilers had been built
in sizes up to 823 horsepower and 300 pounds pressure. . . ."[2] The
company also acquired the United States manufacturing rights for
the French Niclausse boiler, which was adapted for marine use.[3]

We have seen that Stettinius had hardly begun to receive recognition in the company when the economic depression of 1893 set in.
Makers of capital goods like machinery are among the hardest hit
in times of depression. Purchases of heavy equipment can be deferred a long time. The precarious condition of the Stirling Company's finances is shown in Stettinius's letter of August 1893 to
Barber:

Unless money comes in more rapidly than it has come in, it will be
necessary for us to do either one of two things; either shut down or else
pay our men off in some way as other manufacturing concerns in and
around Cleveland, and in the East are doing, viz: by check or some note
recognized by law. . . . It would seem to us that just as soon as the
work upon which our men are now engaged is completed, it would be
advisable for us to shut down and cut off every possible source of expense. We are in a fair condition now, and will have approximately
$4,500 in cash after meeting our pay roll on the 15th, but this amount
will be absorbed by notes maturing between now and the first, provided
the offers that we have made to exchange commercial paper for same
are not accepted. We have a great many promises of money, but the
promises do not seem to materialize.[4]

[2] *The Babcock & Wilcox Story, 1867–1967: 100 Years of Service to Industry*
(New York, 1967), p. 11.
[3] Herbert Manchester, *William Armstrong Fairburn, A Factor in Human
Progress* (New York, n.d. [ca. 1940]), p. 14.
[4] PM 1, ERS to Barber, Aug. 11, 1893.

Stettinius set to work to pull the Stirling Company out of its slump. In addition to assuming the duties of temporary treasurer, he became active in sales. His fortunes improved with those of the company. The minutes of stockholders' and directors' meetings show a steady increase in his responsibilities, salary, and holdings of company stock.[5]

At the stockholders' meeting of February 9, 1894, Stettinius was elected to the office of treasurer at a salary of $300 a month and made a director of the company. The following year he signed the minutes of the annual meeting with the title of assistant secretary. At that meeting the following statement of the condition of the Stirling Company as of January 1, 1895, was presented:

Assets

Patents & Good Will		$397,152.97
Real Estate, Boiler Shop, Fdry., Other Bldgs.		
Cottages, Machinery, Tools & Equipment		150,422.98
Accounts Receivable	145,659.37	
Bills Receivable	10,400	
Cash	20,103.08	
Raw Material, &c per Inventory	50,059.73	226,222.18
		773,798.13

Liabilities

Capital Stock		$500,000
Surplus		79,995.11
Profit for the Year		13,501.23
Bills Payable	151,532.50	
Acc'ts Payable	28,769.49	
		773,798.13

The company was beginning to make a little money.

The directors elected Stettinius secretary-treasurer on February 7, 1896, and raised his salary to $400. In 1899 Stettinius was paid $7,500 a year, while Barber as president received $4,800.

A special stockholders' meeting was called on April 9, 1900, and the capitalization of the company was doubled to one million dollars. Stettinius held 769 shares at this time. The board of directors met the same day and promoted Stettinius to general manager at a salary of $7,500, to be augmented by a bonus of $2,500 for any year in which the profits exceeded $60,000. On July 11, 1900, the directors declared a 2 percent dividend.

Stettinius was elected first vice-president and treasurer at the

[5] Years 1894–1905.

board meeting of February 7, 1901. Later that year a new corporation, the Stirling Company (New Jersey), was established with a capitalization of $1,875,000. On November 12, 1901, the New Jersey company bought the original Illinois company, and two days later the new directors elected Stettinius first vice-president, treasurer, and a director of the reorganized company.

Barber continued to be pleased with the performance of his protégé. In January 1902 he wrote, "I have been thinking over the business of the Stirling Company and the efficient service you have rendered the Company, and I am inclined to believe that we ought to raise your salary to $15,000.00 a year, if that is agreeable to you." [6]

At this time the Stirling Company received an important order for Niclausse marine boilers for the Great Northern Railroad cargo vessels *Minnesota* and *Dakota*. The choice of the Niclausse was made by William A. Fairburn, naval architect and marine engineer for the James J. Hill interests of St. Paul, which controlled the Great Northern. Fairburn subsequently joined Barber and Stettinius's Diamond Match Company as the direct result of this encounter. Fairburn's biographer says that this contract "put the Stirling Company on its feet" and gave it "a new lease on life." He also reports that in 1903 Fairburn again came to the rescue of the company as an expert witness in defending at a naval inquiry the installation of a Niclausse boiler in the U.S.S. *Maine* (successor to the Spanish War *Maine*). He quotes O. C. Barber and Stettinius as having said that "during this period Fairburn twice saved the Stirling Company from collapse." [7]

Stettinius tells us that he "formed Stirling Consolidated Boiler Co., 1905." [8] The Stirling Company bought out Aultman & Taylor Machinery Company of Mansfield, Ohio, an entirely new corporate structure was created, and a new board was elected which made

[6] PM 1, Barber to ERS, Jan. 24, 1902.

[7] Manchester, *Fairburn*, pp. 14, 17, 18. Manchester not only served as Fairburn's biographer, but earlier had been engaged while Fairburn was president of the concern to write a history of the Diamond Match Company (*The Diamond Match Company* [New York, 1935]). Throughout both studies, Fairburn is mentioned only in terms of fulsome praise. Stettinius, who preceded Fairburn as president of Diamond, is barely mentioned in the company history, and in the biography he is brought in mainly as a foil for Fairburn's wisdom or cleverness. In view of the circumstances that Manchester had been on Fairburn's payroll and that Stettinius felt some unfriendliness from Fairburn, as will be seen, caution must be exercised when making use of these studies as sources on Stettinius.

[8] *Who's Who in America*, XIII (1924–25), 3035–36.

Stettinius a director and first vice-president. Four days later the new board elected him treasurer as well.[9]

Stettinius did not underestimate the value of his services to the company. He wrote to Barber in November 1905: "I respectfully submit that it is not unfair that I be paid an additional amount over and above my salary, for the work that I have done, and I, therefore, suggest that I be given the sum of $25,000.00 as a bonus. In regard to my compensation from November 1st, I suggest that I be paid a salary of $20,000 per annum, with the understanding that if the net profits per annum amount to $400,000 or more, that I be paid an additional sum of $5,000 each year." [10]

The Babcock & Wilcox Company

The Babcock & Wilcox Company was a larger and older competitor of the Stirling Company. The company had pioneered in the design and construction of water-tube boilers with a patent granted in 1867 and had received considerable prominence at the Philadelphia Centennial Exposition of 1876. The company was incorporated in New Jersey in 1881 and after a few years specialized in the application of steam to the generating of electricity and to marine transportation. The company's main plant from 1901 on was in Bayonne, New Jersey.[11]

Babcock & Wilcox was interested in buying out the Stirling Company at least as early as 1902. Stettinius reported to Barber in a letter of December 1902 that E. H. Wells, president of the rival company, wanted to merge, and conversations on the subject had begun.[12] It is not spelled out in the correspondence exactly why Wells was so eager for the merger, but we can infer that he was interested in eliminating an active competitor and in gaining control of valuable boiler patents. This last is apparent in the detailed description of the Stirling boiler in the Babcock & Wilcox history published in 1967.[13]

In reporting back to Barber on the progress of his conversations

[9] Scrapbook I, minutes, stockholders' meetings, Nov. 1, 1905; directors' meetings, Sept. 27, 1905, Nov. 9, 1905, and Nov. 13, 1905.

[10] PM 1, ERS to Barber, Nov. 23, 1905. Barber endorsed the proposal by countersigning the letter in the space provided.

[11] Scrapbook I, excerpts, minutes of Babcock & Wilcox and covering letter, Pratt to ERS, Jr., Aug. 18, 1932. See also *The Babcock & Wilcox Story*, pp. 3–10.

[12] PM 1, ERS to Barber, Dec. 29, 1902.

[13] *The Babcock & Wilcox Story*, p. 11.

with Wells, Stettinius revealed himself to be a master strategist. When Wells mentioned an element of strength in Babcock & Wilcox, Stettinius countered with an outline of Stirling's market advantages. But Stettinius's strongest weapon was assumed indifference and the expressed view that a merger would be of no advantage to the Stirling stockholders. As he reported to Barber, "The more I talked down the deal, and the more I said in regard to its being unlikely that anything would be accomplished, the more earnest he became and the more he sought to convince me that I was wrong. Indeed he showed more anxiety to make the deal than he had ever shown before." [14]

Negotiations languished until 1906. Meanwhile, the capitalization of Babcock & Wilcox climbed steadily from one million dollars in 1890 to a million and a half in 1901 to three million in 1904. On January 17, 1906, Stettinius offered to sell the stock of Stirling Consolidated Boiler to Babcock & Wilcox for five and a half million dollars in their stock, if the company were recapitalized at $15,000,000. The Babcock & Wilcox directors agreed to both of these conditions at their January 24 meeting, and on February 26 the stockholders ratified the decision. Two days later the Stirling stockholders met and elected the Babcock & Wilcox directors to their board. The directors then elected O. C. Barber president, E. H. Wells first vice-president, and Stettinius second vice-president. On March 14, 1906, the stockholders of Babcock & Wilcox elected Stettinius a director.

For the balance of 1906 Stettinius directed the destinies of the Stirling Consolidated Boiler Company and Babcock & Wilcox, which continued to do business as separate corporate entities until April 6, 1907. The two companies ran full-page advertisements identical in typography and format on facing pages of the December 1906 issue of *Power*, the journal of the steam engine industry. The relative size of the two concerns was indicated in the text, where Babcock & Wilcox claimed to have supplied boilers currently producing 6,000,000 horsepower, while Stirling took credit for the production of 4,000,000 horsepower by Stirling and Cahall vertical water-tube steam boilers.[15] Following the merger,[16] Stettinius continued to serve as second vice-president of Babcock & Wilcox at $25,000 a year until April 1909, when a series of reduc-

[14] PM 1, ERS to Barber, Dec. 29, 1902.
[15] *Power*, Dec. 1906, pp. 278, 279.
[16] Reported in the *Commercial & Financial Chronicle*, Feb. 23, 1907, p. 451.

tions in salary reflected his progressively greater involvement in another Barber enterprise, the Diamond Match Company.

Nineteen hundred and seven began very well for Babcock & Wilcox. The company did not publish financial reports in those days before the Securities and Exchange Commission, but Stettinius wrote to F. M. Clough of the Chico, California, factory of the Diamond Match Company that Babcock & Wilcox net profits for the year were $2,075,020.93, after charges to reserves of $381,817.25. He stated the assets of the company to be $20,039,315.98, with a surplus of about three million dollars.[17] The panic of 1907 interrupted this prosperity. We shall see this again in the case of the Barberton Savings Bank.

The year 1908 was a time of continued depression, and the boiler industry suffered as it always did. The greater part of Stettinius's energies through 1908 were devoted to the affairs of the boiler company. In November Taft was elected president. Business looked up the following year, and Stettinius was able to report to Barber in March 1909 that "The Boiler business is showing a distinct improvement, but our volume has, of course, not by any means reached or come anywhere near reaching the average for the years 1906 and 1907."[18] By the summer of 1909 the economic recovery was in full swing and Stettinius could announce, "The boiler business is very good and orders for the month of July have been larger than any month since before the panic."[19] The fact is that business for Babcock & Wilcox was too good—from the point of view of the company's competitors!

At the time of the first stages of merger in 1906 the boiler industry was highly competitive. Thirty-four boiler manufacturers advertised in the issue of *Power* that ran the double advertisement for the nominally competing Stirling and Babcock & Wilcox companies. Within less than three years competitors were raising a hue and cry about "the boiler trust," claiming that Babcock & Wilcox was seeking a monopoly of boiler manufacture in the United States and, not content with local triumphs, had been embraced by the British Navy. Stirling had absorbed Aultman & Taylor, it was pointed out, and Babcock & Wilcox had swallowed up both Stirling and in 1909 the Rust Boiler Company.[20]

[17] PM 5, bound letters, No. 178, ERS to Clough, May 19, 1908.
[18] PM 1, ERS to Barber, March 27, 1909.
[19] PM 1, ERS to Barber, Aug. 4, 1909.
[20] *Power,* July 20, 1909, p. 121. (*Power* changed from a monthly to a weekly in 1908).

Babcock & Wilcox expanded their marine boiler operations at this time and developed a new compact, lightweight three-drum boiler for the destroyer U.S.S. *Mayrant* in 1909. In the same year the company introduced an assembly technique which made possible the mass production of marine boilers in World War I.[21]

O. C. Barber was the dominant figure in both the boiler business and the match business. After putting Stettinius in charge of the boiler company, he kept pushing him further and further into the match company, and Stettinius kept resisting, all the while gradually yielding. Barber's motive for wanting Stettinius to direct the affairs of the Diamond Match Company is never stated in so many words, but apparently he had great confidence in the younger man's executive capacity and wanted to take full advantage of his talents. In the summer of 1906, when the problems of the boiler merger were most acute, Barber tried to persuade Stettinius to accept a directorship in the British match company Bryant & May. Stettinius saw through the other's maneuver and begged off for a number of good reasons, concluding,

Again, I believe that if I were to accept a position with the Bryant & May Co. it would merely mean the entering wedge which, in time, would result in my being required to devote more or less time and attention to the Diamond Match Co. . . .

I know that you take the ground that a man is broader and more effective if his interests are diversified and if his work is distributed over two or three Companies, rather than devoted to one. However true this may be in general, it does not work out in my case, for, whatever I have gained in the past has been the result of application and concentration to one thing, and it would be the height of folly for me to attempt now, or at any time in the future, to do active work for more than one Company.[22]

In the light of Stettinius's subsequent career, it is apparent that Barber's estimate of the younger man's capacity was more accurate than his own more modest appraisal.

The real break with Babcock & Wilcox came on May 5, 1909, when he became president of the Diamond Match Company. He remained an officer and a director of Babcock & Wilcox until 1915, when his association with the Allied purchasing effort in World War I created a conflict of interest. He submitted his resignation as second vice-president and director at the board meeting of March 22, 1915, and sold his stock in the company. In a letter of October 1915 to Barber he mentions that he sold out before the

---

[21] *The Babcock & Wilcox Story*, p. 13.
[22] PM 1, ERS to Barber, July 30, 1906.

boom in war industry stocks and therefore lost money on the transaction.[23] After the war, when conflict of interest was no longer an issue, Stettinius became a director of the company again at the insistence of his old friend and sometime adversary, E. H. Wells.[24]

[23] PM 1, ERS to Barber, Oct. 27, 1915.
[24] RS 219, E[dward] H. Wells to ERS, April 28, 1919.

III. *The Diamond Match Company* (*1897–1915*)

W E SAW that O. C. Barber gradually maneuvered Stettinius into assuming greater responsibility in the Diamond Match Company. This dual role of executive in two major concerns was made possible not only by Barber's influence but by the physical proximity of the main plants of the two companies in Barberton, Ohio.

The Diamond Match Company (*1880–1909*)

The Diamond Match Company was the leading producer of matches in the United States. It was formed in Connecticut on December 3, 1880, by the merger of ten of the oldest and largest match manufacturers in the country. The company was capitalized at $2,250,000, divided into 14,000 common and 8,500 preferred shares with a par value of $100 each. The largest stockholder from the outset was O. C. Barber.[1] The original company prospered and on February 6, 1889, was reorganized as the Diamond Match Company of Illinois, with an increase in capital stock of 60,000 shares. Two weeks later Barber became president of the company.[2]

Stettinius had a connection with the Diamond Match Company going back to 1897. He became a director in April 1904 and second vice-president the following December. We saw that in 1906 Stettinius had been uneasy about attempts to draw him into the affairs of the match company to the detriment of his work with Babcock & Wilcox.[3] His fears were confirmed when he was offered the presidency of Diamond Match at the January 1908 board meeting.[4]

---

[1] Material in this chapter, unless otherwise identified, is provided by the minutes of the directors' and stockholders' meetings of the Diamond Match Company. These were made available to me in 1969 by Mr. Anthony Davey, at that time general counsel for the Diamond National Corporation, 733 Third Avenue, New York. In 1971 the company name was changed to Diamond International Corporation.

[2] Manchester, *The Diamond Match Company*, pp. 59–65.

[3] PM 1, ERS to Barber, July 30, 1906.

[4] PM 1, ERS to Barber, Jan. 21, 1908.

The Diamond Match Company was in trouble. Earnings had fallen off badly, and in consequence there were complaints. There was a depression on. The new Oshkosh plant had been a financial drain. The spring of 1908 had been hot and humid, making it "one of the worst years for manufacturing matches in 10 years." [5] The company's lumber operations were going badly.[6] Stettinius was called in to get the company out of its difficulties. He made a final attempt to sever his connection with the match company at the end of the year. On Christmas Eve 1908 he wrote a strong letter of resignation. He stated in so many words that he wanted to quit before he was forced to take the presidency.[7] This last effort failed. At the directors' meeting of May 5, 1909, Barber resigned as president of the company after ten years in office to become chairman of the board, and Stettinius was elected president of the Diamond Match Company at the age of 44.[8] O. C. Barber later commented somewhat patronizingly on Stettinius's election, "Wishing to throw off some of my cares, I used my influence to make him president of the Diamond Match Company." [9]

The presidency of E. R. Stettinius was marked by two important and entirely separate series of events. One was financial, the other humanitarian.

The Rehabilitation of the Company (1909–1915)

Stettinius found two primary causes for the decline in earnings. One was the investment in the unprofitable British match company, Bryant & May. More important was the investment in California timberlands, some of these bought with money borrowed from Bryant & May. This land, he pointed out, had caused the company to be out of pocket $433,281.46.[10] The problem was that the Barber administration had exceeded the limits of prudent vertical integration for the supply of matchwood and gone into the lumber business.

[5] *Commercial & Financial Chronicle*, Oct. 31, 1908, p. 1162.

[6] *Ibid.*, Nov. 28, 1908, p. 1422.

[7] PM 1, ERS to Barber, December 24, 1908.

[8] See the *Commercial & Financial Chronicle*, May 8, 1909, p. 1120. Leon N. Brown, Diamond Match Division, Diamond National Corporation, Springfield, Mass., has kindly shown me his notes for a history of the company, which outline this sequence of events.

[9] J. Willard Ridings, "Missourians Abroad, No. 5—Edward R. Stettinius, Assistant Secretary of War," *Missouri Historical Review*, XIII (Oct. 1918), 39.

[10] President's report, submitted at the directors' meeting of Nov. 26, 1909.

The dividend rate had remained at 10 percent for a number of years. In 1909 the rate fell to 8 percent and at the end of January 1910 to 6 percent.[11]

Disagreements between Stettinius and Barber had developed in recent years. Barber harassed the younger man to the point where it began to affect his health. In the summer of 1910 Stettinius finally confided to his fellow director Edwin A. Potter of the American Trust & Savings Bank of Chicago that he was fed up and wanted to get out but didn't want to let down the company or his associates. Potter urged him to remain, observing that by resigning he would be doing just what Barber wanted him to do.[12] Stettinius did reconsider and went ahead with his program for the company.

Early in his presidency, Stettinius was responsible for hiring William A. Fairburn as a production coordinator. Fairburn was to succeed him as chief executive of the company. As earlier noted, he had come to the attention of Stettinius and Barber when he was a customer for Stirling boilers.[13] As we shall see when we come to Stettinius's direction of the Export Department of J. P. Morgan & Co., one of his administrative gifts was the ability to choose good men and to delegate responsibility to them. Fairburn was unquestionably highly competent, but we continue to be conscious of tension between the two men.

With the surviving company records so scanty, we have to rely on what Fairburn's enthusiastic biographer has to say about Stettinius's instructions to Fairburn and the carrying out of this threefold charge. The assignment was to

(1) clean up and sell the company's New England timber and lumber operation, for which Stettinius had received an offer of purchase of $100,000; (2) discontinue book match manufacture and liquidate that phase of the company's business, then in its infancy, as it was considered by the management to be "an unprofitable nuisance," because, "the book match is no good and will never be popular"; (3) report on the California timber and lumber operation and arrange immediately to discontinue all retail yards and such channels of distribution and methods of merchandising.[14]

Fairburn countered with his own analysis of the situation. While Stettinius was not entirely in accord with Fairburn's subsequent

[11] *Commercial & Financial Chronicle*, Feb. 5, 1910, p. 375.
[12] PM 4, Potter to ERS, Aug. 11, 1910.
[13] Brown, notes for a history of the Diamond Match Company; Manchester, *Fairburn*, pp. 21–22.
[14] Manchester, *Fairburn*, p. 45.

recommendations, he went ahead with most of them. The New England lumber business was retained and turned into a profitable venture. Book matches were continued successfully. California retail lumberyards were held and operated profitably, but California lumber production was continued at a loss over Fairburn's protest and despite Stettinius's own earlier findings.[15]

A drastic shake-up of operating personnel is recorded in the minutes of the August 2, 1910, board meeting. Three members of the Palmer family were quietly purged in what Stettinius described as "the best interests of the company." Such is the frustrating discretion of directors' meeting minutes that we are not told what mistakes of commission or omission were attributed to the Palmers. C. H. Palmer was fired as general superintendent, W. N. Palmer was eased out as assistant general superintendent, and T. A. Palmer was relieved of his job as manager of the Barberton factory. W. A. Fairburn was appointed general superintendent.

The next major step was to pay off the company's notes and allow earnings to be used for working capital. On November 3, 1910, Stettinius proposed to the stockholders a plan for issuing two million dollars' worth of 6 percent convertible debentures, redeemable in ten years, on December 15, 1920. The capital of the company was increased from $16,000,000 to $18,000,000 and the number of authorized shares from 160,000 to 180,000.

Stettinius applied his talents as a salesman[16] to the problems of the ailing Diamond Match Company. In the summer of 1912 he embarked on a limited advertising campaign to see if such techniques could be used effectively to increase the sale of matches. As usual, he carried the board along with him, and they endorsed his proposal at the July 15 meeting. The idea was to spend from $10,000 to $20,000 over the next six months in certain key localities on an experimental basis. The experiment was tried again with the "Safe Home" brand of matches and proved successful, and Stettinius therefore recommended that an advertising appropriation of $100,000 be approved. The board agreed at its meeting of May 5, 1914.

Meanwhile, the company began to prosper, and as its cash position improved Stettinius secured the permission of his directors to pay off the indebtedness to Bryant & May incurred through an earlier agreement to buy out their interest in California timberlands. Diamond paid $637,921.44 after the July 15, 1912, meeting and $330,853.50 after the October 9, 1912, meeting. He was also able

[15] *Ibid.*, pp. 46–48.   [16] A. G. Pratt to the author, June 29, 1970.

to convince the board at their July 9, 1913, meeting of the wisdom of selling the company's holdings of Bryant & May stock.

As the company continued to make money, Stettinius had the debentures retired. It was announced on February 1, 1913, that debentures in the amount of $412,600 had been redeemed and cancelled. The retirement of more debentures was reported at the October 8, 1913, meeting and again on January 23, 1914. By September 1915, debentures of $860,100 had been bought up and retired. At a special stockholders' meeting called on September 24, 1915, Stettinius recommended that the remaining $1,139,900 of debentures outstanding, held by the Continental and Commercial Trust and Savings Bank of Chicago, be redeemed. The measure was approved.

The *Boston Evening Transcript* of September 24, 1915, quoted this statement by H. F. Holman, secretary of the company: "At a meeting of the directors of the Diamond Match Company the officials of the company were directed to take appropriate action looking toward the retirement and payment on December 15, 1915, of the balance now outstanding of the company's issue of $2,000,000 of debentures dated December 15, 1910, and due December 15, 1920."

Holman was further quoted as predicting that company assets would exceed liabilities by approximately $7,500,000 at the end of 1915 as compared to $1,864,727 on December 31, 1908. Since this period corresponds almost exactly with Stettinius's term of office, it is obvious that the company flourished under his direction.

Stettinius commented on the early retirement of the debt: "The authorization of the directors to retire the outstanding balance of its debentures, due in 1920, marks the completion of the task I laid out when I assumed the presidency of the Company in May, 1909. When these debentures shall have been paid, all of the Company's funded and deferred obligations of every character will have been discharged, and its liabilities will consist only of accounts payable for current purchases of materials, amounting in the aggregate to a relatively small sum." [17]

Industrial Statesmanship: The Nonpoisonous Match Patent

A single action separated Edward R. Stettinius from a thousand other competent, shrewd, successful business executives of the

[17] "A Memoir, Edward Reilly Stettinius, 1865–1925," anonymous typescript in the Stettinius Papers, Alderman Library, University of Virginia, pp. 10–11.

prewar era and gained him nationwide recognition. This was his part in the renunciation by the Diamond Match Company of the patent rights to the only nonpoisonous matchhead manufacturing process then known.

Most matches in the first decade of the twentieth century continued to be made of wooden splinters dipped into a mixture of white phosphorus. White phosphorus is an extremely poisonous chemical, and the use of this process in match manufacture led to the high incidence among workers of the industrial disease necrosis of the jaw, known colloquially as "phossy jaw." For many years the Diamond Match Company made white phosphorus matches as did everybody else. Occasional items in the directors' minutes refer to the voting of sums of money for pensions or medical expenses for victims of necrosis of the jaw formerly employed by the company.[18]

Eventually Diamond acquired U.S. Patent No. 614,350 for the manufacture of matchheads out of sesquisulphide of phosphorus, a nonpoisonous substance, and proceeded to phase out the old process and replace it with the new. Stettinius was profoundly concerned about the occupational hazards of match manufacture in his own company and in the industry at large. Following a resolution by the board in August 1910,[19] Stettinius negotiated licensing agreements with eight of his leading competitors for the use of the nonpoisonous Sévène-Cahen process. The directors hoped that by sharing their exclusive rights to the process with their competitors they could overcome Congress's fear of a Diamond Match monopoly and open the way for passage of the Esch Bill to stop the use of the phosphorus process.

At the board meeting of December 22, 1910, Stettinius spoke strongly on behalf of a more liberal policy by the company. The result was that the patent was assigned to an independent group of three trustees, who had the power to grant licenses on whatever basis they thought fair. It was still feared that under the circumstances the passage of the Esch Bill, then before Congress, would create a monopoly. So Stettinius took a drastic step. He and the other officers of the Diamond Match Company renounced the patent and made the nonpoisonous process available without charge to the world, i.e., to their competitors. On February 14, 1911, Stettinius presented the board with a *fait accompli*, pointing out to the directors that notwithstanding Diamond's arrangement for the

---

[18] Directors' minutes of Dec. 22, 1910, and Oct. 9, 1912.
[19] For the text of the resolution see Appendix A.

patent to be available by license, the opinion of men close to Congress was that the Esch Bill would not pass, "And in the event of the bill not being passed by Congress, the cause of the failure would no doubt be charged to this Company. In order to remove all bones for such a contention he deemed it advisable that the Company surrender its patent and stated that such action had been taken with the consent of all the companies that had been licensed by us to use the patented ingredient." The board went along with the action of the president and other officers and voted their acquiescence.

The renunciation of the patent was favorably received by the press and was the subject of a detailed and soberly laudatory article in the *Scientific American* for February 11, 1911.[20] Congress still failed to pass the Esch Bill or other appropriate legislation. However, such laws became less and less necessary as other match companies quietly changed over to the new process.

Stettinius's contribution to industrial safety was not entirely forgotten even after the great events of 1914–1918, the postwar unrest, and the more important role that he played in the business community as a Morgan partner. The following letter appeared in the *New York Herald Tribune* on September 16, 1925, a fortnight after Stettinius's death on September 3:

To the New York Herald Tribune:
   In none of the accounts of his career and the public tributes to him when he passed away does there appear to be any mention of one of the finest things for which Edward R. Stettinius was responsible.
   It was while he was president of the Diamond Match Co. that he opened to the world freely the secrets and patents possessed by this company alone, whereby its operatives were made immune from the horrible results caused by dipping the wooden part of the match in phosphorous. The operatives of every other company were subject to the loathesome disease which attacks the bony structure of the body, eating away the flesh and resulting in frightful maiming and death. The company of which Mr. Stettinius was the head alone knew how to prevent this, and it was his great contribution to a humanitarian cause that led him to take this step, of which the papers of about a dozen years ago will, if referred to, be found to give an elaborate account.
   I trust these data, even if somewhat indefinite, will add a word of appreciation of the life of a singularly modest, gifted and truly resourceful, big man, who was ever mindful of the welfare of his fellows.

                                                            LEE KOHNS

   The writer of the letter, Lee Kohns (1864–1927), was the long-time head of L. Straus & Co., importers and makers of china and

---

[20] Reprinted in Appendix B.

glassware, a vice-president of the Abraham & Straus department store in Brooklyn, and an associate of Stettinius's on the board of the Irving Bank–Columbia Trust Company.

The Monopoly Issue

An awareness of the danger of appearing to hold a monopoly in an industry is a recurring motif throughout this period. We have just seen how it colored Diamond's policy regarding the Sévène-Cahen patent.

In 1911 Stettinius engaged the law firm of Weeks, Battle, and Marshall to make a broad survey of the company's operations relative to the Sherman Act. George Gordon Battle of that firm tells us that Stettinius was as conscious of public opinion and the general emotional and political climate within each state on the antitrust issue as he was of relevant legislation pending or enacted.[21]

The board of directors passed a resolution on September 12 expressing their wish to support the Sherman Act. They ratified past actions by the president leading up to the final renouncing of the Sévène-Cahen patent. The threat of government action—both federal and state—was a very real one in 1911, and as president of the Diamond Match Company Stettinius was continually concerned to keep abreast of statutes and make sure that company practices kept well within the limits prescribed by law.

World War I: Stettinius Resigns the Presidency

The world war broke out in Europe in the summer of 1914, with the Central Powers of Germany, Austria, and their satellites ranged against Great Britain, France, Russia, and their smaller allies. As the war continued and the position of the Allies worsened, J. P. Morgan & Co. assumed an important role in the task of supplying American-produced matériel to the Allies.

These events had a direct bearing on Stettinius and his relations with the Diamond Match Company at the beginning of 1915. The Morgan firm hired Stettinius on a parttime basis to direct their munitions purchasing. As this arrangement continued, it became more and more apparent that the demands of the Morgan assign-

[21] Scrapbook II, George Gordon Battle, "In re Edward R. Stettinius," June 21, 1938.

ment were increasing to the point where Stettinius had to decide
which of the two jobs he would keep. On September 4, 1915, he
wrote to the principal officers and directors of the match company,
summarizing the entire situation and giving his views on resolving
the problems involved:

At the last meeting of the Directors of The Diamond Match Co., I
stated that I had definitely agreed with Messrs. J. P. Morgan & Co.,
to continue in charge of their Purchasing Department for the British
Government as long as they desired me to do so. I called attention to
the fact that in January last I had asked for a leave of absence of 90
days, that this time had subsequently been extended, but that now it was
uncertain when I could resume my work for the Match Co. I, therefore,
suggested that I be relieved as President. The members of the Board,
however, appeared reluctant to accept my resignation and suggested that
the present arrangement be continued and that I return to the Company when and as soon as I could.

Since that meeting, and more particularly during the last week or
ten days, I have learned that some of the German trade of The Diamond
Match Co. were discriminating against the Company on account of my
active connection with the Purchasing Department of the British Government. The competitors of The Diamond Match Co. appear to be
using this fact, and very energetically in some sections. It, therefore, appears that the business of the Company may possibly suffer by reason
of the fact that I am prominently connected with it as President. Moreover, as a result of recent developments, I have come to the conclusion
that for other reasons it is proper that I should retire as President.

The term of my connection with Messrs. J. P. Morgan & Co. as
Manager of their Purchasing Department for the British Government
is, of course, indefinite. It may come to an end in one month or it may
last for a number of years. When that work shall have been completed,
however, I wish to be entirely free to make such connections as may
appear desirable. While I have made no definite commitment of any
character whatever, and am for many reasons unwilling to do so at
this time, nevertheless, suggestions of a tentative character have been
made to me looking toward the future that are so attractive that I cannot but heed them.

Having definitely determined, therefore, that I will not return to the
Company to serve actively in any capacity, and as it appears that my
present connection may possibly operate to the Company's detriment,
I propose now to tender my resignation as President and to ask the
Board of Directors at their next meeting to take immediate action in
respect thereto. I am writing to you and to Messrs. Potter, Barber and
Dr. Bevan along similar lines. I would suggest that you confer with one
another by letter or in person as you may all deem advisable, for the
purpose of deciding upon a definite program to be adopted at the next
meeting of the Board.

I recommend strongly that Mr. Fairburn be elected President to succeed me, and that there be created a position either of Chairman of the Board or Chairman of the Executive Committee, and that some one be elected to either one of the latter positions who can generally direct and keep in touch with the business in the future, and who will be charged particularly with the duty of supervising its finances, etc.

So far as I am personally concerned, I would not be willing to serve as Chairman of the Board. If there is a good reason why I should retire as President, the same reason would apply with equal force against my serving as Chairman of the Board, to which position more or less attention would be directed in the Press and otherwise. If, on the other hand, it was desired that I accept the position of Chairman of the Executive Committee, and it was definitely understood and agreed that no publicity would be given to that fact, but that, on the other hand, an announcement would be made publicly and otherwise, that I had severed my active connection with the Company, I would be willing to accept the position, provided it was clearly understood that I would not be required to give any considerable time to the business of the Company, and that I would act only in an advisory way in respect to its general operations, although having direct charge of its finances. I do not recommend, however, that this program be adopted. I believe, on the other hand, that it would be in the interest of the Company if some one were selected who could give some considerable time to the business of the Company and who, in case of emergency, could give all of the time necessary to deal with any important problem arising that might require a great deal of time and attention. . . .

In brief, my position is that I would like to withdraw altogether from the Company, that I am willing to continue to serve as Director if you all wish me to do so and that I am willing to go even farther and serve as Chairman of the Executive Committee under the conditions named above, if it appears that it is wise that such an arrangement be made. I repeat, however, that I do not recommend such a plan.[22]

Stettinius handed in his resignation at the regular board meeting of September 25, 1915. The minutes record the event under the head "Resignation of Mr. Edward R. Stettinius as President," with the usual resolution.

The ritual expression of the board's regret found more specific confirmation in a letter from Lewis E. Pierson, then president of Austin, Nichols & Co. and later head of the Irving Trust Company, written the very day of the meeting: "In noting your retirement as President of the Diamond Match Company, I cannot refrain from expressing to you my admiration for the remarkable results achieved

[22] RS 4, James A. Patten correspondence, ERS to Francis A. Hardy, Sept. 4, 1915.

in that Company during your short administration of its affairs. To have brought that Company out of chaos with meagre profits and considerable debts into a condition of orderliness—no debts and good profits is a result of which your Directors and Stockholders cannot fail but to feel great appreciation—and prove of deep satisfaction to yourself." [23]

Stettinius, Fairburn, and Barber

Fairburn was strongly opposed to the idea of a chairman of the board to whom he as president would be subordinate. The matter came up before the May 1916 board meeting, and no chairman was named. This was a blow to Stettinius and the cause of considerable embarrassment both to him [24] and to his candidate for the chairmanship, Edwin A. Potter of Chicago. [25]

Stettinius's attitude toward Fairburn was completely detached from personal considerations. His primary concern was the good of the company and the stockholders. He had recommended that Fairburn be elected president to succeed him. He continued to support him. He had earlier written, "Fairburn is a very efficient man, and in point of fact is largely responsible for many of the improvements that have been made in manufacturing methods during the past four or five years, and has, moreover, contributed quite a little in the Sales Department." [26] Stettinius believed that Fairburn had turned Barber against him,[27] although he had tried to help Barber out of his serious financial difficulties [28] and stood by him when disgruntled stockholders wanted to oust him from the Diamond board.[29]

In May 1916 Stettinius returned his salary cheque of $7,309.14 for the period from January 15 to April 30, observing that he had done "little or no work for the company since January 15th, 1916." Six weeks later he resigned from the board of directors.[30]

[23] PM 4, Pierson to ERS, Sept. 25, 1915.
[24] RS 268, ERS to Hardy, May 11, 1916.
[25] RS 343, Potter to ERS, May 31, 1916.
[26] PM 3, ERS to A. H. Marks, Nov. 6, 1915.
[27] RS 7 (2), ERS to James P. Sneddon, Nov. 26, 1917.
[28] PM 4, ERS to Potter, April 21, 1915; PM 1, ERS to Dr. Arthur D. Bevan, Dec. 10, 1915.
[29] PM 4, James A. Patten to ERS, Sept. 17, 1915; ERS to Patten, Sept. 18, 1915.
[30] RS 268, ERS to Fairburn, May 11, 1916, and June 27, 1916.

IV. *Miscellaneous Business Concerns before World War I*

B ETWEEN 1892 and 1915 Stettinius was primarily occupied with the management of the Stirling Consolidated Boiler Company, its successor company, Babcock & Wilcox, and the Diamond Match Company. Around the edges of his work in the steam-boiler and match industries, Stettinius invested money and sometimes took an active part in a number of enterprises of assorted sizes and degrees of risk. Sometimes he went into these ventures on his own; at other times he went in with one or more associates. It might be argued that these miscellaneous undertakings were an outlet for Stettinius's repressed gambling instinct.

This is a tantalizing and frustrating chapter in Stettinius's business life because the surviving materials are so scanty and incomplete. Most of the companies have long since disappeared and their records with them. We are left with a few notes and letters in the Stettinius Papers and, when the events were important enough to be recorded, reports published in the financial journals. From the fragmentary accounts it would appear that Stettinius's chief sources of income were his salaries and returns from the securities of the companies he worked for. Some of the peripheral concerns were profitable but many were not; in most cases the amount of money involved was not very great.

Barberton Savings Bank

In 1905 the First National Bank of Barberton, Ohio, failed. Barberton, an industrial suburb of Akron, was another O. C. Barber project. Barber laid out the town in 1891 and developed it as a manufacturing center, moving to the new town the plants of the companies he dominated.

The collapse of the First National created the threat of a run on the Barberton Savings Bank. To protect the latter, Stettinius and Barber made a substantial loan to the bank. The bank was unable to repay the loan and as a result the creditors took control, with Stettinius as president.[1] Stettinius then became a banker throughout his critical years with the boiler and match companies.

The panic of 1907 caused a widespread lack of public confidence in banks, and a number of depositors withdrew their money from the Barberton Savings Bank. Stettinius's calm handling of the situation prevented these withdrawals from becoming a run on the bank.[2] The day-to-day affairs of the bank were managed by J. A. Artley, the secretary-treasurer,[3] but the arrangement with Artley collapsed when it was discovered in 1908 that he was taking advantage of the absentee management of the bank to embezzle the funds. Stettinius, just back from Europe, promptly called an emergency directors' meeting at Barberton for April 28.[4] After this, Isaac Harter, an executive with Babcock & Wilcox, became Stettinius's principal man on the ground.

The bank did business with a number of important concerns including the Diamond Match Company, which was located in Barberton, the Goodyear Tire & Rubber Company of nearby Akron, and the Berghoff brewery of Fort Wayne, Indiana. The only surviving records of these connections are letters in a bound file of Stettinius's correspondence for 1908. We learn, for example, that in April 1908 he directed the bank to send the Diamond Match Company a draft for $25,000 on the Empire Trust Company of New York. A month later he wrote to Harter about the Goodyear account, "I do not recall exactly how much of their paper we have at the present time, but am under the impression that we have in the neighborhood of $12,000. In that event, I think it might be well for us to hold them down to this limit for the time being at least." This lack of confidence in the young rubber company is also revealed in a later letter, "I notice that you have an item 'Goodyear Tire & Rubber Co. Protest $2.76.' Does this mean that one of the notes they gave us went to protest?"

The Berghoff brewery borrowed $15,000 for six months at 6 percent in March 1908 and renewed the note the following September.[5]

A somewhat irrelevant but historically interesting inquiry reached

[1] RS 758, Agreement of June 23, 1905.
[2] PM 1, ERS to Barber, Nov. 21, 1907.
[3] PM 5, bound letters, No. 43, ERS to Artley, March 17, 1908.
[4] PM 5, bound letters, No. 79, ERS to Barber, April 13, 1908.
[5] PM 5, bound letters, No. 103, ERS to Barberton Savings Bank, April 15, 1908; No. 142, ERS to Harter, May 11, 1908; No. 349, ERS to A. H. Kirkland, secretary-treasurer, June 23, 1908; No. 2, ERS to Stephen B. Fleming, March 13, 1908; No. 661, ERS to Kirkland, Sept. 18, 1908.

Stettinius in the fall of 1910 because of his Akron connections. He was approached by a representative of Lotta Crabtree, the actress associated with the years after the Gold Rush in pioneer California, for advice about her real-estate holdings in Akron. By this time Stettinius was out of touch with the situation there, so he forwarded the letter to Barber with the request, "Will you not be good enough to give me such information as you can in regard to this property, and such advice as you are disposed to offer as to whether Miss Crabtree should hold or sell the property?" [6]

As his interests became centered in New York, Stettinius felt, and Barber with him, that it was not feasible to continue to run the Barberton Savings Bank as an absentee executive. Barber sounded out possible buyers for the bank.[7]

Meanwhile, the Central Savings & Trust Company of Akron was expanding and looking for an outlet in Barberton. They offered to buy out Stettinius and his associates, and on November 12, 1910, an agreement was signed under which the group sold 72 percent of the stock of the Barberton Savings Bank to the Akron bank.[8] Accordingly, Stettinius resigned as president and director, and Barber and Harter resigned as vice presidents.[9]

Mining Ventures

Consolidated Flagstaff Mines Company

In 1906 Stettinius lent $15,000 to the proprietors of a gold mine in Alta, Utah, with an option to accept 9,000 shares of stock in payment of that loan if the engineer's report on the mine proved favorable. His partner in this agreement was Robert Pringle of Pringle, Fitch & Rankin on the Chicago Board of Trade.[10] Pringle's brother Thomas J. Pringle was president of Flagstaff.[11]

Stettinius learned that an attempt had been made by the proprietors to bribe the mining engineer who had previously examined the mine to alter his report. His reaction was predictably explosive. He

[6] PM 1, ERS to Barber, Oct. 1, 1910.
[7] PM 1, Barber to ERS, April 14, 1908.
[8] RS 758, Agreement of November 12, 1910.
[9] RS 758, ERS to Babcock & Wilcox, Nov. 12, 1910.
[10] PM 2, Flagstaff Mines file, ERS to Robert Pringle, July 31, 1906.
[11] PM 2, Flagstaff Mines file, P. D. Durant to ERS, Aug. 6, 1906; ERS to D. Edgar Kidwell, Nov. 17, 1906.

wrote his own mining engineer, Edgar Kidwell, "I would not touch the property on the basis of 2¢ a share payable in Confederate money." [12] Stettinius got his money out [13] and Kidwell subsequently discovered that the situation was even more chancy than suspected; the shaft had not even reached an ore deposit! [14]

Dolly Varden Mine

Stettinius entered into an agreement on October 14, 1907, in Reno with O. C. Barber and W. H. Landers as his associates and R. W. L. Stevenson as the grantor. This document set up the Dolly Varden Leasing Company to take over the lease of mining claims in Churchill County, Nevada. [15]

Charles C. Moore, the Babcock & Wilcox representative in San Francisco, wrote in late December 1907 to say that the mine at Rawhide, Nevada, had shut down. Further, gossip had it that Stevenson had gone to New York in a private railroad car and was staying at the plush Waldorf Astoria Hotel! [16] Moore wrote to Stettinius again three weeks later and announced that Stevenson was indeed a crook, [17] but the final blow came with the news from Landers, one of the partners, that now that the lease had been cancelled, the mine had begun to produce again. [18] Happily, Stettinius had only paid in $3,333.33. [19]

Streetcar Line Syndicates

The Indiana Syndicate

A factor in the success of the Stirling boilers was the proliferation in the first decade of the century of electric trolley-car companies in the United States. Otto von Schrader, reminiscing to the younger

---

[12] PM 2, Flagstaff Mines file, ERS to Kidwell, Nov. 17, 1906.
[13] PM 2, Flagstaff Mines file, ERS to the Germania National Bank, Milwaukee, Nov. 30, 1906.
[14] PM 2, Flagstaff Mines file, Kidwell to ERS, Dec. 20, 1906.
[15] PM 4, R. W. L. Stevenson file, agreement of Oct. 14, 1907.
[16] PM 4, Moore to ERS, Dec. 27, 1907.
[17] PM 4, Moore to ERS, Jan. 18, 1908.
[18] PM 4, Landers to ERS, June 12, 1908.
[19] PM 4, Stevenson to ERS, Oct. 13, 1907.

Stettinius, remembers that "I with some friends built and owned an Interurban Electric Road in Wisconsin and, as I recall, we equipped our power plant with Sterling [*sic*] boilers." [20]

It is difficult for us to realize from this distance in time the extraordinarily ambitious schemes and projects of these entrepreneurs. With a zeal comparable to that of the Dutch tulip speculators of an earlier century, they built a sprawling network of electrified tracks over great sections of the United States.

Stettinius, together with Stephen B. Fleming of Fort Wayne, put some money into this popular and financially fashionable business and participated in a syndicate whose lines included routes radiating from Indianapolis to Terre Haute, Lafayette, New Castle, and Richmond; the city lines in Terre Haute; and outlying lines to Martinsville, Brazil, and Danville, Illinois.[21] Their trolley cars not only plied the streets of urban Indianapolis and Terre Haute, but ran clanging and rattling through the cornfields and thin forests of the countryside. One reads of this era in Indiana with gentle nostalgia in the picnic chapters of Booth Tarkington's *Seventeen.* This enterprise, which Stettinius and his associates referred to as the Indiana Syndicate, appears in the financial periodicals as the Schoepf-McGowan Syndicate. W. Kelsey Schoepf of Cincinnati, a vast bulk of a man, was a major figure in midwest street railway financing in the period before World War I. Hugh J. McGowan represented the syndicate in Indianapolis. On March 23, 1907, the Terre Haute Indianapolis & Eastern Traction Company was incorporated to take over the various Indiana properties controlled by the syndicate.[22]

In 1908 Stettinius and Fleming grew restless and tried to sell their interests in the syndicate through Hugh McGowan.[23] They were apparently unsuccessful, but in 1910 the outlook for the syndicate improved.[24] The investors did not make a killing on trolley-car lines. Their original joint subscription was $25,000. On July 16, 1909, they sold $2,500 worth of shares to Charles Werner. On December 14, 1911, Fleming wrote Stettinius that as of that date each had an investment worth $7,467.57.[25] This is the last mention of their Indiana flier in the correspondence. Since they habitually

[20] Scrapbook II, von Schrader to ERS, Jr., April 9, 1938.
[21] PM 2, Fleming to ERS, Nov. 16, 1907.
[22] *Commercial & Financial Chronicle*, Supplements, "Street Railways," Oct. 19, 1907, p. 46.
[23] PM 2, Fleming to ERS, June 22, 1908.
[24] PM 2, Fleming to ERS, Jan. 29, 1910.
[25] PM 2, Fleming to ERS, Dec. 14, 1911.

discussed the Indiana Syndicate and the Ohio Syndicate in the same letter, and since only the Ohio Syndicate is mentioned in Fleming's letter of February 19, 1914,[26] we can infer that they had sold their Indiana interest before that date. The holding company, the Terre Haute Indianapolis & Eastern, continued to exist until the properties were sold to Midland United Subsidiaries at a foreclosure sale on June 23, 1931.[27]

The Ohio Syndicate

During this same period Fleming and Stettinius were also involved in the street railways of Ohio.[28] They invested in the Ohio Syndicate, another Schoepf-McGowan venture, whose principal holdings were combined in the Ohio Traction Company, which was formed May 22, 1905, and controlled a transportation network in and around Cincinnati.[29]

The managers of the syndicate were Ervin & Co., an investment house in Philadelphia.[30] As with the Indiana Syndicate, Stettinius became disenchanted with the undertaking and tried to sell out early in 1908. Fleming received assurances from Schoepf that he would try to find a buyer for their interest.[31] The attempt to unload the stock was not successful and the assessments continued to come in from Ervin & Co.[32]

In May 1912 Stettinius inquired of Fleming, "Is there any opportunity of cleaning up the Ohio Syndicate and getting our money out of that, even though at a loss?"[33] Two years later Fleming wrote summarizing the joint investment in the syndicate. They had paid in $13,192.68. Fleming was prepared to sell out for $7,500 cash.[34] Further information on Stettinius's participation in the Ohio Syndicate is lacking. But we do know that the Ohio Traction Company received permission to sell its assets to a stockholders' committee in June 1926.[35]

[26] PM 2, Fleming to ERS, Feb. 19, 1914.
[27] *Commercial & Financial Chronicle*, July 11, 1931, p. 288.
[28] PM 2, Fleming to ERS, Jan. 7, 1908.
[29] *Commercial & Financial Chronicle*, "Street Railways," p. 25.
[30] PM 2, Ervin & Co. to Fleming, Dec. 31, 1907.
[31] PM 2, Fleming to ERS, Jan. 7 and Jan. 14, 1908.
[32] PM 2, Ervin & Co. to Fleming, July 11, 1911; list of assessments, 1906–1910.
[33] PM 2, ERS to Fleming, May 9, 1912.
[34] PM 2, Fleming to ERS, Feb. 19, 1914.
[35] *Commercial & Financial Chronicle*, Supplements, "Power, Light and Railways," Oct. 30, 1926, p. 136.

Berghoff Brewing Association (Berghoff Products Company)

Another unsuccessful venture shared by Stettinius and Fleming was their 1908 investment in the Berghoff brewery, which was located in Fort Wayne, Indiana, Fleming's home town.[36] Apparently the company looked promising at the outset, because Stettinius induced a number of his friends to invest in it. On March 1, 1913, the stock was valued on Stettinius's private books at $150 a share. The books show holdings of 500 shares common and 500 shares preferred. Early in 1916, when Stettinius was consolidating his securities portfolio after election to partnership in J. P. Morgan & Co., he thought of selling his Berghoff stock, but there was no market for it.

Prohibition was being talked about but Fleming pooh-poohed the possibility. With remarkable foresight, Stettinius saw Prohibition coming and began urging the company to prepare for the inevitable by considering the manufacture and distribution of a substitute drink. In February 1916 he wrote to Harry B. Lusch, another stockholder:

There ought to be some way of putting the Company in shape so that they will be in a position to manufacture and put upon the market something that can be sold in lieu of beer. If people don't drink beer they will drink something else. There is quite a demand in England for what, I think, they call "tonic water." It is put up by Schweppe, and it is not only used extensively in England, but largely in the tropical countries. I have always thought that a big trade in a drink of this kind could be built up in this country.[37]

Several decades later the popularity in the United States of Schweppe's bore out the validity of this suggestion.

By March 24, 1917, the shares had declined in value and Stettinius wrote to the friends he had advised to invest in Berghoff and offered to take the stock off their hands. All refused the offer except Mary Winter, his long-time secretary at Diamond Match.[38]

Prohibition finally came in 1919, and with this the bottom dropped out of the stock. Ten shares of common were sold at auction on December 27, 1922, for twenty cents.[39] Stettinius commented on the state of Berghoff shares in a vein reminiscent of Mark Twain: "If you know of anybody in the western country,

[36] PM 2, Fleming to ERS, Jan. 14, 1908.
[37] RS 140, ERS to Lusch, Feb. 17, 1916.
[38] RS 515, memorandum of J. J. Bennett, Jan. 30, 1924.   [39] *Ibid.*

who has a yellow dog, or cow, or any live stock, or any other property that he wants to get rid of or would like to trade in, bear in mind that I have a very choice high-grade investment in the form of preferred and common stock of the Berghoff Products Company that I would like to get rid of." [40]

National Salvage Association

The most romantic of Stettinius's ventures was his investment in a company set up in Glasgow in 1911 to raise H.M.S. *Lutine*, a ship lost off the coast of Holland on October 9, 1799, with a cargo of treasure.[41] Earlier attempts had been made to recover the vessel, and one such adventure had even brought up the ship's bell, which hangs to this day in the main underwriting room of Lloyd's in London, where it is struck in a ritual gesture whenever a ship insured by Lloyd's is lost.

They might well have rung the *Lutine's* bell for the National Salvage Association before it ever put to sea. From the outset, the reports of misfortune under water sent out by the captain in charge of the expedition are masterpieces of tragic literature, as are the requests from the home office for more money from the stockholders. Stettinius was not a heavy investor. A list of his holdings in the company as of April 18, 1916, shows 560 shares of stock, £200 in debentures, and £300 in company bonds.[42] By May the company was in receivership.[43]

The International Agricultural Corporation

In 1913 the International Agricultural Corporation, a large-scale producer of fertilizers in which J. P. Morgan & Co. had an interest, was in trouble. C. J. Fay of White & Case, attorneys for the Morgan firm, tells how Stettinius became involved in this situation:

Our firm had met Mr. Stettinius in a business way while he was a receiver (with Mr. William H. Woodin as a co-receiver) of the Mc-Crum-Howell Co., which was reorganized as the "Richmond Radiator Company." In that matter my partner, Mr. Hartfield, was active.

Mr. Stettinius made contact with my partners, Mr. White and Mr.

---

[40] PS 27, Bartlett Hayward file, ERS to Lusch, Feb. 5, 1921.
[41] RS 351, National Salvage Association correspondence.
[42] RS 351, H. C. Cranz to W. A. Smith, April 18, 1916.
[43] RS 351, Smith to Cranz, May 3, 1916.

Case, about the middle of March, 1913. At that time I had been asked by Mr. Case if I knew anyone I could recommend for consideration by the International Agricultural Corporation directors for president of that corporation. I told Mr. Case I could think of only one person who would meet his requirements and that [was] Mr. Stettinius. I was doubtful whether Mr. Stettinius would feel free to leave the Diamond Match Company at that time, for I understood he had not completed his program for that company, to which he had come in 1907. However, I said to Mr. Case perhaps we could get him for a director and that *that* would be enough; for Mr. Stettinius was a "director who directed" and who insisted upon knowing everything about a company of which he was a director. I felt sure that if Mr. Case could secure Mr. Stettinius as a director, Mr. Stettinius could find someone who would be a desirable person for president. Mr. Case was sympathetic with my suggestion, and so I arranged for a luncheon meeting at the Down Town Association on March 18, 1913, at which Mr. Stettinius met Mr. Case. Mr. Case at once appreciated Mr. Stettinius' knowledge of the requirements for successful business management. Mr. Stettinius told Mr. Case he did not feel free to leave the Diamond Match Company, but said he might consider becoming a director. He also said he thought he could submit a name as a candidate for president. Mr. Stettinius asked Mr. Case for the balance sheets and the operating statements which he might study, and they were furnished promptly. The incident led to Mr. Stettinius becoming a director of International Agricultural Corporation, and his recommendation of Mr. Stephen B. Fleming, of Fort Wayne, for president was carried out.

During 1913 and 1914 Mr. Stettinius was very active in the councils of the International Agricultural Corporation and its rehabilitation. This led to his close association with Mr. Thomas Lamont and Mr. Henry P. Davison. The corporation took a turn very much for the better during that time.[44]

Fleming was apparently more effective as an executive than as an investor in breweries and trolley cars. Stettinius remained a director of the International Agricultural Corporation for the rest of his life.

This contact with Thomas Lamont led directly to Stettinius's engagement by J. P. Morgan & Co. to take on another "temporary" outside assignment two years later.

The materials remaining to us about Stettinius's private financial ventures are highly unsatisfactory in their incompleteness. On the other hand, it is only from them that we learn of the man's ap-

[44] Scrapbook II, C[harles] J. Fay, "Some Recollections of 'E.R.S.,'" Dec. 22, 1936, written at the request of ERS, Jr.

parently unlimited energy, and the multiplicity of his business interests and find out who his associates were.

There is one piece of evidence relating to Stettinius's finances during this period, however, that is extremely baffling in view of the modest amounts accounted for in his private files and the corporate records of the boiler and match companies. This evidence is contained in the account of Lewis E. Pierson, long an associate of Stettinius in the affairs of the Irving National Bank, of his own temporary departure from the Irving to accept the presidency of the grocery distributors Austin, Nichols & Co. and his attempt in 1912 to interest Stettinius in investing in the expansion of that concern:

As such a program would require the intensive, intelligent application of a number of able men, LEP mentioned to his associates the possibility of Mr. Stettinius being interested, and with one of his associates LEP lunched with Mr. Stettinius at his beautiful home in Dongan Hills, Staten Island, and discussed the matter.

Mr. Stettinius was interested and frankly stated he had about eight hundred thousand dollars and was looking for a place to use some of that money and his services to advantage, and that the grocery line rather attracted him and the program in mind seemed feasible.

Due, however, to opposition amongst LEP's associates, who as little men were fearful of dominating personalities, the invitation was not pressed and the opportunity for another close business association between LEP and Mr. Stettinius was lost.[45]

Could Pierson have exaggerated the amount of money Stettinius had available to invest in 1912? If the figure of $800,000 is accurate, we can only conclude that more of the miscellaneous concerns prospered than we know about.

[45] Scrapbook II, "Lewis E. Pierson's Recollections of Edward R. Stettinius," p. 1. Covering letter, Pierson to ERS, Jr., Aug. 27, 1937.

V. *Staten Island* (*1905–1916*)

WHILE major manufacturing plants of both Babcock & Wilcox and Diamond Match remained in the midwest, and Chicago continued to be an important business center for the two corporations, the executive offices were finally moved to New York City. Stettinius came to New York in 1905.[1]

The Stettiniuses and their four children settled at Dongan Hills on Staten Island, in the Borough of Richmond. Staten Island was rural and unspoiled in those days before the Verrazano Narrows Bridge opened it up for speculative real-estate "development," and the Stettinius family liked it. On his return from England in the spring of 1908 Stettinius wrote to Charles T. McCormick, "My wife and children are quite well and I think are so well pleased with their surroundings here that they would be unhappy at the mere suggestion of being compelled to go back to Chicago." [2]

Staten Island was an ideal place for a commuter to downtown Manhattan, with the trip to the city requiring only a scenic ferry ride and a short drive in a carriage [3]—later in the chauffeur-driven Peerless [4]—to and from the landing at St. George. C. J. Fay, a friend and neighbor, talks about this period in his reminiscences:

Mr. Stettinius once told me that his first visit to Dongan Hills was on a Saturday afternoon, on some occasion, and at the time of that visit he was about to settle upon a residence in Long Island. The visit that day to Dongan Hills was at the Cromwell place, and Mr. and Mrs. Stettinius were so charmed with the locality that before leaving Dongan Hills that day Mr. Stettinius arranged to lease the Cromwell place. From then on Mr. Stettinius was very fond of the locality. I recall very distinctly years later, when the family had removed to Locust Valley, he was disinclined to hear from me the story of how beautiful Dongan Hills looked that May morning; everything was in full bloom, even the apple tree which had been brought up from Stapleton for his children

---

[1] PM 3, ERS to Arthur Man, Dec. 19, 1905.
[2] PM 5, bound letters, No. 84, ERS to McCormick, April 14, 1908.
[3] PM 3, ERS to Man, Dec. 19, 1905.
[4] PM 5, bound letters, No. 23, ERS to Peerless Motor Car Co., March 16, 1908.

to climb. He stopped me, saying "Don't talk to me about that. Dongan Hills is the most beautiful spot in the metropolitan district."

At that time Mr. Stettinius was President of the Diamond Match Company and was extremely active in and out of business hours. He was the life of any group of which he was a member.

I recall the attention he gave to his children in making sure that they acquired the art of riding. It used to be a very pleasant sight to see him and his four children out riding together.

Mr. Stettinius was very active in the Country Club at that time (1907). He played some golf, but not very well. In fact, he told me one time that he had asked his caddy if there was anyone who played worse than he did and the caddy had said, "Yes, Mr. Fay." [5]

In 1908 Stettinius decided to build a house on property he had bought at the corner of Todt Hill and Four Corners Roads. He engaged the architect Charles W. Leavitt, Jr., of 230 Broadway, to draw plans and sketches for the new house. But things went badly and in July 1908 Stettinius fired Leavitt. He asked for all the drawings to date and for a bill.[6] He had already found a new architect, Percy Griffin of Fifth Avenue and 26th Street, who pleased him more. There was no pause in the proceedings. The designs for the house were completed and construction began almost at once.[7]

The Stettinius house stood in thirteen acres of lawn and garden; it overlooked the Richmond County Country Club and had, in the words of a later sales brochure, "a commanding view of New York Harbor." [8] When completed, it cost between $75,000 and $80,000.[9] The house was Georgian in style. Brick with white trim, three stories high, and T-shaped in plan, it would have been exceedingly handsome had not the façade been marred by a balustraded two-story semicircular portico too tall for its own breadth. There were spacious living rooms on the main floor and nine master bedrooms and five baths on the two upper floors, with seven servants' bedrooms. The walls of the entrance hall were decorated with the classic Zuber scenic wallpaper "El Dorado," which shows characteristic views of Egypt, Germany with a ruined castle, Italy with umbrella-shaped stone pines and cypresses, Istanbul with minarets and a kiosk, and a forbidding bold, dry landscape that might

[5] Scrapbook II, Fay, "Recollections."
[6] PM 5, bound letters, No. 442, ERS to Leavitt, July 6, 1908.
[7] PM 5, bound letters, No. 486, ERS to Griffin, July 16, 1908.
[8] *A Gentleman's Home* (New York, n.d.). This eight-page brochure was lent to me kindness of Mr. Vasa K. Bracher of Staten Island.
[9] PM 1, A. B. Ashforth, Inc. file, ERS to W. P. Belknap, Nov. 21, 1913.

be Mexico or Spain. The living room was panelled in dark wood and furnished mostly in massive seventeenth-century English style, with an upright piano, some oriental rugs, and—characteristic of the first decade of the twentieth century—a pair of reproductions of Renaissance bronzes, one of them Giovanni da Bologna's *Hermes.*

Fay recalled, "Mr. and Mrs. Stettinius lavishly landscaped the place with shrubs and trees, converting what had been wasteland into a park."[10] Under the direction of the gardener Fred MacMaster, the place was a mass of flowers.[11]

A succession of cars in the garage reflected the changing styles and the gradually increasing financial success of their owner. The 1907 Peerless was replaced with a new Peerless the following year. Stettinius complained to the Peerless Motor Car Company about an ill-fitting mudguard and the excessive charge of $7.50 for monograms on the doors.[12] In 1911 a Delaunay-Belleville was added. Two years later Stettinius bought a Packard car, and in 1915 a Stevens-Duryea.[13] The following spring he bought a landaulet body to replace the original body on the Stevens-Duryea, but the car ultimately came to grief at the corner of 52nd Street and Madison Avenue on October 2, 1916, in a collision with the horse and cart of one John Zambricky.[14]

In 1907 Stettinius was running a boiler company and a small-town bank, helping to run a match company, managing his own private investments, and travelling to Chicago, to Barberton, and to London. Naturally, with his irrepressible energy, he could not resist the temptation to engage in business activity at Staten Island, even though it was theoretically the place he escaped to at night from the business worries of Manhattan. With Arthur Man, manager of the Cromwell Property, he invested in the Dongan Hills Realty Company in 1907 and began a long association with that concern.[15] Upon becoming a member of the Dongan Hills community Stettinius also threw himself into the affairs of the Dongan Hills Improvement Society and the Richmond County Country Club with his usual zest. He was nominated as a director of the

[10] Scrapbook II, Fay, "Recollections."

[11] RS 358, Frederick MacMaster correspondence.

[12] PM 5, bound letters, Nos. 23, 446, ERS to Peerless Motor Car Company, March 16, 1908, and July 8, 1908.

[13] RS 451, Automobiles file, Ashforth, Inc. to ERS, April 20, 1915; Ashforth bill, May 26, 1913; ERS to Ashforth, Inc., May 11, 1915.

[14] RS 451, Automobiles file, Ashforth, Inc. to ERS, April 21, 1916; PM 1, O. H. Droege to ERS, Nov. 1, 1916.

[15] PM 3, ERS to Man, May 31, 1907, and following letters.

Country Club for the first time in March 1908.[16] Fay tells us that he became president of the club in 1911 and proceeded at once to reorganize it, revise the constitution and bylaws, form a corporation to buy up and preserve the neighborhood, and expand the club's facilities.

In July 1913 Stettinius wrote to Fred W. Abbot, a former neighbor, "You ask how the Club is getting on and if I am as popular as ever. The Club is all right, but if there ever was an unpopular man on Dongan Hills, it is yours truly. I have had the hardihood to insist upon certain rules being followed and, as a result, am looked upon as a stern, unyielding and brutal task master. It would be truly a pleasure to run a man's Club. I hope God will forgive me for ever having undertaken to run a Club in which the gentler sex plays as active a part as they do in the Richmond County." [17]

The following month he reported on the family—the Stettinii, he sometimes called them: "We are all fairly well at home, although the Madam is not in very good shape. I am trying very hard to make arrangements to take her away for two or three weeks, and will do so next week if I can secure accommodations at White Sulphur Springs. Carrington returned last week from a trip through Colorado Springs, Cripple Creek, Salt Lake City, Butte, Montana, Yellowstone Park, Glacier Park, etc. He is in fine shape. He and Isabel are spending the week with some friends in their camp and will then go to Southampton for a week or ten days and will join us on the 1st of Sept." [18] Stettinius planned to take them all to Europe in the summer of 1914. Passage was reserved on the *Mauretania* for July 7, with the thought of coming back on the same vessel on August 22 or on the *Lusitania* a week later.[19] The war altered these arrangements.

Life on Staten Island continued its pleasant course on the eve of war. Stettinius wrote to Abbot on June 17, "Carrington is back at Pomfret and is delighted to be with his friends and in the country again. Edward is the same as ever, getting along fine. He went to the Polo game yesterday and was as proud as a peacock over the possession of a Polo ball on which Capt. Cheape had written his name with a Fountain pen. He met all the fellows on the English team and was literally bursting with pride. He was very much tickled that Lord Wimbourne addressed him as 'Old Top'. He says the American team were 'beefy', and that Larry Waterbury was a

---

[16] PM 5, bound letters, No. 44, ERS to Charles C. Bowring.
[17] PM 1, ERS to Abbot, July 8, 1913.
[18] PM 1, ERS to Abbot, Aug. 13, 1913.
[19] PM 1, ERS to Abbot, June 17, 1914.

'bounder'. I guess he is right. Isabel is fine and keeps me moving. You can always gamble that that young woman will have her own way and the joke of it is that other people don't know it."

He added a sprightly comment about a neighbor: "Everything is about the same at Dongan Hills. Your friend, Mrs. W., carries her nose as high as ever and is apparently just as proud of the wart on her knee as she was when you used to know her. Of course, I don't know that she has a wart on her knee, but she must have some concealed charms to justify so much self-satisfaction. The Lord knows she hasn't any charms that are visible to the naked eye." [20]

When the war came Stettinius wrote: "Even if I did not sympathize with the English because I love them and, moreover, because I think they are right, I would do so because I believe that if any harm comes to them this country will surely suffer, and will be compelled to either suffer indignities (or even worse) at Germany's hands, or will be forced into war, for which it is not in any way prepared. I believe the sooner this country as well as England, adopts a policy of involuntary service in the Army and Navy, the better will it be for the entire civilized world." [21]

Stettinius was busy with financial matters and his young family during the Staten Island period, but he always seemed to have some energy to spare. He became interested in the career of John Powell, the pianist, and managed his business affairs and tried to get him concert engagements, while the Steinway firm acted as his concert managers.[22]

William Carrington Stettinius was a student at Pomfret School in Pomfret, Connecticut, before he went to the University of Virginia. As a result of this connection, the directors of the school invited Stettinius to join the board, and he served in 1915 and 1916.[23]

---

[20] *Ibid.* [21] PM 1, ERS to Abbot, Nov. 12, 1914.
[22] PM 4, John Powell file, Ernest Urchs, Steinway and Sons, to ERS, June 17, 1913, and April 26, 1916.
[23] PM 4, ERS to William B. Olmsted, Oct. 22, 1914, and following letters.

VI. *The War: J. P. Morgan & Co. and Munitions Buying for the Allies* (*1915–1917*)

IN THE fall of 1914 the European War, which had begun in the late summer, was going badly for the Allies. Only the unexpected and brief resistance of the Belgians had prevented the success of the German general staff's carefully devised von Schlieffen Plan for the rapid conquest of France.

Particularly pressing were the problems of financing Allied purchases abroad and of supplying the armies in the field with munitions. The Allies were dependent on two sources of funds for their foreign buying. The first was the shipping of gold, and more than a billion dollars in gold was transferred to the United States up to the time of this country's entry into the war. The second source was the selling in the United States of American securities held by private investors in the Allied nations. This also was undertaken on a large scale. J. P. Morgan & Co. were large-scale participants in the financing of the Allied cause. The partners soon saw that the two immediate sources of money could not be counted on indefinitely. They proposed that the Allies borrow from the American financial community and that the firm assume the responsibility for this borrowing.[1] An agreement was finally reached in principle, but it was agreed that the offering of a large bond issue would best be postponed until the time was ripe.[2]

The problem of the actual purchasing with the credits to be provided was still unresolved. The memorandum outlining the history of their purchasing activities for the Allies which was distributed by J. P. Morgan & Co. in April 1922 describes the confused situation in munitions procurement in 1914:

The sudden outbreak of war in 1914 found the Allied nations completely unprepared in material and supplies. In the confusion which followed, England, France, Italy and Russia turned to the United States as the one great neutral power from whose resources prompt assistance might be expected.

[1] Thomas W. Lamont, *Henry P. Davison: The Record of a Useful Life* (New York and London, 1933), pp. 186–87.
[2] *Ibid.,* pp. 189–91.

At the outset requirements were limited. Raw materials, such as copper, foodstuffs, etc., were eagerly sought, as were horses and mules. There was also urgent inquiry for such manufactured goods for military purposes as clothing, equipment, etc., which were required in excess of home production. But a large trade in munitions did not develop, and was not even foreseen, during the last four months of 1914. Some orders for rifles and small arms ammunition were placed in the United States by the British and French within that period, and the British also ordered some field artillery and artillery ammunition. The Russians, too, carried on negotiations looking toward the purchase of rifles, but it was not until late in the year that the demand became urgent for munitions and particularly for explosives. Even then the policy of the Allies as to purchases of munitions in the United States was necessarily vague, as their military and industrial programmes had not been determined. When these military programmes were finally fixed, it was uncertain as to what deliveries could be expected from home production. Accordingly, the various Allies were unable at that time to be at all specific as to what was required from America in the way of finished munitions.

As time went on, however, and as it became apparent that the War would be of long duration, the British, French and Russians began to compete actively in the American markets for all kinds of commodities as well as munitions. Representatives of these Governments visited the United States to make purchases; in addition purchases were being made in Europe by the respective War Offices from dealers in American supplies and from representatives of American producers. Inquiries which originated abroad, and those which were set on foot by Government representatives in the United States, were frequently passed along to brokers and middlemen who multiplied rapidly in numbers, and many of whom endeavored to anticipate requirements which had not even been expressed by the Governments themselves. The duplication of inquiries and the extreme activity of the vast horde of "war brokers" was having a demoralizing effect upon prices and deliveries and was increasing the confusion which was, to a certain extent, unavoidable under any circumstances.

Not only did complete lack of co-operation exist between different governments, but there was frequently active competition, sometimes in evidence between different departments of the same government. The Allied Governments and their representatives experienced all the difficulties caused by ignorance of American markets, of American concerns and their standing, credit and ability to perform. Also, they lacked acquaintance with business usages, customs and procedure in the United States, and the French, Italians and Russians had the additional handicap imposed by the use of a foreign tongue.

On their side, the American manufacturers were unfamiliar with the problems of munitions production. But the excessively depressed industrial conditions of 1913 and 1914 made many so eager for business that some were disposed to undertake munitions contracts without a full realization of their inherent difficulties.

From every standpoint the situation had become serious, and the conditions were rapidly growing worse as the intricacies of commerce in munitions became more pronounced, with the increasing complexity of requirements, specifications, deliveries, etc. Every factor tended to encourage highly speculative prices, to demoralize American industries, to curtail production and to delay deliveries.[3]

The radical and unexpected departure of the banking house of J. P. Morgan & Co. into the field of munitions purchasing evolved slowly. The firm had already taken part in conversations relating to the Allied war effort. As early as September 1914 Willard Straight received an inquiry from the French government: Would J. P. Morgan & Co. purchase ten thousand horses in the United States?[4] The specific subject of munitions buying came up in the course of Davison's conversations in London about financing. David Lloyd George, Chancellor of the Exchequer, put forward the bold suggestion that J. P. Morgan & Co. undertake the task of purchasing the materials of war for the British government. Edwin S. Montagu joined Lloyd George in urging Davison to discuss this suggestion with Sir George Gibb of the Army Council, the body in charge of procurement for the British Army. Henry Davison, the Morgan emissary, went along most reluctantly with this idea. He held that J. P. Morgan & Co. were financiers, were not looking for business, and had neither the experience nor the organization for going into the purchasing field.[5] On the other hand, his prime worry from the outset was the chaos that had developed in the American market to the detriment of both the United States economy and the Allied purchasers frantically bidding for supplies as their situation worsened. He was finally convinced that this confusion could best be resolved by concentrating Allied purchases in the Morgan firm. Accordingly, he entered into negotiations with the British government to establish an agency agreement. The drastic proposal that the firm take on the new and unfamiliar function of munitions procurement set the partners in New York to looking for a man to run the new program if and when it was agreed to.

[3] RS 773, memorandum, "Regarding Activities of J. P. Morgan & Co. as Purchasing Agents for the British and French Governments," April 17, 1922.
[4] [F. Carrington Weems], *America and Munitions*, 2 vols. (New York, privately printed, 1923), I, 27.
[5] *Ibid.*, I, 30.

Stettinius and the Export Department

At this time Stettinius was approached by representatives of J. P. Morgan & Co., with Thomas Lamont as their spokesman. Lamont told Stettinius that Davison was then in London discussing with the British government plans for helping the Allies to finance the war and to coordinate their purchases in the United States. If the negotiations proved fruitful would Stettinius be willing to direct the coordinating activity?

Lamont later described the encounter: "When I explained the situation to him I found him greatly in sympathy with the idea and eager to coöperate." [6]

It was not until January 15, 1915, that the British Commercial Agency Agreement with J. P. Morgan & Co. was signed.[7] F. Carrington Weems says that the signing did not come a moment too soon: "On the sixth of January, 1915, more than a week before the Agreement was actually signed, the first official inquiry had arrived. It indicated the urgent importance of obtaining early deliveries of trinitrotoluol, the standard British explosive. Other inquiries had to do with picric acid and its availability. With such inquiries Mr. Stettinius began at once to deal." [8]

On the day of the signing Stettinius moved into the Morgan Building at 23 Wall Street and went to work. Fay gives an account of this beginning: "He had an office on the third floor, opening out on the inner court. He at once took off his coat and vest and plunged into the work. He was perfectly tireless. I recall his remark to me that Mr. Lamont had not appreciated how much work there was to be done. He said to me, 'Tom Lamont said I could come over from the Diamond Match at eleven o'clock and be out early in the afternoon. Look at me! I come here at nine o'clock every day and stay until nearly midnight.' " [9]

Stettinius described his new routine in a letter to George W. Paton of Bryant & May, the British match company: "I have . . . so arranged my program and organization that I feel that I can handle the situation all right if I can stand the strain physically. My hours are pretty long. I manage to dispose of a good deal of the match business by 9 or 9:15 in the morning and then go to my offices with J. P. Morgan & Co. where I remain until almost any

[6] Lamont, *Davison*, p. 227.   [7] Weems, *Munitions*, I, 33–36.
[8] *Ibid.*, I, 52.   [9] Scrapbook I, Fay, "Recollections."

hour in the evening or night, as circumstances require. Of course, during the day I am in touch with the offices of the Match Company and meet my colleagues for discussion and conference whenever necessary." [10]

Fay noted, "It was remarkable how immediately Mr. Stettinius made his strong personality felt at 23 Wall. I recall distinctly how, when we were working under high pressure on a picric acid contract for the French Government, early in February, 1915, Mr. Stettinius was pressing for completion of the contract. It was already after 7:30 P.M. and we were working at full speed. Suddenly the door opened and Mr. Davison looked in and said, 'Mr. Stettinius, may I leave now [?]' For one of the heads of the firm of Morgan so to address Mr. Stettinius after his very short stay there revealed how soon the firm recognized Mr. Stettinius as already in complete charge and leadership of that stirring work." [11]

Stettinius's grasp of problems and gifts for handling the job impressed the partners at once, as Davison wrote to Morgan, Grenfell & Co. on February 3, 1915:

All the orders that have thus far been received for the British Government have been handled through the organization of Stettinius. This organization consists at present of Stettinius, who is occupying a room in our building, assisted by W.E.S. Strong and such secretaries, stenographers, etc., as are necessary. . . . Stettinius is acting in the capacity of a broker with a commission not yet agreed upon. It has been our idea that some time in the future we would determine the amount of compensation to Mr. Stettinius and his associates, which will be figured in the way of a commission to be paid by the British Government. . . . we are more than pleased with the way the work has progressed thus far, and particularly pleased with Stettinius, who has shown himself to be quite a remarkable man. He places himself entirely in our hands, and we can conceive of no question with him regarding proper remuneration. . . .[12]

The joke was current at the time on Wall Street that this brokerage arrangement with a percentage—though still undetermined—of the gross amount of purchases going to Stettinius was potentially so advantageous to him that the partners of J. P. Morgan hastily re-

---

[10] PM 1, ERS to Paton, Feb. 2, 1915.
[11] Scrapbook I, Fay, "Recollections."
[12] RS 679, "Memorandum Setting Forth in Outline Such Information as is Available in the Files in Regard to Mr. Stettinius' Relations with the Commercial Agency," n.d. pp. 2–3. This document (hereafter cited as "Commercial Agency Memorandum") was almost certainly prepared by F. Carrington Weems.

vised the agreement lest he earn more than they.[13] An examination of Stettinius's federal income tax returns for the years 1915 and 1917 gives support to this contention. Federal income tax figures are available for 1914, 1915, and 1917. In 1914 Stettinius's net income was reported as $97,173.49. The largest item was salary, $46,000 from the Diamond Match Company and $10,000 from Babcock & Wilcox, totaling $56,000. Dividends received amounted to $45,041.08, interest received to $15,287.79. The following year was the first of his tour of duty as head of the Export Department of J. P. Morgan. In 1915 his net income rose to $858,856.84, of which the largest single item was $500,000 from the British Government Commercial Agency as a share in purchasing commissions. From the French he received $97,500. Profit realized from the sale of securities came to $153,130.67. Other items were salary, $48,033.33; dividends, $42,535.50; profit from the Watson syndicate of the International Agricultural Corporation, $13,108.70; interest from bonds, $1,705.22; and interest from notes and bank accounts, $1,232.80.

The figures for 1916 are missing. In 1917 Stettinius had a net income of $448,320.22. This year he received an income from his partnership in J. P. Morgan & Co. and Drexel & Co., its Philadelphia house, of $265,690.65, with no commissions so labelled from the Allied governments. Salary and director's fees from the same source amounted to $30,000. The other figures were: dividends, $129,-522.03; profit from the sale of stocks, $33,251.05; bond interest (tax free), $4,472.50; interest and rent, etc., $1,408.80.[14] Stettinius took the relaxed position throughout this whole period that whatever the firm wanted to do, whatever compensation they cared to give him, would be entirely acceptable to him.[15]

He built up his staff as he went along. Early associates in the newly created Export Department of J. P. Morgan & Co. were William E. S. Strong, consulting engineer, in charge of heavy equipment purchases (steel billets, airplanes, locomotives, chemicals); Francis H. McKnight of the Morgan firm, financial officer (comptroller); Frank Enos, in charge of correspondence with prospective contractors and brokers; and Walter L. Clark of Niles-Bement-Pond Corporation, a machine-tool man, who developed sources of supply for rifles and advised shell manufacturers.

By May 1915 it became apparent that everyone had underesti-

[13] ERS aide James F. Mimnaugh, interviewed April 22, 1968.

[14] PS 1, federal income tax returns for 1914, 1915, and 1917. Gross income 1914 was $116,648.37; 1915, $869,510.64; 1917 form shows only net figure.

[15] RS 679, "Commercial Agency Memorandum," p. 4.

mated the magnitude of the task at hand and the pressures that
would build up within the Export Department. The staff of the department was greatly expanded. George A. Graham of John H.
Graham & Company, the hardware company, was hired to look
after hardware purchases; Leland L. Summers, consulting engineer with his own firm, an old associate of Stettinius from Babcock & Wilcox, joined the staff to look after shell manufacture, and
with him came Thomas J. White of Yale & Towne Manufacturing
Company. Waddell Catchings was hired as assistant to Stettinius;
George B. French, a railroad executive from the Pacific Northwest,
became food and livestock buyer; and Harry B. Prindle, engineer,
was engaged as Strong's assistant and James D. Rennick as assistant
to Graham.[16]

Stettinius organized the staff of the Export Department in such a
way as to utilize the particular experience and gifts of each member. To each was assigned responsibility for inquiries and requisi-
tions in areas with which he was familiar.[17] B. C. Forbes described
this group in the *American Magazine* of September 1917:

Around him Stettinius had drawn a score or more of large-caliber
engineering, manufacturing and commercial experts, and a total organization of a hundred and seventy-five men, not one of whom, not even a
single clerk, had been selected haphazardly, but because of his enthusiasm, his aptitude, and his indifference to the clock. Some of the
men in the organization formed what they termed the "S.O.S." which,
translated, means, "Slaves of Stettinius."

"Yes," admitted Mr. Stettinius, "that is what they have called themselves, but there never was a more willing and more cheerful body of
slaves. Every one of us worked all day and late into the evening. If any
fellow quit at nine o'clock at night he was usually congratulated by the
others on being able to take a half-holiday. I have seen something of
different organizations of workers, but I have never in my life known
such sustained, white-heat enthusiasm, such determination to get things
done, such disregard of personal convenience and comfort, such self-
sacrifice.

"Only once did I receive a mild shock, and that was when one of our
most promising young men came and asked me if he could have the next
Saturday off. This was an unprecedented request. I asked him if it was
absolutely necessary. He became confused, but repeated that he would
like very much to go if it could be arranged. 'Can't you postpone what
you have in mind?' I asked. 'Not very well,' he said, blushing furiously.

[16] Weems, *Munitions*, II, Appendix III, "A Summary of the Formation of
the Export Department."
[17] *Ibid.*, I, 54.

'What do you want to do?' I asked. 'I am going to get married!' he blurted out. I hastened to assure him that he must take not a day, but a week or two off. 'No, sir,' he replied, in a tone of finality, 'my fiancée and I are both too strongly pro-Ally in our sympathies to be willing to take our honeymoon until the war is over.'

"That reveals the *esprit de corps* which permeated the whole force from bottom to top." [18]

C. J. Fay added to this picture: "We all called Mr. Stettinius, 'Chief'. That very word reflected our absolute loyalty to and our affection for him. No one worked harder than he did. No one was more just than he was. He made tremendous demands and expected us to fulfill them. We reveled in our work, for we were working for one who worked harder than any of us and one who was our leader by 'Divine right'. The dinners Mr. Stettinius used to give the whole organization were wonderful. I recall one dinner Mr. Stettinius gave at Sherry's, where we were placed around an enormous circular table. Each one of us was 'adorned' with an iron chain necklace from which hung an Iron Cross, a l'Allemande." [19]

George E. Foley, secretary to Morgan partner Dwight Morrow, recalled his initiation into the "Slaves of Stettinius," his first encounter with the new man in the Morgan office: "He grinned as I entered, and shook hands and asked me to sit down. He said, 'I understand Mr. Morrow has turned you over to me while he is away. When can you start?' I replied that I had a great deal of cleaning up to do for Mr. Morrow, although probably by working tonight and tomorrow (Sunday) I could finish by Tuesday. He said: 'Can't you make it sooner?' – 'Well, perhaps Monday.' – 'Can't you do better than that?' I said, 'Hell, yes! I'll start now,' and he laughed and said, 'That's what I wanted you to say all the time!' "

Foley provided another personal detail in describing Stettinius at work: "When dictating, he would pace the floor nervously, invariably smoking a cigar, which he always inserted into a paper and quill holder." [20]

By the summer of 1915, J. P. Morgan & Co. decided that the brokerage arrangement with Stettinius and his organization was not a satisfactory way to handle matters and they would, according to their letter of June 8, 1915, to the London firm, themselves pay the

[18] B. C. Forbes, "The Biggest Buyer in the World," *American Magazine*, Sept. 1917, pp. 15–82.
[19] Scrapbook I, Fay, "Recollections."
[20] Scrapbook I, Foley to ERS, Jr., Sept. 18, 1933.

expenses of the purchasing organization.[21] By the fall it was obvious that Stettinius could not carry on several jobs simultaneously, so he handed in his resignation as president of the match company and withdrew from Babcock & Wilcox.

In his interview with Forbes, Stettinius gave a vivid picture of the situation at the Export Department:

"The Morgan office was overrun, not with hundreds, but thousands of people anxious to sell all kinds of things. There were manufacturers, both responsible and irresponsible, of clothing, machinery, hardware, chemicals, surgical instruments, automobiles and what not; there were merchants, commission agents, horse dealers, inventors, and war brokers by the score. After listening to the stories of the typical war broker, you would have thought that four or five million rifles, one or two billion rounds of rifle cartridges, and millions of pounds of picric acid and powder could be picked up almost anywhere for immediate delivery. Everything was in a state of chaos.

"Obviously, the things to be undertaken at the start were to ascertain the requirements of the British Government, to determine just what munitions or materials could be furnished by America, and, finally, to separate the responsible from the irresponsible offerers of goods here.

"How to determine the needs of the British Government and arrive at a decision as to what work should be done at home and what work attempted here, how, in short, to straighten out the thousand and one matters at the other end, and convey detailed information to us with the brevity demanded by cable dispatches was a task calling for a rare order of ability. Fortunately, one of the Morgan firm in London, Charles F. Whigham, rose to the occasion splendidly, and whatever success has attended the work here has been due in large measure to the services he rendered and has rendered persistently throughout. His grasp of the whole situation, his ability to understand the needs of the different departments in London, his skill in suggesting what could be done here, resulted time after time in enabling us to forge a link in a chain which otherwise would not have been made effective.

"We thus had right off the first essential factor for securing intelligent coöperation between the British War Department and us."[22]

Relations between J. P. Morgan & Co. and the British War Office were a model of mutual understanding and accommodation and forbearance for the duration of their close association.[23] The Export

[21] F. Carrington Weems, an untitled typescript of thirty-six pages in the possession of Mrs. Weems (hereafter cited as Weems, *Memorandum*), p. 4.
[22] Forbes, "The Biggest Buyer in the World," p. 15.
[23] Weems, *Munitions*, I, 73–75.

Department did relatively little purchasing for the British Admiralty, which had developed its own sources of supply.[24]

Relations with the French government, while largely amicable, were never as close as those with the British. Davison, who was handling the negotiations, suggested a purchasing agreement similar to the agency agreement with Britain. Nothing came of these discussions at the time.[25] Finally, on April 30, 1915, the French government asked J. P. Morgan, the senior partner, if the firm would take over their purchasing in the United States. The arrangement became effective on May 3, 1915, but there never was any formal commercial agency contract between the firm and the French government.[26]

The general mechanics of the Export Department's business under Stettinius's direction were worked out early, but procedures remained flexible throughout. The Allied governments cabled their inquiries about the availability of specific war materials. The Export Department provided the necessary information on sources of supply, prices, market conditions, the reliability of suppliers, and offers to sell the commodities in question. Upon receiving authorization, the Export Department negotiated with the suppliers, secured the best possible terms for the Allies, and placed the orders. Orders were reported back to Europe and the formal execution of the contract followed. Finally, the Export Department acted as disbursing agents for paying the suppliers.[27] But these somewhat obvious functions comprised only the visible tip of the iceberg. The Export Department did much more. They encouraged the creation of new productive capacity for needed items. They helped prime contractors find subcontractors. They helped locate financial backing for suppliers. They maintained an exhaustive file of information on all existing and potential sources of supply. They expedited the gathering of competitive bids for contracts. Although specifically relieved of the responsibility for transportation of goods purchased, they found cargo space on carriers by land and sea. They made countless useful suggestions about technical cooperation between the buying governments and suppliers.[28]

Forbes drew from Stettinius a detailed description of how the Export Department worked:

"A large proportion of the stuff the British wanted here during the first twelve months of the war had never been produced in the United States before, outside of our own arsenals, except on a very limited

[24] *Ibid.*, I, 73, 77.   [25] *Ibid.*, I, 39–43.   [26] *Ibid.*, I, 45.
[27] *Ibid.*, I, 53–72.   [28] *Ibid.*, I, 349–54.

extent. Our initial problem was how to start up the wholesale manufacture of munitions. Existing plants were totally inadequate; but how and where should we begin to develop others? To what extent could concerns making other things transform their machinery and equipment into plants for the output of munitions? Would steel plants be the most suitable, or automobile factories, or locomotive works, or car building works—or what?

"We were embarking on an uncharted sea. We had no compass, no precedents, to guide us. It was an absolutely new industrial problem. It not only involved many millions of dollars, but possibly the lives of thousands of men; serious mistakes would occasion delays and dangers of far more moment than the heavy money loss. Some plan, some principle, some policy had to be adopted, and adopted quickly.

"After careful study, we decided that in placing war contracts we would have to be guided less by the nature of any concern's product than by the character of the men at its head. We figured that the layout of any plant, the design of the buildings or the kind of machinery in it was of minor importance to the degree of success that had been exhibited in running it. In other words, bricks and mortar, machines and tools, were not what we went by, but the brains that administered these things.

"Through the knowledge and experience and ramifications of those in the Morgan firm, we had a good idea of who was who and what was what throughout the manufacturing world. We knew the men who had demonstrated unusual ability in different lines, and we got into touch with them, no matter what they were producing. Meanwhile, we were selecting men to negotiate for the purchase of the varied materials we were required to purchase; and in three months had perfected an organization."

Forbes went on to ask, "What qualities and qualifications did you particularly seek in the men you gathered around you to look after the buying of materials?"

"First of all, we made sure of a man's absolute integrity, loyalty, and ability to keep his mouth shut.

"We believed that men who had had practical experience along engineering and manufacturing lines could more effectively negotiate for the purchase of munitions than a man with a purely commercial experience. A man of technical training who has successfully supervised or conducted manufacturing operations in any line, and who has learned how to handle men, is usually able to deal successfully with new problems.

"As we negotiated, say, for shells, we interviewed the concerns who had applied for contracts—we had been flooded by requests for orders. Also, we communicated with companies and firms whom we knew had the right kind of management.

"Usually we invited each concern to bring in its technical man, the man who would have direct charge of the work. An important part of our duty was to size up each of these technical men, to determine whether or not they had the earmarks of success.

"In many cases where contracts had been solicited, we found that the would-be manufacturers knew little about what the work called for. Brokers and middlemen of all sorts and conditions plagued us; but we abolished all this bother by refusing to deal with any but principals, for we concluded that the broker was a handicap to the Government, and that any company that was not strong enough to rely on its own position and its own record to come and get businesss was not likely to merit confidence." [29]

The daily schedule of the Export Department began with an exhausting morning and afternoon of receiving the multitude of manufacturers' representatives, brokers, and others wanting war contracts. The staff dined at the office. After dinner the real work began. The detailed cablegrams to the British and French governments were composed. These dealt with the whole range of business: inquiries, negotiations, contracts, purchases. Stettinius wrote the important cables himself and edited those prepared by his staff, who lined up to submit their draft cables for his inspection. He also read the incoming cables and distributed them appropriately among his subordinates. It was very much a one-man show, with the concentration of purchasing in Stettinius's hands. The authority and responsibility were further concentrated in that it was Stettinius who maintained contact with the members of the Morgan firm on the larger questions raised by the Allied governments and the financial problems arising from the buying operations.[30]

F. C. Weems preserves for us Henry Davison's comments on Stettinius's statesmanlike approach: "If, in the course of negotiations, Mr. Stettinius felt convinced that the price was not sufficient to enable the contractor to perform his work faithfully without financial loss, Mr. Stettinius had insisted upon increasing the price set by the prospective contractor in his offer. Sometimes he advised the British Government to buy; sometimes he advised it against buying, and sometimes to increase voluntarily the price which it was to pay. Frequently he pointed out that the course the firm's clients wished to pursue was unwise, even though its results represented profits to the firm." [31]

Stettinius had times of deep depression about the work. He re-

[29] Forbes, "The Biggest Buyer in the World," pp. 15–16.
[30] Weems, *Memorandum*, pp. 5, 6.   [31] *Ibid.*, pp. 6, 7.

vealed a moment of low spirits to Colonel Wilfred Ellershaw at the British War Office. Ellershaw had just written him a friendly letter of appreciation on the job he was doing and Stettinius was deeply grateful. He replied:

The work has been arduous, the hours long and the strain severe—sometimes almost to the breaking point, and I have wondered whether the game was worth the candle and whether, in point of fact, I was justified in not only giving up so much of myself to the business, but also in continuing to occupy a position by reason of which I am unable, of course, to participate, directly or indirectly, in or derive profit from any of the operations having to do with the manufacture of munitions of war. Moreover, I have often felt and feel that the work we are doing for the Government and the efforts that we are making in its behalf are not and, in point of fact, cannot be appreciated, for, indeed, we do a great many things which, by reason of the conditions under which the business is handled, cannot be explained or understood fully by the people on the other side.[32]

Stettinius a Morgan Partner

Stettinius made a tremendous impression at Morgan's. There were intimations as early as June 1915 that they wanted to take him into the firm. He wrote:

I do not know what will be the final outcome of my present engagement with Messrs. J. P. M. & Co. Mr. Morgan has been good enough to invite me to make my home permanently with him, and his associate, Mr. Davison, has told me on several occasions that they had no idea of parting company with me when the war is over. Up to this time, I have not committed myself to any permanent arrangement with them. Indeed, I am very reluctant to do so. I am very happy in the Match Co., and business conditions here are such as to render it possible for me to attend to business, and at the same time to enjoy life. Were I to become permanently associated with Messrs. J. P. M. & Co., I am very much afraid that the magnitude and importance of the work that would be assigned to me would render it impossible for me to do anything else but work, and I am beginning to realize that after all there is something more in life than work.[33]

Lamont recalls the next episode in the story:

One morning late in December, 1915, Davison and I were on our way to call on Mr. Morgan at his town house. Prior to this time neither of

[32] PM 2, ERS to Ellershaw, Oct. 22, 1915.
[33] PM 1, ERS to G. W. Paton, June 29, 1915.

us had discussed at length with each other the relation of Stettinius to the Morgan firm. But on that morning Davison said to me suddenly: "Are you ready to join with me in recommending Ed for membership in the firm?" "I am," I responded. But when we took the matter up with Mr. Morgan, we found that he already had the same plan in mind.

Thus it was that Stettinius came to enter the Morgan firm of which he was a valued member up to the time of his death, in 1925.[34]

Years afterwards, Lamont's son sent Stettinius's son a memorandum he had found among his father's papers. This was a list of Stettinius's talents and qualities scribbled in soft pencil in the elder Lamont's handwriting. This brief catalogue may well have been an inventory of characteristics to support Stettinius's candidacy for admission to the Morgan firm. That would have been a logical time for Lamont to set down on paper his thoughts about the other man. The note reads:

E.R.S.—High character
 Perfect integrity
 Wonderful head—better *business* man than any of us
 Splendid and long experience
 With our backing great money maker
 An industrial doctor
 A finder of men—IAC [International Agricultural Corporation]
 A terrific worker—beats us all
 A cool negotiator
 Indescribably loyal
 Born & reared in the west—just the side where we are weak
 JPM hse must not ignore that fact
 For world wide trade ERS wd be a wonder
 To end contract he is the only man
 What other qualities count? [35]

The partnership became effective on January 1, 1916. The *New York Times* announced his admission on January 4, 1916, and noted that he was the eleventh partner. The news story gave the names of all the partners. They were J. P. Morgan, Charles Steele, Henry P. Davison, William P. Hamilton, William H. Porter, Thomas W. Lamont, and Edward R. Stettinius in the New York office and Edward T. Stotesbury, Horatio Gates Lloyd, and Arthur E. Newbold at Drexel & Co., the Philadelphia house. The article also listed Stettinius's corporate directorships: Diamond Match Company, American Gas and Electric Company, American Power and Light

---

[34] Lamont, *Davison*, p. 229.
[35] PS 34, Misc. Family file, covering letter, Thomas S. Lamont to ERS, Jr., Feb. 10, 1949.

Company, Babcock & Wilcox Company, Fidelity-Phenix Fire Insurance Company, International Agricultural Corporation, Irving National Bank, Model Fireproof Tenement Company, and American Surety Company.

Stettinius was profoundly moved by his election to partnership.

> Tomorrow I enter the firm of J. P. Morgan & Co. This connection means more to me, probably, than it does to other people, because, during the past year I have come to know the members of the firm pretty intimately, and have had an opportunity of seeing them in all kinds of situations and working under all kinds of conditions. I have never met any men at any time in my life whose moral and business standards were as high and, entirely apart from the financial phase of the situation, I consider that no greater honor could be given me than that which is involved in the invitation to become a member of the firm. Perhaps I ought to feel elated; as a matter of fact, a very keen appreciation of the magnitude of the work and of the responsibilities attached to it rather sober me. I am forming the new connection in a serious, rather than in a joyful, mood.[36]

The partners do not seem to have regretted their action. In a memorandum to Stettinius written some years later, Henry Davison paid him a gracious tribute. In asking him to talk with Seward Prosser of the Bankers Trust Company, he wrote, "No one can give him as sound advice as you on this particular subject, as you have a sense of the value, including a psychology, which none of the rest of us have." [37]

Stettinius did not change his demeanor or his way of life on becoming a partner in the most famous business organization on earth, nor did he slacken his work for the Allies. But he did change his investment pattern. On January 4, 1916, he acted to sell some shares and spoke of "a policy that I have adopted of disposing, as far as possible, of all scattered interests, and of consolidating my investments." [38]

Temporary Misunderstandings:
Conversations in London and Paris

Late in 1915 the relations between the Export Department and Great Britain took a new direction. Just when matters were running

[36] PM 1, ERS to Miss Lucy Lee Brownlee, Dec. 31, 1915.
[37] RS 392, memorandum, Davison to ERS, Nov. 18, 1919.
[38] PM 4, Northern Insurance Company file, ERS to W. S. Brown, Jan. 4, 1916.

smoothly between the Commercial Agency and the British Munitions Board, Lloyd George, the Minister of Munitions, drastically altered the arrangement. He appointed Ernest W. Moir (later Sir Ernest Moir, Bart.), a director of S. Pearson & Son, the British firm of engineers and building contractors that had built railroad tunnels under the river into New York, to bring in a team of men to replace the Board.[39] The Moir-Pearson group proceeded to move in and engage in actual purchasing, thus disrupting the delicate mechanism so carefully built up by the Morgan firm.

On February 19, 1916, after putting George W. Bacon in charge of the office, Stettinius sailed for London on the S.S. *St. Paul.*[40] One of his primary objects was to meet with Lloyd George and offer to have J. P. Morgan & Co. withdraw from the purchasing agreement, though continuing to help Moir where possible. Lloyd George was emphatic in urging that J. P. Morgan & Co. not drop out. He instructed Moir to cooperate fully with the Morgan firm. Later in 1916 we find Moir's energies channelled toward solving the problems of inspection and transportation of supplies bought in the United States, so the difficulties were resolved.[41]

Sir Ernest Moir and Stettinius became good friends. After the war, Moir asked Stettinius to find out how much it would cost to send his two nephews, lately demobilized from the Australian forces, to the University of California, Berkeley. The report came back that it would cost a thousand dollars a year each. Moir immediately sent the boys to California.[42]

The Russian problem was another subject of conversations with the British on the European visit. The Russian government was never a client of the Commercial Agency, but the Export Department placed large orders for Russia on behalf of the British and French governments.[43] The Russians were not easy to do business with. The Morgan memorandum of April 17, 1922, speaks of the smooth relations between the Export Department and the British authorities and adds: "The experience with Russian contracts for complete artillery ammunition afforded sharp contrast. There was difficulty with the drawings and designs from the outset. Frequent and arbitrary changes were made. No assistance was available from a suitable government production organization, and the inspection of the Russian Mission was unsympathetic and sometimes even hos-

[39] Weems, *Munitions*, I, 80.
[40] Weems, *Memorandum*, p. 7; *Journal of Commerce*, Feb. 21, 1916.
[41] Weems, *Munitions*, I, 80–82.
[42] RS 252, ERS to Moir, July 18, 1919; Moir to ERS, Aug. 1, 1919.
[43] Weems, *Munitions*, I, 91–93.

tile. The results were frequent delays, unsatisfactory product, and eventually a partial cancellation.[44]

Stettinius tried to ameliorate this situation on a personal level without success.[45] The British tried even harder. Weems writes, "In March, 1916, Lord Kitchener impressed upon Mr. Stettinius in conferences in London the anxiety the Russian situation was causing and the necessity of obtaining prompt aid from America." [46] This anxiety was to lead to the deaths of both Kitchener and Ellershaw. They finally decided to go to Russia to try to straighten out the difficulties. They sailed from Scapa Flow on H.M.S. *Hampshire* on June 5, 1916, and were lost with the ship.[47]

Still another important question was the matter of French shell steel for 1916. The French kept changing their requirements and shilly-shallying about whether they would buy through the Export Department or through their own French Mission.[48] Stettinius got no satisfaction from the French authorities, but on his return went ahead anyway to protect the Allies from the steel famine which he saw was coming.[49]

It is impossible to separate the tangible, immediate results of the European trip from the subtler long-range effects. Certainly, the value of the face-to-face meetings with the London and Paris staff of the Morgan organization and with the British and French government officials was very great. In London, Stettinius in effect renegotiated the agency agreement with Chancellor of the Exchequer McKenna and Lord Reading, securing an interpretation and clarification and determining the business on which the firm was to charge commissions.[50]

In Paris he gave Herman Harjes, the senior partner of Morgan, Harjes & Co., his personal cheque for two ambulances for the American Ambulance Corps.[51]

Stettinius returned to the United States on April 14, 1916.[52]

Hostility toward J. P. Morgan & Co.

The whole job of supplying the Allies would have been a great deal easier and more congenial if it had not been carried on in an atmos-

[44] RS 773, memorandum, "Regarding Activities of J. P. Morgan & Co. as Purchasing Agents."

[45] PM 2, ERS to Ellershaw, Oct. 22, 1915.   [46] Weems, *Munitions*, I, 91.

[47] *Encyclopaedia Britannica*, 14th ed., s.v. "Kitchener, Horatio Herbert"; Weems, *Munitions*, I, 92.   [48] Weems, *Munitions*, I, 152.   [49] *Ibid.*, I, 159ff.   [50] Weems, *Memorandum*, p. 8.   [51] RS 187, Harjes to ERS, April 7, 1916.   [52] Weems, *Memorandum*, pp. 7–8.

phere of suspicion and hostility from large sections of the press, groups favorable to the Central Powers, disappointed speculators, and that ever-present segment of the population that is envious of material success in general and of J. P. Morgan & Co. in particular. Harold Nicolson in his life of Dwight Morrow says, "The odium entailed upon J. P. Morgan & Co. by this task was extreme." [53] Stettinius was acutely aware of the attacks on the Morgan firm. In his letter to Charles C. Moore about his own avoidance of a conflict of interest he added, "What I have done in retiring from and disposing of my interests in The Babcock & Wilcox Co. is merely a repetition in a very small way of what J. P. Morgan & Co. have been doing in a much larger way in respect to other Companies. The public will never know and, if they did know, probably would never believe what sacrifices of profit J. P. Morgan & Co. and the members of that firm have made in acting for the Governments they represent. It is a damnable outrage that men whose standards are as high as the members of that firm, are so calumniated and abused by some of the papers in this country." [54]

But a more sinister force was involved than the pro-Germans, the envious, the frustrated greedy, and miscellaneous critics. This was the German government, whose agents were active in the United States. J. P. Morgan & Co. had reason to fear for the very lives of Stettinius and his family and whisked them away from Staten Island early in 1916. The correspondence with Captain Guy Gaunt, the British naval attaché (later Admiral Sir Guy Gaunt), gives us a tantalizing awareness of the web of espionage that surrounded those who were involved in helping the Allies. Gaunt wrote to Stettinius in August 1916:

there is a certain lovely lady in New York who receives considerable presents from one of the leading men in the Austrian Secret Service. It may be purely platonic—I don't know. This lady also has another friend who is an official of a foreign government—this show is certainly not platonic. *He has been carrying letters which have been seen on the table there addressed to E. R. Stettinius.*

Some day when you have five minutes I will come and talk with you, mentioning names which I do not wish to put on paper. The inference, of course, is that these *official envelopes* are opened during their stay in this house.[55]

Three weeks later Gaunt wrote again, enclosing a calling card with the legend: "The Count Frederick Moltke, Director of Army

[53] Harold Nicolson, *Dwight Morrow* (New York, 1935), p. 181.
[54] PM 4, ERS to Moore, Oct. 28, 1915.
[55] RS 281, Gaunt to ERS, Aug. 25, 1916.

Contracts attached to the Danish Legation." Gaunt's note said: "The bearer of enclosed card I rather think I told you about some-time ago. The dope is that he is simply a German agent. He was run out of London as such. Will you pass the glad news everywhere you can for he, of course, is only trying to get details as to munitions for the enemy?" [56]

Summary of the Purchasing Program

Stettinius summarized the achievements of the highly complex purchasing program in a letter of January 1918:

Contracts were closed here by the Allied Governments for over 6,000,000 rifles, and plants were built and equipped with a daily capacity of from 15,000 to 20,000 British Enfield and Russian rifles. Although the construction of these plants was begun in the winter and spring of 1915, it was not until the end of 1916 that they were capable of producing anything like their estimated output. All of this time was saved to the United States Government, the net result having been that in July, 1917, there were available to and were acquired by the United States Government three plants which had been producing Enfield rifles and which were capable of producing 10,000 rifles daily, while two additional plants, which until recently have been making Russian rifles, will be released shortly for the manufacture of machine guns for our troops.

The production of rifle cartridges was similarly developed. In 1914 the output of military cartridges by private plants was practically negligible. In the spring of 1917 a capacity had been created sufficient to produce 2,250,000,000 cartridges per annum.

The capacity of privately owned powder plants prior to the war did not exceed 15,000,000 pounds per year, whereas in the spring of 1917 it had increased to approximately 360,000,000 pounds per year.

Shell production was developed on a huge scale. Upwards of 45,000,000 shells of various sizes were manufactured in the United States for the Allies. An annual capacity was created of upwards of 20,000,000 rounds of 3-inch high explosive and shrapnel complete rounds, including cartridge cases, fuses, primers, etc., approximately 5,000,000 shells of sizes between 3-inch and less than 6-inch of 5,000,000 6-inch, 3,250,000 8-inch, 3,000,000 9.2-inch and 350,000 12-inch.

Fuse manufacture was practically unknown before the outbreak of the European war. In the spring of 1917, however, there had been created plants and organizations capable of producing between 40,000,000 and 50,000,000 time and detonating fuses per year.

Similarly, plants were built and equipped and organizations created

[56] RS 281, Gaunt to ERS, Sept. 13, 1916.

for the manufacture of machine guns, picric acid, trinitrotoluol, gun cotton, benzol, and the innumerable other things required for the prosecution of war.[57]

The United States Enters the War:
The End of the Export Department

On February 3, 1917, President Wilson broke off diplomatic relations with the German government in response to the unrestricted sinking of neutral shipping by German submarines. On April 6 the United States entered the war on the side of the Allies.

Stettinius and his partners saw immediately the desirability of coordinating the munitions purchases of the British and French with those of the new member of the Allies, the United States. They knew also that the Allied cause and their clients would be best served if they could share in the advantages of government price control and priority allotments. Accordingly, on May 25 they urged the cancelling of the purchasing agreements in identical letters to Sir Cecil Spring-Rice, British Ambassador to the United States, and André Tardieu, French High Commissioner in this country.[58] The British and French were in no hurry to sever the connections with the Export Department of J. P. Morgan, which had been so successful in matériel procurement for so long. Eventually, on August 22, 1917, the French and Italian representatives in the United States met and agreed that it would be prejudicial to their dealings with the Wilson administration to continue the close ties with J. P. Morgan & Co. The firm realistically pointed out to the British the essential validity of the fears expressed by the French and Italians, noting that the same risks applied to them.[59]

The shifting of Allied purchasing in the United States from the Export Department to separate national missions was a gradual and confused process. The great days of the Export Department were over, but a greatly reduced staff was retained to ease the transition and to continue to handle inquiries and negotiations already in progress and conduct other business, such as the extending of existing contracts. Stettinius wrote to his associate, Charles F. Whigham of Morgan, Grenfell & Co. in London, a few days after the new British purchasing organization was formed:

[57] Scrapbook I, ERS to John R. Rathom, Jan. 15, 1918; see Appendix C, Chief Categories of Matériel Purchased by the Export Department.
[58] Weems, *Munitions*, I, 243.   [59] *Ibid.*, I, 251.

Well—our activities in our Export Department on behalf of the British and French Governments have come to an end; the new organization under Sir Charles Gordon has been set up and all fresh orders will be filled by it in the future. I must confess that, although I am, of course, relieved in one way that the burden has been lifted from our shoulders, I am, nevertheless, more than sorry to retire from the work. The Export Department has become so much a part of me during the past two years and a half that the day before yesterday, when the work was turned over to Gordon, I felt as if I were parting with one of my own children.

He added wistfully, "I expect to leave here tomorrow afternoon for ten days' or two weeks' rest in the mountains. I am pretty well tired out and, in any event, there does not appear to be anything for me to do here at the present time.[60]

Whigham was deeply distressed by the abandoning of the Export Department. He wrote:

I cannot help thinking that if our Authorities had shown a little more oversight and energetic grappling with the new conditions arising out of America coming into the war, they might have preserved the wonderful organization which you had built up, instead of allowing things to drift until there were so many loose ends to be gathered together again. Even if the conditions made it impossible for you personally to continue as a moving spirit of the organization, a great deal more of the structure which you had built up with so much labor might have been preserved than is now the case. However, when all is said, you and your partners and assistants have done a marvelous work for the British Government, and at a time when it was even more needed than now. In any case, the more material side of your labors, such as organizing up of American industry into a huge war department, will continue to bear fruit, not only for this country, but for your own. At any rate, those of us who have been closely in touch with you realize the magnitude of your task and the marvelous results which you have attained.[61]

[60] WY, ERS to Whigham, Aug. 30, 1917.
[61] Weems, *Memorandum*, p. 14.

VII.   *The War: The American War Effort* (*1917–1918*)

GIVEN Stettinius's extensive experience in supplying the Allied armies with munitions, it would seem to have been most logical for him to transfer this knowledge to the service of his own country. This transfer never did take place. Stettinius was willing, even eager, to take an active part in the American war effort. There were rumors in the press from time to time that he would be offered this or that important post, but nothing came of these stories. When he was finally given some war work to do, it was given grudgingly, in response to public clamor, and the much-heralded job would turn out to be a post of minor significance. He wound up as a high-level trouble shooter for the Secretary of War.

Why was Stettinius never given a job worthy of his talents, or one that made real use of his great familiarity with the problems of procurement and supply? The answer is partly political, partly ideological. Woodrow Wilson was president of the United States, and he was profoundly mistrustful of the business community and actively antagonistic toward large business concerns and their leaders. The chief accomplishments of Wilson's first term were measures to restrict, regulate, and reduce the power and profits of business. He approached this task with an almost evangelical zeal, speaking of his program as "absolutely necessary to satisfy the conscience of the country and its perception of the prevailing conditions of business." [1] When Wilson was finally convinced that the administration's conduct of the war was going badly and help was needed from the business community, he ran into opposition from politicians in the Democratic party, including his son-in-law, Secretary of the Treasury William Gibbs McAdoo.

One of Stettinius's young associates at this time was Edgar W. Smith, subsequently the chief executive of the overseas operations of General Motors. He was later active in the Baker Street Irregulars, the Sherlock Holmes society, and was the undisputed authority on the career of the late and unlamented Professor James Moriarty.

---

[1] Ray Stannard Baker, *Woodrow Wilson, Life and Letters*, 8 vols. (Garden City, N.Y., 1927–39), IV, 376.

He recalls this period in writing to the younger Stettinius: "I
have quite a few notes in my diary . . . covering the period from
January, 1918, to July, 1918, when I was with your father down in
Washington . . . they deal with the uncertainties and misunderstandings which attended his original appointment to a high post in
the War Department, and in connection with which he won, finally,
a splendid, clean-cut victory over the devious political forces which
were attempting to ham-string him." [2]

"Big Business" and "Wall Street" were phrases with strong emotional overtones. It is not at all surprising, then, to find Stettinius, a
partner in the most important firm on Wall Street, one associated
with the very biggest of the country's businesses, being passed over
by the Wilson administration. Nor was he himself surprised, though
he was bitterly disappointed. Another factor in limiting Stettinius's
usefulness in the prosecution of the war was the prevailing outlook
of the War Department. The real authority for procurement and
supply was tightly held by generals in the regular army. Secretary
of War Baker eventually made Stettinius his personal agent in dealing with the other Allies, but at no time gave him any authority that
might conflict with that of the military hierarchy.

Stettinius and Preparedness

The story of Stettinius and the American war effort begins with his
purchasing munitions for the Allies. Stettinius had already armed
the United States before this country entered the war.

In January 1918 Stettinius wrote to the editor of the *Providence
Journal*, taking issue with an editorial which suggested that the
United States was defenseless:

Those who are disposed to take a gloomy view of the munitions situation lost sight entirely of what was accomplished in this country in
the way of preparedness before the United States entered the war. The
manufacturers of America created an absolutely new industry in the
United States between the Fall of 1914 and the Spring of 1917. Not only
were enormous plants constructed, but hundreds of thousands of men
were trained in manufacture.

All this was accomplished through the orders and at the expense of
the Allied Governments. As a result the United States has saved not
only hundreds of millions of dollars that were spent directly or indirectly by the Allies for the construction and equipment of plants but

[2] Scrapbook II, Smith to ERS, Jr., April 22, 1933.

also months in time, which in the last analysis may well mean the lives of thousands of our American boys. Had nothing been done in the development of the manufacture of munitions in this country, the position of the United States would indeed be serious. . . .

With all these plants in existence, with hundreds of thousands of men trained in the production of munitions and explosives, it is difficult to find warrant for the suggestion so frequently made that the resources of the United States for the production of munitions were wholly undeveloped when a state of war was declared on April 3rd [*sic*], 1917.[3]

Stettinius had also established a connection with the United States military which enabled him to share his specialized knowledge of military supply before this country entered the war. He was in constant contact with Brigadier General William Crozier, chief of the Ordnance Department of the army.[4]

The tragic events in Europe were not lost on the American Congress, which passed the National Defense Act, signed into law on June 3, 1916. The act established a commission to investigate and "report upon the advisability, desirability, and practicability of the Government manufacturing arms, munitions, and equipment and certain other allied questions."[5] On December 19, 1916, Stettinius testified before the Kernan Commission, appointed in accordance with this section. The commission's report stated how important to the defense of the United States was the productive capacity for munitions developed in the process of supplying the Allies, observing with a poetic fervor not often found in public documents that "in our day of need a benevolent Providence has stood between us and our peril."[6] These sentiments were subsequently forgotten when postwar zealots accused the agents of that benevolent Providence of selfish motives and possibly criminal acts.[7]

Throughout 1917 Stettinius continued to be in touch with the United States authorities, military and civilian, advising them on preparations for war and then on the conduct of munitions procurement.[8]

On April 6, 1917, Congress declared that a state of war existed between the United States and the Central Powers.

Congress had already set up the Council of National Defense on August 29, 1916, but it was March 3, 1917, before this body was fully organized. At a meeting of the council to which Stettinius was invited, Secretary of War Newton D. Baker asked him point-blank

[3] Scrapbook I, ERS to Rathom, Jan. 15, 1918.
[4] Weems, *Memorandum*, pp. 8–9.
[5] Cited *ibid*.   [6] Cited *ibid.*, p. 9.   [7] See Preface, above.
[8] Weems, *Memorandum*, pp. 9-11.

what he would do if he were faced with the problem of providing munitions for the United States. Stettinius gracefully evaded the too-comprehensive question, instead he outlined for the Council the two factors that he had found most likely to cause delay in munitions production. They were, first, the lack of experience on the part of American manufacturers in producing the items that they would be called upon to make and second, the difficulties that would be experienced in designing the products—there were no standardized designs, and there were inevitable sudden demands from the military for changes as military needs in the war shifted.[9]

Colonel E. M. House, the unofficial confidant of the President, asked Stettinius to prepare a memorandum giving his recommendations on the whole problem of munitions procurement, with particular attention to the purchasing activities of the Allies and the effective coordination of military supply. This memorandum was submitted on May 19, 1917.[10]

Stettinius on the Sidelines

There had been reports in the American newspapers immediately after the United States declared war that Stettinius's knowledge and experience would be shifted over to the service of his own country. However, he himself was astute enough to recognize the political realities from the outset. He wrote Edward Walsh of St. Louis in May 1917:

There is not a particle of warrant for the statements that have been made in the press to the effect that I will take charge of buying for the United States and Allied Governments. As a matter of fact, no arrangements whatever have been made as yet by which the United States Government will take over the buying for the Allied Governments and until such arrangements have been actually made, it would, of course, be quite impossible for me to even consider anything that would affect my obligations to the British and French Governments.

In any event, I am afraid that my political affiliations are such that I would not be acceptable to the present Administration.[11]

Tentative feelers kept coming from official Washington. On October 24, 1917, Stettinius wrote to his old Babcock & Wilcox associ-

---

[9] *Ibid.*, pp. 10–11.
[10] Weems, *Munitions*, II, Appendix XII (text of the memorandum); *Memorandum*, p. 12.
[11] RS 431, ERS to Walsh, May 9, 1917.

ate James P. Sneddon to say that he expected to be called to Washington to take charge of the buying and production of ordnance for the army. He added, sensitive as always to the political climate, "All of the conversations that I have had have been informal and were strictly confidential. Again, there are certain political objections to my appointment which may not be overcome. . . ." [12] Nothing came of these negotiations.

Stettinius expressed his interest in doing his bit and his concern about Washington's mismanagement of the war in a letter to his old business associate at the Diamond Match Company, Francis A. Hardy of Chicago:

I find myself completely rested and ready physically, as well as mentally, for whatever task may be assigned to me. We are necessarily in fairly close touch with what is going on in Washington and I must say that I am a good deal disturbed about the situation, owing partly to the inefficiency of some of the appointments and partly to the lack of coordination between the various departments of the Government, as well as between the United States Government and the Allied governments. Apparently we are repeating all of the mistakes that were made by England during the first months of the war; perhaps it is because the form of autocratic control which the British finally found it necessary to adopt is as offensive to our democratic ideals as it was to our friends across the water. Be that as it may, the fact remains that confusion and overlapping will continue until all of the war activities of the Government are centralized in a war council under which appropriate departments will be established which will co-operate one with the other.[13]

Stettinius was not optimistic, but he felt that the War Industries Board, created on July 28, 1917, offered possibilities. He wrote about it to General F. F. Minchin, first observing, "I . . . find it very hard to be comparatively idle at a time when there is so much to do."

Mr. Willard, whom you will remember having met last spring, has recently been appointed chairman of the War Industries Board and I believe he will make it go if anybody can. After all is said and done, the form of organization that may be employed to do the work doesn't cut much figure; that which really counts is the man directing and controlling the organization. Willard certainly has the experience and the ability, and the only thing that makes me fearful about the

[12] RS 7, ERS to Sneddon, Oct. 24, 1917.
[13] RS 376, ERS to Hardy, Oct. 27, 1917.

outcome is the inefficiency of some of the men who are associated with him.[14]

Dissatisfaction with the Conduct of the War

Meanwhile pressure was building up in the American press, and the public was demanding to know why Stettinius's knowledge and experience were not being used. At the same time a similar reaction was developing abroad. Thomas Lamont reported from Europe that sentiment was strong for the appointment of Stettinius as chairman of an Inter-Allied Advisory Board to deal with the whole question of Allied munitions.[15]

Senator George Earle Chamberlain, Democrat from Oregon, introduced a bill in Congress which would have established a cabinet post and department comparable to the British Ministry of Munitions. The industrial preparation for war had bogged down. There was widespread discussion and approval of this plan in Congress and in the country at large late in 1917, and Edward R. Stettinius was frequently mentioned as the logical Secretary of Munitions. The administration was unalterably opposed to this, so nothing came of it. Stettinius was no less opposed to the idea than the Democrats, but for a different reason. In his letter of January 1918 to John R. Rathom, editor of the *Providence Journal*, he explained why he would be unwilling to serve as Secretary of Munitions:

I feel compelled to say that if such a position as that which would be created by the Chamberlain bill were offered me, of which there would not be even a remote possibility, I would unhesitatingly decline to accept it, as I am convinced that the creation of such a ministry to make all purchases for all Departments of the United States Government and for all of the Allies is thoroughly impracticable, and, if attempted, would produce an absolutely chaotic condition. The problems with which such an organization would be required to deal, involving not only munitions but clothing, food, motor transport, merchant ships, battle ships, torpedo boat destroyers, aeroplanes, horses, mules and the thousand other articles and materials required for our army and navy, would be so varied and complex that it would be utterly impossible to find a man, or even a board, that would be competent or able physically to deal with all. Again, the size of such an organization would be so huge that its very bulk would render it ineffective and the time required for its development would be so great that it would be months

[14] RS 199, ERS to Minchin, Nov. 24, 1917.
[15] Weems, *Memorandum*, p. 16.

before it could function at all, while, in the meantime, existing departments would necessarily become demoralized and their efficiency destroyed.[16]

Official Recognition: Surveyor General of Supplies
(February–April 1918)

In mid-January 1918 Stettinius was invited to confer with the War Department about a proposal to create the post of Surveyor General of Supplies, to which he would be appointed. It was never clear just what the duties of the new position would be, but they were to be related to the Office of the Director of Purchases.[17] News of the conversations leaked to the press, and the papers announced prematurely that Stettinius had accepted the job. The *New York Times* carried the story on January 26.

William McAdoo, President Wilson's Secretary of the Treasury, was not happy about the report. Wilson's biographer R. S. Baker relates the circumstances:

Secretary Baker's appointment of Edward R. Stettinius, of J. P. Morgan & Co., as Surveyor General of all army purchases was made public. Secretary McAdoo wrote the President by hand on the 27th: ". . . . Confidentially I think the Stettinius appointment very unfortunate. As I have been going over the country I have been impressed with the suspicion of and feeling against the big interests—and J. P. Morgan & Company—particularly as they are believed (and justly, I think) to have made enormous sums through financing and purchasing for the allies prior to our entrance into the war. This is one of the reasons I was so anxious to create the Inter-Ally Purchasing Commission here and to get away from the Morgan connection and influence. . . . Recently Mr. Baker made Mr. McRoberts (vice-president of the National City

---

[16] Rathom was a consistent critic of the Wilson administration. On Oct. 28, 1920, Franklin D. Roosevelt announced that he would sue Rathom for $500,000 damages for libel, alleging that Rathom had charged Roosevelt with criminal misconduct while Assistant Secretary of the Navy and had stated that Roosevelt "had persistently favored and actively forwarded in the Navy Department a policy of returning to the service in the United States Navy persons actually guilty of unnatural crimes, had deliberately falsified the facts with reference to his official conduct after abstracting and secreting documentary evidence thereupon and prostituted his public office for personal and political advancement, regardless of the public interest and had been guilty of falsehood, deception and other dishonorable conduct" (*Commercial & Financial Chronicle,* Nov. 13, 1920, p. 1911). After a brief flurry in the newspapers, the threatened suit was forgotten.

[17] Weems, *Memorandum,* p. 19.

Bank) a Colonel & put him in charge of very important matters. Mc-
Roberts is a protege of Armour & Co., I am told, and was put in the
National City through their influence. McRoberts & Stettinius are Re-
publicans, and while this alone does not disqualify them, it is not possible to count on their complete loyalty, I fear, when bitter partisan
attacks are under way by their party. . . ."[18]

The actual offer was made on January 29, 1918, in a letter from
Colonel Palmer E. Pierce, Director of Purchases.[19] Stettinius's letter
of acceptance of February 12, 1918, was tentative. He undertook to
assume the duties of the appointment on a provisional basis, "while
I endeavor to ascertain whether I can render a useful service in that
position." [20]

The news that Stettinius had finally been given a position in the
government and a challenge worthy of his steel was greeted with
enthusiasm all over the United States and among the Allies abroad.[21]
Lord Northcliffe cabled on January 26, with characteristic enthusiasm: "Joy. Victory now assured." [22] And in a newspaper interview
of the same date he was quoted as saying that the appointment of
Stettinius was "a piece of world news of the highest importance,"
adding, "In my considered opinion he is easily the ablest business
organizer in the ranks of the Allies or the enemy." [23] Sir William
Wiseman, later of Kuhn, Loeb & Co., wrote to Stettinius: "I know
enough of our people to say that the news of your appointment will
spread from our Government circles to our Army in France like
the news of a victory for the Allied cause." [24]

The general satisfaction with the Stettinius appointment was premature. The skepticism reflected in Stettinius's tentative acceptance
was soon justified. Offering him the job amounted to no more than
a grandiose political maneuver to relieve public pressure on Baker
to give Stettinius an important role in the prosecution of the war.
One of the first evidences of the hollowness of his position was the
Goethals episode. Major General George W. Goethals was appointed Quartermaster General to replace Major General Henry G.
Sharpe. Frederick Palmer, Baker's biographer, notes that "Goethals,
with characteristic directness, immediately declared that either Stettinius must yield in a conflict of authority, or he himself would retire. Stettinius gracefully yielded." [25] One surmises that Stettinius
yielded so readily because he saw the essential weakness of the

---

[18] Baker, *Woodrow Wilson*, VII, 499.   [19] Weems, *Memorandum*, p. 19.
[20] *Ibid.*, p. 20.   [21] *Ibid.*, p. 21.   [22] *Ibid.*
[23] *New York Tribune*, Jan. 27, 1918.   [24] Weems, *Memorandum*, p. 21.
[25] Frederick Palmer, *Newton D. Baker: America at War*, 2 vols. (New
York, 1931), II, 3.

whole supply structure. He was not a yielder by nature where the issue was important.

The position of Surveyor General was never important because it was never made specific. Stettinius never knew what he was supposed to do or what the limits of his authority were. A conference was finally held on March 30, 1918, to discuss the status of the Surveyor General of Supplies and the function of his office. It was agreed that the position was an organizational anomaly and a source of confusion and duplicated effort.[26] On April 1 Stettinius wrote to the newly promoted Bridgadier General Pierce, Director of Purchases, and to Acting Secretary of War Benedict Crowell asking to be relieved of his duties as Surveyor General of Supplies, since those duties had turned out to be almost entirely statistical.[27]

The War Industries Board: Stettinius and Baruch

A major issue in the supply situation has already been hinted at: Should there be military or civilian control? The civilian committee which had been set up to supply the armed forces was the War Industries Board. The War Industries Board had been created to replace the earlier General Munitions Board and Munitions Standard Board, but many months passed before it became a successfully working body.

In his study *Industrial America in the World War* G. B. Clarkson charges: "Perhaps in despair of the Board's lack of vigor, Mr. Baker found his promise (of full army cooperation) invalid, surrendered to the steam roller of the Army's eager will to dominate, and thus came to seek a way out in that plan of military replacement of the War Industries Board by an organization within the Army with which Mr. E. R. Stettinius was connected." Later in the book he claims: "Secretary Baker was letting the Army run wild through the supply pastures and was planning, with the aid of Mr. Stettinius, to create the needed agency through a munitions department within the army, that would have left the War Industries Board a shell." [28]

The suggestion that Stettinius was party to a plan to abolish the War Industries Board or keep the civilian organization subordinate to the military is nonsense. We saw in his letter of November 24, 1917, to General Minchin that he welcomed the establishment of

[26] Weems, *Memorandum*, p. 21.   [27] *Ibid.*, p. 22.
[28] Grosvenor B. Clarkson, *Industrial America in the World War* (Boston and New York, 1923), pp. 41–42, 84.

the War Industries Board. The fact is that the Board was not very effective and the needs of the army were immediate. Stettinius as Surveyor General of Supplies conferred with Bernard Baruch on cooperation between their two groups and after the discussion wrote to him on March 18, 1918, apparently at his request, outlining organizational changes which would strengthen the Board.[29]

Writers have tried to stir up ill-will in retrospect between Stettinius and Baruch without much evidence to go on.[30] It is doubtful that the two men were close friends. Each was aloof and strong-willed, but they acted toward each other with consistent courtesy, even friendliness, over many years. They corresponded on such matters as the Inter-Allied Munitions Council,[31] the affairs of the Texas Gulf Sulphur Company,[32] in which both were interested, and such personal matters as Baruch's present of a brace of ducks to Stettinius.[33]

Second Assistant Secretary of War
(April–August 1918)

Official Washington accepted the fact that Stettinius was too able and knowledgeable to be excluded from taking an active part in the American war effort. As professional politicians they knew that to keep him out for partisan or ideological reasons would be to invite further criticism. On April 9, 1918, President Wilson appointed him Second Assistant Secretary of War. He took the oath of office two days later.[34] Again there were loud hosannas in the press at home and abroad. André Tardieu, French High Commissioner in the United States, sent a telegram of congratulations. Sergei Ughet of the Russian Embassy wrote on April 10 and expressed his "hearty joy that at last you will be able to be helpful to your country in the full extent of your capacities." [35] Again these expressions of relief and gratification were premature. As before, Stettinius was given no real authority; this was reserved for the office of the chief of the army.

The public picture of Stettinius's job was further confused by the

---

[29] Baruch Papers, Princeton University, ERS to Baruch, March 18, 1918.
[30] Clarence W. Barron, *More They Told Barron* (New York, 1931), pp. 255–59.
[31] Baruch Papers, Princeton University, ERS to Baruch, July 14, 1918.
[32] RS 466, ERS to Baruch, Jan. 28, 1922; Baruch to ERS, Feb. 6, 1922.
[33] RS 78, ERS to Baruch, Jan. 15, 1923.
[34] Weems, *Memorandum*, p. 22.   [35] *Ibid.*

newspaper report that he was the new "Gun Dictator." This brought further unjustified reassurance to a sector of the public that felt it could now relax and be assured of an adequate supply of artillery. Stettinius tried to clarify matters with a published statement on May 9, 1918, explaining that he would be as helpful as possible to the Army's Acting Chief of Ordnance, General C. C. Williams, but that the furnishing of guns was strictly the general's province.[36]

Matters continued to drift. The supply situation became more chaotic as more American troops were sent overseas. Meanwhile, Stettinius tried to do a constructive job under impossible conditions. At length Baker suggested that he go to France as the personal representative of the Secretary of War and a sort of upper-echelon trouble shooter. Stettinius welcomed the idea.

On July 6, 1918, Baker wrote General Pershing: "Mr. Stettinius will leave very shortly for Europe; I enclose you a copy of a letter which I have given him, outlining the inquiries which I desire to have him make. You will find him a very considerate man in the matter of demands upon your time, as he is accustomed to dealing with busy men and not prolonging conferences beyond their useful limit." [37]

At this time Baker also alerted General Tasker H. Bliss, recently retired chief of staff, to Stettinius's coming, observing, "He is a man of great exactness and of an almost terrifying sense of responsibility." [38]

The Secretary's letter of July 6, 1918, directed Stettinius as Second Assistant Secretary of War to:

(1) act as representative of the War Department on the Inter-Allied Munitions Council, (2) inquire into the financial relations of the United States established by the American Expeditionary Forces in matters of European purchases, with a view to formulating and rendering definite those relations so that current accounts would at all times be kept in which would appear all obligations of the United States, and obligations of other governments to the United States growing out of purchases by and from the A.E.F., so that subsequent controversies and misunderstandings might be avoided, and (3) examine into the systems of finance and accounting between the A.E.F. and the Bureaus in the United States with a view to establishing such systems of reports as would keep the War Department in the United States constantly advised of the amount of its financial obligations.[39]

---

[36] *Ibid.*, p. 23.   [37] Palmer, *Baker*, II, 334.   [38] *Ibid.*, II, 396.
[39] ERS to Baker, Jan. 8, 1919, Record Group 213, National Archives, Washington, D.C.

Stettinius Overseas

Stettinius sailed for France on July 14, 1918, and immediately set to work to carry out the mandate from Secretary Baker.[40]

Mention has already been made of Edgar W. Smith, later of General Motors, who kept a diary during the time he worked with Stettinius. Thanks to him, we know more about Stettinius's mission to Paris in 1918 than about any other period in his life. He provides a detailed account of those days:

In this present memorandum I shall confine myself . . . to the story from the date of our sailing abroad to the date of our return to America.

Your father sailed from New York for Europe on July 14, 1918, as you undoubtedly know, on the steamship "Great Northern", which had formerly been plying between Seattle and San Francisco, and which was called over to troop transport service because of the great speed that she and her sister ship, the "Northern Pacific" possessed. . . . The voyage across was uneventful, although the going was very rough. Your father showed his well-known propensity to keep right on working, even when he had to sit around with his life-jacket on, as he did when we were going through the submarine zone. There was one scare when we were two days out, and I understand that your father was led, like those of us in the rear ranks, to really believe for a while that we were going to abandon ship, when a boat just visible over the horizon was seen to start firing. It developed that it was simply another transport doing some target practice, however, and we all went back to our quarters without getting damp. A day out from Brest, there was another scare, of a "periscope" nature, this time, but it was a false alarm of short duration. The time made in the run across was excellent, especially as the ships stopped twice for several hours to indulge in submarine target practice, each ship in turn maneuvering over a dummy periscope trailed by the other ship. At this dummy the other ship charged at full speed, blazing away with her two forward six-inch guns, passing directly over the target, dropping a depth bomb from the stern when the target appeared there, and then taking up the battle again with a pair of six-inchers aft. These were the standard maneuvers for anti-submarine fighting, and were supposed to be kept up until the "sub" was left behind, sunk or disabled — or until something unpleasant happened to us.

We were convoyed into Brest by five destroyers — British, I think — docking at this point of entry for American troops on July 22nd, and leaving after only two hours delay on a special train for Paris.

---

[40] Weems, *Memorandum*, p. 24.

The Mission reached Paris early on the morning of July 23rd, and went immediately to the Hotel Westminster on the Rue de la Paix, where the offices were to be located, and where most of us were to live. Mr. Stettinius, however, and two or three of the higher ranking members of the Mission, went to the Ritz on the Place Vendome.

On July 25th your father left for a visit to the American Grand Headquarters in Chaumont. I did not go along so I do not know what happened there, but I suppose it was largely a matter of courtesy contact and establishment of the necessary liaison.

This initial period of the Mission's stay in Paris was concerned mainly with the establishment of temporary offices in the Hotel Westminster, and with the building up of the necessary contacts among the various A.E.F. organizations in Paris. No sooner had the temporary offices been successfully established—on August 1st—than we moved out of them to permanent office quarters in the Elysée Palace Hotel on the Champs Elysées near the Etoile. This building is still standing and in use as an office building, I believe, and a photograph of it would be readily obtainable. Most of the crowd which had been staying at the Westminster moved at the same time to the Hotel Dominion, and I think it was about this time, or a little later, that your father took his apartment on the Avenue Henri Martin.

On August 5th came the first intimate contact with war which I think your father experienced. Shortly after our arrival in the office a periodic "booming" was heard, which we took at first to be a French gun being proof-fired, but it suddenly dawned on us that it was the German Big Bertha which was favoring us with her attentions. Paris had had none of it since the middle of July, and we had almost forgotten that sooner or later it must come again to greet us. Several of the shells fell uncomfortably near the Elysée Palace—one less than half a block away—and during the day over fifteen were sent on their seventy mile course, all of them falling somewhere within the metropolitan area. Work went on as usual, of course, and I remember your father indulging in some very forceful uncomplimentary expressions relating to the doubtful ancestry of the gunners, when I was sitting alongside of him and one of the explosions went off not half a mile away.

The bombardment continued on August 6, 7, 8 and 9th. It was on the 8th that a shell shattered the wall of the Hotel Westminster almost exactly at the spot where your father's desk had been situated when our offices were located there.

I have a note that on August 14th your father attended the first official meeting of the Inter-Allied Munitions Council. . . .

It was about this time that efforts began to be exerted to get your father to relinquish his civilian status and "join the Army". They wanted to make him, I recall, a Brigadier General, but he was quite scornful of the whole idea—it would have been a frightful mistake, of course, and he would have lost prestige enormously. By maintaining his civilian status in the War Department he was actually superior to any of the numerous Generals that abounded on every side, no matter how high their rank, and perfectly able to tell them to go chase themselves, without fear of being court-martialed. I remember his laughing one day and saying to me "They'll never get me in a yellow suit!"

Another interesting development about this time was the injection of Brigadier General Charles G. Dawes into the picture. General Dawes was head of the S.O.S., and had about as close contact with your father as any of the American officers, as a consequence of the close relationship of his work with the Allied Coordination work your father was doing. I have a distinct recollection of having been closeted with your father and General Dawes several times for hours on end, with General Dawes doing most of the talking (and the accounts of the vividness and picturesqueness of his dialog are by no means exaggerated!), but with your father jumping in at the appropriate point, time after time, and dictating the keynote of the thought they were attempting to agree upon, with the General readily, if profanely, accepting the definitions laid down for him.

On August 21st, because of an extreme crisis in the aircraft end of the Allied equipment program, your father moved his office into the Air Division Headquarters at 45 Avenue Montaigne, to be right on the spot in the controls he was exercising.

On August 29th your father went to Tours to carry his Air Equipment findings to the S.O.S. headquarters, and to develop the forward program from that point in line with the specifications he had prepared. It was while he was away on this trip that a little-known reporter by the name of Isaac Marcosson came in to interview him, and I became quite well acquainted with him—a contact I have kept up ever since. Marcosson saw your father some time later, and I suggest that if we can get a copy of the interview he had with him from his old files it would make a very interesting bit for a side-light.

On September 6th we moved our offices back to the Elysée Palace hotel, the special Air Division liaison work having been completed, and your father assumed his general activity again in connection with co-ordination of all Allied Supply functions.

Secretary Newton Baker arrived in Paris September 9th, and one of the first contacts he made was with your father. They were closeted for several hours.

On September 14th your father went over to London to consult with the British officials. George Foley went with him and I was not sufficiently party to the things that happened to be able to report what was done. As a consequence of his absence from Paris, however, he missed the last air raid which the Germans made on the city. It was quite a bad one, and Walter Gifford and I sat huddled through the most of it in the lobby of our hotel. I think he was the only man in Paris who was more frightened than I was.

Your father returned to Paris on September 18th with Secretary Baker.

On September 21st your father went down Chaumont way to see Carrington, who was in the hospital there from the gassing he had received.

On September 28th your father went over to London again, with Foley accompanying him. It was just at this point, according to a note I have, that the German armies began to crack. Bulgaria collapsed on September 30th, you will recall, and in anticipation of the victory that was in sight, I remember that the discussions in London were already being pointed to the steps to be taken after the Armistice. Your father was gone until October 4th.

Beginning October 8th your father was ill for two or three days, and it was then that I had the experience I mentioned to you of taking dictation from him while he was flat on his back in bed, unable even to lift his head, so that I had to hold papers in front of him for him to read and dictate the reply to.

Again on October 16th your father made a trip over to London, where he stayed much longer than usual. I find a note in my diary "The Chief has been doing real work in London, and the results are beginning to show"—but I cannot for the life of me remember what, in particular, the conversations had to do with. His return was on October 21st.

Incidentally, there was nothing even approaching a five-day week in your father's office: we always worked all day long on Saturday, just as on other days, and frequently came in Sundays as well. The same pressure kept up even when the Allied victory was in sight and, if anything, due to the negotiations that were commenced then for liquidation of the military commitments, a little additional pressure was put on at this time.[41]

Stettinius and Pershing

Stettinius and Pershing established a working relationship almost at once and soon developed a friendship that was to last the rest of their lives. Stettinius was especially helpful in aircraft, artillery, and

[41] Scrapbook II, Smith to ERS, Jr., April 22, 1933.

artillery ammunition procurement and in advising the general on the financial problems of the Expeditionary Force. Pershing had looked forward with pleasure to Stettinius's coming, as he told Secretary of War Baker in a postscript to a letter of June 18, 1918:

With reference to sending over Mr. Stettinius as a member of the Munitions Board, the more I think of the proposal the more it appeals to me. Mr. Stettinius' broad acquaintance among Inter-Allied countries and his experience in handling just this line of work seems to me to fit him especially as your representative on the Munitions Board.

This is a very broad subject which seems to me will become more and more complicated as time goes on. Board after board, and committee after committee are being piled one on top of the other and a state of confusion exists that only a man of Mr. Stettinius' abilities can straighten out, so far as we are concerned. I hope that you may send him over.

His presence here would give great strength to our end of the program, which is destined to be a very important one. I have seen the telegrams sent by Mr. McFadden and Mr. Cravath, who were evidently brought into this by Mr. Loucheur. In the meantime, I have appointed General Wheeler as our representative until the question could be decided by you.[42]

Scattered entries in Pershing's diary show that he was not disappointed:

Paris, Tuesday, July 23, 1918. . . . Met Mr. Stettinius, Assistant Secretary of War, to-day and am certain he will be very valuable in handling munitions and financial questions.
     Chaumont, Sunday, July 28, 1918. . . . Conferred with Mr. Stettinius on Friday. Tardieu wants priority on Liberty motors; Stettinius will handle.
     Chaumont, Tuesday, August 13, 1918. . . . King George visited the Division Headquarters Monday and decorated General Bliss, me, and several men of the 33d. Went to see Field Marshal Haig to arrange release of three of our divisions. Returned to Paris and saw Winston Churchill, Lord Weir, and Stettinius about artillery and aviation. British can provide us with additional artillery.
     Souilly, Thursday, November 7, 1918. Had long talk with Stettinius about ordnance on Monday.[43]

After the war there was a continuing association between the two men. Pershing was Stettinius's guest at White Sulphur Springs in

[42] John J. Pershing, *My Experiences in the World War* (New York, 1931), p. 103.
[43] *Ibid.*, pp. 169, 177, 214, 377.

1921, and shortly afterwards Stettinius invited him to watch the Dempsey-Carpentier prize fight.[44] Stettinius advised Pershing frequently about his personal securities portfolio. In February 1922 he did some trading on the market for Pershing which netted the General a profit of $10,000. He subsequently opened an account for Pershing with James B. Colgate & Co., stockbrokers, and bought shares in Texas Gulf Sulphur in his name.[45] He continued to advise the General about his affairs for some years. He performed the same service for the General's aide, one Lieutenant Colonel George Catlett Marshall.[46] The following year Stettinius was unable to accept Pershing's invitation to sit in his box at the Army-Navy football game. He addressed his regrets to that same aide, the future author of the Marshall Plan.[47]

Miscellaneous Duties

Stettinius's first duty abroad was to take part in the deliberations of the Inter-Allied Munitions Council, about which he later observed, "when all is said and done there is not very much opportunity in the inter-Allied Munitions Council for really effective work." [48]

A more important job was to establish some sort of orderly contractual relationship between the United States and her allies. Benedict Crowell, Assistant Secretary of War, later discussed this in a book he wrote with Robert Forrest Wilson: "The numerical expansion of the A.E.F. in the spring and summer of 1918 resulted in a greatly increased demand by the A.E.F. for French artillery and ammunition. America supplied schedules of raw materials which she could furnish, and the French made estimates of the numbers of guns they could deliver monthly to the A.E.F. But this was all understanding and mutual agreement—no formal contract was drawn. When Mr. Stettinius reached Paris in the summer of 1918, he immediately began to press to get this agreement down in black and white, so that America might know exactly what her obligations were." [49]

[44] RS 143, ERS to Thomas Cochran, April 25, 1921; RS 108, ERS to Pershing, May 24, 1921.

[45] RS 108, ERS to Pershing, Feb. 9, 1922.

[46] PS 29, Marshall correspondence.

[47] RS 108, ERS to Marshall, Oct. 22, 1923.

[48] RS 237, ERS to Irving S. Olds, Sept. 5, 1918.

[49] Benedict Crowell and Robert Forrest Wilson, *Demobilization: Our Industrial and Military Demobilization after the Armistice, 1918–1920* (New Haven, 1921), p. 305.

It is fortunate that Stettinius, though frequently irascible, was flexible in matters of organization, because his titles and duties shifted often. On August 21, hardly a month after Stettinius arrived in France, Secretary Baker cabled that he wanted to form a new Air Service which would combine the Production and Aircraft Departments: "There is no easy way to do this, except by using the Second Assistant's place for Mr. Ryan (John D. Ryan), having Mr. Crowell take over your work in Ordnance on this side and maintaining you in Europe for the present as the Special Representative of the War Department with all powers and duties you now have, of which Generals Pershing, Bliss, and others would be advised. Before leaving you suggested that I should feel free to suggest this alteration in your relations if the situation at any time justified it." [50]

Baker hastily added that his final decision on shifting the title of Second Assistant Secretary of War to Ryan would depend entirely on Stettinius's own wishes in the matter. Naturally, Stettinius resigned by cable two days later, on August 23. The public announcement of the shift in the secretaryship appeared in the newspapers on August 29, 1918.[51]

Special Representative of the War Department
(August 1918–January 1919)

In resigning, Stettinius made it clear that he would be willing to remain in Europe as Special Representative of the War Department, but he would appreciate specific information defining his authority and his duties.

Secretary Baker wrote to Stettinius on October 4 to tell him what he was expected to do:

I am anxious to make a clear record of the relation you have been generous enough to undertake to the War Department and its work in Europe, since the acceptance of your resignation as 2nd Assistant Secretary of War. That relation, shortly stated, is that you remain the direct representative of the Secretary of War in France and elsewhere in Europe, to advise with General Pershing and his assistants on the financial, procurement and supplies questions arising between the Expeditionary Forces and the European Allied Governments and European controls, individual and corporate. I use the word advise only because you and I realize that good administration requires the authority to flow from General Pershing through his subordinates in the actual business

[50] Weems, *Memorandum*, p. 24.   [51] *Ibid.*, p. 25.

relations established, but General Pershing and General Harbord will call upon you to advise with them and to aid them in negotiations and business arrangements and when you are so asked by them, you will speak as I would be empowered to speak if I were there.

In addition to this General Pershing and General Harbord will welcome suggestions from you as they would from me which in your judgment will tend to systematize, simplify and expedite our accounting, exchanges of opinion with Washington, the formulation of requirements programs and generally the efficiency of service of munitions and supply. . . . You will, of course, continue to represent the War Department as the accredited delegate upon the Inter-Allied Munitions Council.[52]

The specific job assigned to Stettinius was to buy artillery and ammunition from the British and French governments. He negotiated these purchases and reported the quantities and calibers to Baker.[53]

In the fall of 1918 it became apparent that the Central Powers could not hold out against the Allies indefinitely. Torn by revolutions at home and suffering defeats in the field, Germany and her associates were clearly losing the war, but it was obvious that they could continue fighting effectively for many months to come. The Western Allies were conscious of this decline in the strength of the Central Powers and reacted accordingly in their relations with their American colleagues. Stettinius became aware of this new sense of impending victory in the course of his negotiations for munitions to supply the A.E.F. for 1919 and reported his findings to General Tasker H. Bliss, who summarized the account in a letter to General Peyton C. March: "He tells me that he is now running up against a decided indisposition on the part of the British and the French to give us the help which they promised. This is not surprising to me because, from various little indications that have come to my notice, it seems to me somewhat evident that the European Allies will attempt to minimize the American effort as much as possible. They think that they have got the Germans on the run and that they now do not need as much help as they were crying for a little while ago." [54]

Stettinius continued to press for orderly and businesslike arrangements with the supplying countries and was successful in dealing with Britain. The *Final Report* of the United States Liquidation Commission says: "From time to time during the spring and sum-

[52] *Ibid.*, p. 26.
[53] ERS to Baker, Jan. 8, 1919, Record Group 213, National Archives.
[54] Palmer, *Baker*, II, 366.

mer of 1918 America placed orders with Great Britain to manufacture or cause to be manufactured and delivered to America certain quantities of artillery and artillery ammunition. All such agreements, some of which were vague and indefinite and might have been so construed as to have given them far-reaching importance, were merged and superseded by a certain agreement, dated October 19, 1918, entered into between Mr. Stettinius, Special Representative of the Secretary of War, and Mr. Churchill, British Minister of Munitions." [55]

It was now the Americans' turn to be vague about prior commitments: "About the 1st of November, however, it became evident that an armistice was drawing near, and immediately the Americans grew lukewarm on the subject of a formal contract. The reason was evident. Under the terms of a formal contract, America's termination obligations would be questions of fact; with the affair left as an unwritten agreement, our obligations would be questions of equity, to be negotiated, and we were likely to emerge from such negotiations in better case financially than we should be if held by the set and rigid conditions of a formal contract." [56]

From Edgar Smith's diary we know what Stettinius was doing as the long war drew to a close:

On November first, in anticipation of the Armistice which was then beginning to be confidently expected, your father went to Advance Headquarters at the front to visit General Pershing. These headquarters were in front of the Allied artillery line, and I remember George Foley told me when he came back of the whistling "curtain" of shell-fire which blanketed their heads all the time they were there. The stay was of two days' duration, and I recall that George told me it was his most interesting experience of the war, and that your father enjoyed it equally intensively.

The Armistice came on November 11th, and after making a futile attempt to work at the office that day, your father told us to shut up shop and sent us on our ways. I did not see him until about ten o'clock that night when, wandering into Ciro's, we spotted him with a very hilarious group over in one corner and beat a quick retreat, so that our own style would not be cramped.[57]

[55] *United States Liquidation Commission—War Department, Final Report* (Washington, D.C., 1920), p. 44.

[56] Crowell and Wilson, *Demobilization*, pp. 305–6.

[57] Scrapbook II, Smith to ERS, Jr., April 23, 1933.

VIII. *Liquidating the War (1918–1919)*

WITH the signing of the Armistice came an entirely new set of problems. All efforts had been devoted to building a great mechanism for winning the war; now the brakes were suddenly applied. Secretary of War Baker immediately cabled Stettinius his new instructions: "It is of course important to cut down expenditures as rapidly as possible. Please get into immediate communication with General Harbord and with General Pershing's headquarters and represent me in working out with them a program for the cessation of all construction and procurement which can be stopped without prejudice to the situation as it now is. Contracts in process of making, both in England and in France, should be suspended, and generally every effort made to narrow our obligations as far as possible." [1]

The following day, November 12, Chief of Staff March cabled Stettinius that reductions and cancellations of contracts or commitments which he had made would be his own responsibility to negotiate. [2]

Baker's biographer tells of the Secretary's dependence on Stettinius at this critical time: "Since Baker was not going to Paris he had to depend upon Stettinius, the American member of the Inter-Allied Munitions Council, to act for him in looking after the disposition of the two billion dollars' worth of American property in France until a liquidation commission should be formed. . . . Stettinius, whose son was in the Army and had been gassed, had no second thought about doing his duty when summoned in war's aftermath, as well as in war." [3]

Baker wrote to Stettinius expressing his confidence in him: "I am anxious to have you know how grateful I am to you for staying there, and how much comfort and consolation it is to me to know that you are on the ground. . . . The whole problem is so vast and complex that I frankly do not see how I can hope for a com-

---

[1] Palmer, *Baker*, II, 283.   [2] Weems, *Memorandum*, p. 27.
[3] Palmer, *Baker*, II, 396–97.

fortable time in having it all adjusted without asking this service at your hands." [4]

Trip through the Battlefields

On November 15, barely four days after the Armistice was signed, Stettinius found it necessary to go to Brussels by motor. We have his hastily written longhand account of the drive through the area that had so recently been fought over.

Saturday
November 16, 1918

We started off early yesterday morning on our trip to Brussels. Our course had been laid out partly with a view of saving time and partly in order to take us through the country which had been most bitterly fought over. Leaving Paris we motored through Senlis, Compiègne, Noyon, Ham, St. Quentin, Bohain, Le Cateau, Solesmes, Valenciennes, and Mons and as far as Casteau where we were halted and ordered to return to Mons as instructions had been given that no one should be permitted to cross the line from the South or East. Although I have sought to ascertain the reason, I have been unable to satisfy myself whether it is because of a decision reached by the Supreme Command in order to prevent intercourse with the Huns, or whether it is due to the trouble that has been broken out in the German Army,—for the reports all along the line are to the effect that the army is in a state of absolute chaos, that the soldiers have revolted, attacked and in some instances killed their officers: other rumors indicate that the civil population has turned upon the Huns,—and has sought revenge for the wrongs and cruelty suffered during the last four years. Certainly some of these reports are true. I had it last night in Mons on the authority of General Loomis commanding one of the Canadian divisions, that only a few days ago as some German prisoners were being brought in by the British, they were attacked by Belgian peasant women, beaten over the heads with their wooden shoes with such violence that three were killed. And when one hears of what all these poor people have suffered and borne during the past four years, there seems to be ample justification for their anger and violence.

It is impossible to adequately describe the ruin and devastation of the country north of Compiègne. Compiègne itself has suffered relatively not at all. True there are great numbers of houses that are mere heaps of bricks and stone,—the Hotel de Ville—the town hall, has been vastly scarred by shell or bombs,—but in the main the City is intact. When I passed through there first six weeks or two months ago it did not con-

[4] *Ibid.*

tain a living creature—except a few lonely sentries stationed here and there and numbers of desolate and unhappy looking cats, but yesterday houses were being opened up, men and women were at work trying to put their homes in order and repair the damage that had been wrought.

Compiègne is fortunate in that it was never in the possession of the Bosches except for a short time in 1914 nor was it within range of his guns. Such damage as it suffered was mainly if not altogether the result of bombs from planes. But Noyon just to the North, Ham, St. Quentin, Le Cateau and all the intervening villages are practically all mere shapeless masses of broken stone. The walls of many houses are still standing,—the Cathedral at Noyon, for instance still retains its shape but there are great shell holes in the walls, parts of the steeple have been carried away and, of course, the windows have been blown into atoms. The country all along from just beyond Compiègne to Solesmes is but a succession of trenches, barbed wire entanglements, shell holes and craters. I wish I could describe it to you, but I cannot and I doubt whether any pen or picture can possibly convey fully any idea of the ruin and desolation that has been wrought in this country extending over fifty miles from one point to another. Of course the towns and cities that have been but recently evacuated by the Germans have not in most instances suffered to anything like the extent as these that have been in the zone of the fierce fighting that has been going on since the summer of 1914. Mons for instance is in relatively good shape and better than Valenciennes a few miles to the South, but if you were to see these towns only and had not seen those that I have mentioned and others like Soissons, Rheims, too, you would say the ruin was horrible.

As we approached Compiègne in the early morning, we passed battalion after battalion of French coming back from the front, and now another long line of German prisoners, but as we came into Valenciennes we saw a military movement but of an entirely different character. Here two Canadian divisions were forming to march to the Rhine. Never as long as I live will I forget the appearance of these men or the picture they made. All the way from Valenciennes to Mons, a distance of fifteen miles or more, there was a solid procession of troops. The Canadians and Scotch in kilts marching with literally flying colors to the music of bagpipes played as I have never heard them played before, batallion after batallion of Canadians in regulation uniform with bands playing and men and women hurrahing, long lines of artillery drawn now by horses, now by trucks, and sometimes by caterpillar tractors, —officers, some mounted on horseback others in motors,—and everywhere there was the note of victory,—the men bore themselves proudly and marched not as if they had fought months and many of them years, but as if they were going out fresh to battle. While this was the inspiring and wonderful picture on one side of the road, that presented on the other was just as unusual, but it was a very sad one and conveyed as nothing else has conveyed to me since I have been in France what the war has really meant to some of these poor people. In long lines they came, returning to their homes which they had left to the Huns four years ago. Most of them were walking, but now and then an old man or woman or someone sick was seen riding; and nearly all were tugging away drawing carts, wagons and all kinds of makeshift contrivances on wheels, all loaded with the poor belongings,—clothing, furniture of the cheapest sort, and all kinds of household furniture or utensils. Only a very few had horses and such as they had seemed hardly able to stand. This contrast of the splendor of way on the one hand, on one side of the road, and on the other the misery and sorrow of it, brought home as nothing else could what it all had meant. And as our motor made its way slowly along, passing sometimes on one side, and sometimes following the troops, we came to village after village in ruins,—now and then a grave of a soldier who had fallen by the roadside, and occasionally a graveyard hastily laid out by the Germans to receive their dead. As we neared Mons evidences of destruction deliberately precipitated by the Germans in their retreat became more frequent. At one point the road had been mined apparently, for it had been literally blown away for a distance of one hundred or two hundred feet and nothing but a huge crater remained. The railroad which paralleled the highway had been totally destroyed. Bridges had blown up, the rails themselves were twisted into a fantastic shape by the force of the explosion that had been used, and here and there a freight car or locomotive was lying on its side torn into a twisted mass of steel and splitting wood.

Mons had been captured by the Canadians but five days before. The British finished the war where they had begun it. And as the Huns drove the first British Expeditionary Force, England's contemptible little army, to the West, so now four years and three months later on the same spot England's sons drove the Hun to the East utterly and hopelessly defeated it.[5]

Munitions Contract Renegotiation

Stettinius would have preferred to come home and be with his family now that the war was over, but he saw what had to be done and remained in France until a few days before Christmas 1918. He became virtually a one-man liquidation commission. He hurled himself into the new task of undoing his earlier labors with all of the vigor and keen perception that he had shown in negotiating the original agreements. He wrote Baker: "Immediately after the conclusion of the armistice, acting upon authority contained in cablegrams sent by you . . . I undertook to make settlements of the

[5] PS 34, unsorted family correspondence.

contracts or arrangements for artillery and artillery ammunition, which I had negotiated, including also pre-existing contracts which had been covered into my negotiations." [6]

The story of the renegotiation of the British contract is taken up by the *Final Report* of the Liquidation Commission:

Immediately after the armistice, Mr. Stettinius gave notice of the cancellation of the contract and at once began negotiations with a view to reaching a fair and equitable settlement for losses occasioned thereby. The negotiations which were merged in the agreement of October 19, 1918, covered a considerable period and it was clear that the British manufacturing operations had been maintained, and that she had made plans for increased production, in order to meet America's demands. A large part of the material contracted for had already been produced and a majority of the remainder was in process. Mr. Stettinius conducted his negotiations on the assumption that, as a large part of these materials were already in being and were in excess of the British requirements, it would be to America's interest to accept completed guns, equipment, and ammunition rather than to pay large indemnities and receive nothing in return.[7]

In the case of the ordnance agreements with France, the report of the Liquidation Commission says, "Immediately following the armistice, Mr. Stettinius began negotiations looking to a fair and equitable settlement of these obligations to the French, with a view to reducing our investments to a minimum, yet at the same time getting, in the form of completed artillery units, as nearly as possible value received for the money invested. In the first conference held with the French authorities it developed that France could not, for economic and social reasons, suddenly cease production, and that they were inclined to hold us responsible for accepting large deliveries."

In other words, Loucheur, the French Minister of Munitions, resisted the cancellation of contracts because it would throw men and women out of work.

The report resumes: "Mr. Stettinius took the position, which he steadfastly and consistently maintained, that the United States ought not to pay for any materials which had been produced as a result of continuing the operation of French factories beyond the war period in the interest of the social and economic welfare of France, and for the benefit of her people. The French authorities finally acquiesced in this position and in December, 1918, Mr. Stettinius had in con-

[6] ERS to Baker, Jan. 8, 1919, Record Group 213, National Archives.
[7] *Final Report*, p. 44.

ference with M. Loucheur, representing the French Government, agreed in principle upon the terms of a settlement." [8]

Edgar Smith's firsthand report of the French settlement is more vivid: "After the Armistice the work took on new pressure due to the rapid preparations that were being made for withdrawal of all troops, and for disposition of the American materials and commitments. It was during this period that, following a session your father had had with Louis Loucheur, he came back to the office about eight o'clock at night with his face wreathed in smiles, and remarked to George and me as he walked through the outer office 'Well, I crucified that ———!'" Smith adds a note on the departure from Paris: "On December 3rd orders were received for all members of the party to return to America, the date and port of embarkation being left to your father's discretion. Movement began on December 10th with Mr. Stettinius going with the main party for London, to sail from England, leaving me and one of the sergeants to convoy the 'office' back to America." [9]

After he got back to the United States, Stettinius wrote at length to Secretary Baker on January 8, 1918, reporting on the completion of his mission and making recommendations of policy and procedure for the demobilization effort. He indicated the need for an early decision on the disposition of aircraft and related items, as well as for prompt legislation to enable the United States to liquidate its assets. He urged a broad-gauge approach in the settling of claims as opposed to a narrow legalistic one:

I call your attention particularly to the fact that most of the claims of the United States against cobelligerents which are based on arrangements made in the United States are unliquidated, that many of them originate in informal understandings and that some of them may be contested either in principle or amount. I need hardly say that such claims can almost certainly be most profitably settled in connection with the claims of our cobelligerents against the United States—particularly claims of the same sort—by way of set-off. Such matters must be the subject of quasi-diplomatic treatment for they must be carried to a forum in which the standing and sanction of a purely moral claim are as good as those of a claim which would possess a more definite and self-sufficient standing in an ordinary tribunal.

Stettinius's most far-reaching proposal was that a Liquidation Commission be established:

In view of the number and magnitude of the matters requiring settlement, and the great value and more or less involved situation of the

[8] *Ibid.*, p. 62.   [9] Scrapbook II, Smith to ERS, Jr., April 23, 1933.

property requiring liquidation, I have advised (and now repeat the recommendation) that a commission be appointed consisting in larger part at least of civilians, who shall be charged with this work, and shall possess full power to act in the premises on behalf of our Government.

It seems to me important that the members of such a commission shall not only be men of sound judgment, but that one or more of them shall possess legal training and experience; that all of them shall be able to devote their time to this work for a considerable period, and consequently that they shall be properly compensated; that they shall in a sense, at least represent the various Departments of our Government which are more immediately concerned (such, for example, as the War Department, Treasury and State Department); that they shall be able to command access to the American Members of the Peace Commission or their close representatives, so that they may keep in touch with the purposes of the Commissioners which may affect their work and that the Commissioners themselves may keep in touch with the activities of the Commission, and above all that they shall be men of such character and position that not only the Executive Departments concerned, but Congress and the people at large shall have confidence in their judgment, capacity and integrity.

He concluded his recommendations by bowing out.[10]

Stettinius spent the rest of December and all of January and February 1919 in the United States getting reacquainted with his family, catching up on accumulated business, and conferring with government officials and with his partners at J. P. Morgan & Co.

On February 13 it was formally announced that for his services in the American war effort Stettinius had been awarded the Distinguished Service Medal.[11]

Return to Europe: The Objectives

The upshot of his conversations with Washington and New York was that he returned to Europe with four objectives in mind. He wanted to help the United States government clean up the unfinished business left by the sudden end of the war. He also wanted to wind up the dealings of the Export Department of J. P. Morgan & Co. with the British and French governments. Two other, more general and less immediate objectives, set by his partners at J. P. Morgan, are considered in a later chapter: to study the operations of

[10] ERS to Baker, Jan. 8, 1919, Record Group 213, National Archives.
[11] *New York Times*, Feb. 14, 1919, p. 12; RS 679, Thomas Nelson Perkins to ERS, Feb. 13, 1919.

their Paris house, Morgan, Harjes & Co., with a view to reorganizing
it to make it more effective and profitable; and to analyze the European economic situation to discover what goods were needed, how
they could be paid for, and how J. P. Morgan & Co. could profit
by the situation.[12]

So on March 1, 1919, Stettinius sailed from New York for South-
hampton on board the *Olympic*, arriving on March 8.[13]

Personal Observations

His partner Dwight Morrow sent a bon voyage present of a box of
cigars. Stettinius was a great cigar smoker. He bought cigars in large
quantities, especially Esperanza cigars from J. V. Flanagan and, in
his later years, Punch brand from Grosvenor S. Nicholas & Co.[14] He
was a plain man, almost a homespun figure in the austerity of his
private life. It is pleasant to find him indulging in a few small
extravagances such as good cigars and silk-tricot union suits,
elbow-length sleeves, ordered from the Colonial Knitting Mills in
Chicago.[15]

Grayson Murphy and their mutual friend Nelson Dean Jay of
Morgan, Harjes sent a more imaginative going-away present to
the ship. Stettinius's letter of acknowledgment is a pleasant bit of
whimsy and reveals the man at his most charming: "I was tremen-
dously pleased to receive the wonderful box of roses which you and
Jay sent me aboard the 'Olympic.' I thank you sincerely, not only
for the gift itself, but more particularly for the graceful compli-
ment that the character of the gift implied. For while others sent
me such vulgar things as cigars and booze, and one had even forwarded a huge consignment of eggs, butter, cream and fresh vege-
tables, you and Jay were the only ones who recognized the highly
aesthetic side of my nature and appreciated that I loved the beautiful, as well as the purely material, things of life." [16]

Stettinius went first to London. He was astonished by the temper
of the British. He described the scene in a letter to his wife written
on March 22:

The whole atmosphere in London has completely changed since I was
there three months ago. There is now everywhere an air of gaiety which

[12] See Chapter X, below.
[13] RS 257, ERS to C. L. McKeehan, March 21, 1919.
[14] RS 308, cigar correspondence.
[15] RS 309, ERS to Colonial Knitting Mills, Oct. 27, 1917.
[16] RS 243, ERS to Murphy, March 27, 1919.

is almost hilarious. The restaurants are filled to the overflowing and I have never seen more beautiful or elaborate gowns than I saw at the Ritz where I dined two evenings. All classes are said to have gone "dance mad." Young people and old people are equally carried away by the craze. It may be, and no doubt is, a perfectly natural reaction, but it seemed strange to me in view of the fact that England is faced with the most difficult industrial and financial problems which must be solved before the normal activities of life can be resumed.

Everyone, of course, was talking about the coal situation, and generally the opinion was expressed that the scale of all wages would have to be materially raised and that English workmen would never be content to work for as low rates as were paid in pre-war times.[17]

After four days in London, he went over to Paris. He wrote to F. W. M. Cutcheon:

It is impossible to describe adequately the confusion that exists generally in Paris as well as in France. No plans whatever have been made for reconstruction, and, if the reports are true, little, if anything, has been done for the care, that is to say for the housing and feeding, of refugees who have returned to their former homes in the devastated regions. No plans have been made, so far as I can learn, for the readjustment of the finances of the Government. The best classes of French appear to agree that more and higher taxes are necessary, but no proposal of any kind appears to have been made except that presented recently by Klotz to the effect that taxes should be imposed on capital. Prices are literally soaring. Beef is selling at $2.40 per pound, butter $1.60 per pound, eggs at from $1.50 to $1.80 per dozen, and chickens at from $3.60 to $4.00 each. In stating these figures, I have computed the franc roughly as being worth 20 cents,[18] so that some allowance should accordingly be made, but even with this allowance, I am sure you will agree that the prices appear high. Rooms at hotels are said to be almost impossible to obtain and generally the profiteer is running rampant. Taxis are cheap during the day, but I am told that at night it has not been unusual for a charge of from 25 to 35 francs to be demanded for a fare from the theatre district to my apartment.

I came over, as you know, with the idea of remaining until the Fall. I am now beginning to plan on returning at a very much earlier date. I of course feel obligated to remain here as long as my partners desire, but under the present circumstances, it seems a waste of time. I would be much happier if I were to feel that I could return to the United States about the middle of June even if I were to come back again in September.[19]

[17] RS 677, ERS to Mrs. ERS, March 22, 1919.
[18] The French franc was quoted in the *New York Times* on March 21, 1919, at 5.71 to the dollar.
[19] RS 149, ERS to Cutcheon, March 21, 1919.

In September 1918 Stettinius had taken an apartment in Paris at 26 Avenue Henri Martin, which he still retained.[20] Shortly after his return to Paris in March 1919 he became ill. He was still tired from his years of work without rest, and London and Paris in March are notoriously cold and damp. Henry Davison, who had been staying on the Riviera, came to Paris for a few days as a guest in the apartment. On March 27 Davison returned by the night train to Cannes and Stettinius went with him, hoping to find warmth and sunshine.[21]

After visiting Davison at Cannes for several days, Stettinius took his car, which he had sent on ahead, and motored along the Riviera, stopping at Monte Carlo. He drove as far as San Remo on the Italian side. He had hoped to get to Florence, but the car broke down.[22] Instead he wandered through Provence and enjoyed seeing Avignon, Arles, Nîmes, and Orange. In Burgundy he became acquainted for the first time with the wine. He returned to Paris in mid-April in good health after an absence of a month.[23]

The Liquidation Problem

Stettinius had returned to Europe hoping to be of some use to the United States in clearing up the chaotic tangle of problems left over from the war. He soon became discouraged, as we see from a letter written a fortnight after his arrival:

The situation in England, so far as the financial and business activities of the Army are concerned, is very unsatisfactory. All of the good men, with the exception of Simpson, have returned home, and Simpson insists upon returning about the middle of April. The Liquidation Board, which was formed last November, has literally gone to pieces and all that remains of it is General Wheeler. He was unable to act because, about a month ago, an order was issued directing that no further sales of property, or settlements or cancellations of contracts should be made, except with the approval of the Liquidating Commission. As no members of the Liquidating Commission were in Europe but Dawes, and as Dawes was unwilling to act, the net result was that nothing was done.

I am sorry to say that the Liquidation Commission is getting under way very slowly. There is a vast amount of talk, but very little action. About all that they have done up to the present time is to confirm the

---

[20] RS 734, Paris—26 Avenue Henri Martin file.
[21] RS 243, ERS to Grayson M.-P. Murphy, March 27, 1919.
[22] RS 149, ERS to Cutcheon, May 24, 1919.
[23] RS 162, ERS to Martin Egan, May 6, 1919.

settlements I had tentatively made with the British for artillery, ammunition and for tanks.

In Paris he resolved to steer clear of the problem. The letter continues: "I am occupying, temporarily, General Rogers' old office on the fourth floor of the Elysee Palace as I have been unable to get a room with Messrs. Morgan, Harjes & Company, but am promised an office in their new building which will be ready for occupancy about the first of the month. At that time, I will move downtown and hope to have little, if anything, to do with the work of the Liquidation Commission." [24]
He reported to Martin Egan on May 6 that he was taking advantage of his recent illness to sever all connection with the Liquidation Commission.[25] But he found it difficult to remain disentangled. On May 24 he wrote F. W. M. Cutcheon:

Of course you are interested in the Liquidation Commission. I am sorry to say that it has made practically no progress. While its problem is of course very difficult, the real trouble lies in the fact that the members of the Commission have never been able to agree among themselves on anything without innumerable meetings and hours of discussion, and indeed, as to the most important questions of policy, have been unable to agree at all. Parker, if left to himself, would, I believe, do good work, but Johnson is simply impossible and of course neither Dawes nor Hollis are of any assistance at all. Indeed, they are a detriment rather than a help to the situation, as they both insist upon talking, but neither ever say anything. The French have shown a willingness to buy all of our moveable and immovable property, but have not stated at what prices or on what bases they will take over the moveable property. Their object apparently is to buy on time at a low price and sell for cash at a high price. Parker prepared what appeared to me to be a very well-worked out plan to deal with the French. It was first proposed at a meeting held the latter part of April which I attended, at which time I was asked to submit my views as to what should be done and as to what kind of an arrangement should be made. Nearly a month was consumed in developing the plan and putting it on paper, and when it was finally presented to the Commission, Johnson, Dawes and Hollis voted against the proposition of submitting it to the French. None of them, however, had any alternative plan to propose. The net result is that nothing further has been done. I attended one or two meetings the earlier part of this week, but in view of the fact that no attention whatever has been paid to any of my suggestions, I have of course made up my mind to

[24] RS 149, ERS to Cutcheon, March 21, 1919.
[25] RS 162, ERS to Egan, May 6, 1919.

have nothing further to do with the Commission, even in an advisory way.[26]

His unofficial advice continued to be available and was listened to more often than he admitted.[27] It is a tribute to Stettinius's tact and diplomacy that Liquidation Commissioner Homer H. Johnson, described as "simply impossible" in the letter to Cutcheon, later wrote a most appreciative letter to Stettinius, concluding: "Let me add, at the probable termination of our relations, an expression of my appreciation of your unfailing courtesy to me in the rather troublesome job that I got into. I am going to put on record to the Department when opportunity offers, my acknowledgment of the fact that the setting up of the Liquidation Commission was due entirely to you; the scheme as outlined, with the necessary legislation, and the beginning of the liquidation itself, had all been done under your conception and direction. All we had to do was to go ahead with the business, which was a much more simple matter than outlining its course."[28]

As the *Final Report* testifies, the Liquidation Commission eventually did get to work and accomplished a great deal in cleaning up the mess left by the war. But this was after Stettinius had gone.

A postscript to the story is added in the election year 1924. Calvin Coolidge's running mate for the vice-presidency was Charles G. Dawes. Stettinius and Dawes had long been acquainted. Both had been active in the Chicago business community. Both were involved in matériel procurement for the American Expeditionary Force during the war. Both were concerned with the abortive attempt to nominate General Pershing for the presidency of the United States in 1920. On top of these other connections, Dawes was a client of the Morgan firm.[29] Stettinius had no personal animus toward Dawes, but he thought him totally unfitted for the presidency of the United States. He questioned the soundness of his judgment. That he felt strongly on this score is seen in the telegram he sent to Martin Egan in the spring of 1924: "Have found it is impossible to vote for president and not for vice president stop Accordingly will either return to faith of my fathers and vote Democratic ticket and if this is not possible will not vote at all stop Helen Maria what a shocking situation."[30]

[26] RS 149, ERS to Cutcheon, May 24, 1919.

[27] RS 243, ERS to Murphy, July 20, 1919.

[28] RS 205, Johnson to ERS, Dec. 2, 1919.

[29] RS 162, ERS to Egan, Sept. 20, 1919; RS 108, ERS to Dawes, Aug. 20, 1920; RS 156, Dawes to ERS, May 5, 1921.

[30] RS 162, ERS to Egan, June 13, 1924.

"Helen Maria" is a sly reference to Dawes's favorite expletive, "Hell and Maria."

Winding Up the Export Department

Meanwhile, the work of settling the accounts of the Export Department with the foreign governments continued. Stettinius found the British ready to negotiate, as we learn in a roundabout way. While he was on the Riviera holiday, Stettinius had an exchange of cables with E. H. Wells of Babcock & Wilcox in New York. The directors of that company wanted him back on the board.[31] Stettinius wrote to Wells on May 23 that he had finally resolved the problem of conflict of interest that would have prevented him from accepting election to the board. "I am glad to say that last week I made a final settlement with the British Government of all matters that would have had any bearing upon the renewal of my association with you, but nevertheless, I would of course prefer that a reasonable period should elapse after the completion of these negotiations before going back into the B. & W. Company."[32] Stettinius finally took his seat at the meeting of February 26, 1920.[33] He remained a board member for the rest of his life.

The French were more difficult. Stettinius wrote from Paris to Raleigh Hansl, the head of the surviving remnant of the Export Department at the Morgan office:

Of course, I have not a particle of doubt that, as far as the War Office is concerned, they will claim everything and anything in sight, and if it were necessary finally to make a settlement with the War Office, I would have little hope of reaching an agreement that would be in the slightest degree satisfactory to us. Fortunately, however, the final settlement will be made by the Treasury and the man with whom we are dealing there appears to be an exceptionally clean and good type of Frenchman who naturally wishes, however, in coming to an agreement with us, to have the support of the various departments affected, and it is for this reason that I find it necessary to spend so much time in discussion with one of the bureaucrats of the War Office.

But Stettinius was tenacious. He added: "However, one of the things I mainly had in mind when I came over was to settle up all

[31] Minutes of stockholders' meeting of April 2, 1919 (company archives, New York); RS 219, Wells to ERS, April 28, 1919, and ERS to Wells, April 28, 1919.
[32] RS 219, ERS to Wells, May 23, 1919.
[33] Minutes of directors' meeting of Feb. 26, 1920 (company archives, New York).

of our Commercial Agency matters with the British and French
Governments, and I have no idea at all of returning to the United
States until they shall have been settled and settled satisfactorily,
and in view of the fact that I am making my plans to reach New
York some time in November, I expect to make a settlement
soon." [34]

He wound up the Export Department business somewhat earlier
than expected and sailed for New York on the *France* in October.

[34] RS 190, ERS to Hansl, July 18, 1919.

IX. *In Town (1916–1925)*

THE Stettinius family was living at Dongan Hills, Staten Island, in the spring of 1916 when they were suddenly uprooted with no warning, rushed out of the house into automobiles, and driven to an unknown destination. The Morgan firm had learned that German agents, seeking desperately to slow down the flow of American munitions to the Allies, threatened the personal safety of Stettinius and his family.

After seeing the others comfortably settled on Long Island in a house that had been engaged for them by the firm, Stettinius himself was installed by Morgan representatives on the power cruiser *Margaret* in New York harbor.[1] There are surprisingly few references in the correspondence to this unusual living arrangement. Stettinius does allude to it in a letter of June 1916 to Sir Guy Gaunt, where he mentions coming across a letter from Gaunt in "running through my papers on the yacht yesterday." [2] Five years later Stettinius wrote to F. K. Pulsifer of New York, "Many thanks for your kindness in sending me descriptive matter of the Yacht 'Hourless.' I myself am not interested as I have had all the yachting that I want and would not accept the boat as a gift." [3]

The *Margaret* remained a simple, utilitarian floating house for Stettinius until the summer, when he chartered the vessel on his own account.[4] This time the family was invited to join him, and his colleague Henry Davison took charge of putting the cruiser in shape for more comfortable living. Such amenities as flower vases and marked linens were added, as well as complete sets of china and plated silver "to take the place of the odd lot of crockery and silver" with which Stettinius had been making do while "batching" on the boat.[5] The demands of the Allied purchasing job were too heavy to have allowed much of a seagoing holiday that third sum-

---

[1] Recalled by Mrs. John B. Marsh (Isabel Stettinius Marsh) in conversation with the author, April 1970.

[2] RS 281, ERS to Gaunt, June 19, 1916.

[3] RS 139, ERS to Pulsifer, March 17, 1921.

[4] RS 280, Captain A. L. Haskell to J. P. Morgan & Co., Jan. 13, 1917.

[5] RS 280, J. S. Pettit to ERS, June 2, 1916.

mer of the war, but the evidence of a toll charge on the Cape Cod Canal for early June 1916 suggests at least a weekend trip.[6]

The very week of this short cruise Stettinius made arrangements for living in New York City that fall and the following winter and spring. He leased a house at 16 East 73rd Street from October 15, 1916, to May 1, 1917.[7] Meanwhile he was looking for a house in New York to buy. He finally settled on the Amos Pinchot house at 1021 Park Avenue, on the northeast corner of East 85th Street. The *New York Evening Post* announced the purchase on November 4, 1916, but noted that actual possession would not be taken until "next spring," when the existing lease expired.[8]

The house at 1021 Park Avenue was built for the Pinchots earlier in the century by the architectural firm of Hunt and Hunt.[9] It was a handsome, formal townhouse in the Italian High Renaissance Revival style introduced by McKim, Mead, and White at Chicago's 1893 Columbian Exposition. The building was rectangular and rose four stories from a strongly rusticated or banded first floor to the typical massive cornice of the sixteenth-century Roman palazzo. The front door was flanked by Tuscan columns; above it was a balustraded balcony onto which the second-floor conservatory opened through three arched windows.

An interesting element of the interior was the spiral stairway, which wound up the full four stories and was indicated on the outside back wall by a semicircular recessed bay. The disposition of rooms was fairly typical for the time. The kitchen and service areas were in the basement, the dining room was on the street floor, and the living room and library were on the second floor or "piano nobile" of the Italian townhouse. Family bedrooms were on the third and fourth floors, and staff bedrooms were in the attic. Stettinius engaged the architect Lewis Colt Albro of 2 West 47th Street to remodel the interior. The remodelling seems not to have been an unqualified success. Stettinius wrote to the architect, "Frankly, I was astonished afterwards, that you would have permitted such abominable work to be done."[10]

---

[6] RS 280, "S.D." (in ERS's office) to J. Beaver-Webb, June 12, 1916.

[7] RS 734, 16 East 73rd Street file, lease, June 12, 1916; ERS to E. C. Gruver, July 9, 1917; W. H. Baiz to ERS, July 25, 1917. The rent was $1,250 a month. There was a charge of $250 for damage to portières and rugs, the latter attributed to the children's dog.

[8] RS 734, 1021 Park Avenue file, warranty deed, June 8, 1917. The house cost $260,000. Stettinius gave it to his wife.

[9] *The Brickbuilder*, XIX, No. 3 (March 1910), plates 41 and 42.

[10] RS 734, 1021 Park Avenue Redecorating file, ERS to Albro, Nov. 16, 1922.

The years when the Stettinius family was based in New York coincided with the period when the four children ceased to be children and were becoming young adults.

In 1917 Carrington was an undergraduate at the University of Virginia, though his father had hoped that he would go to Princeton.[11] His father saw that American involvement in the European war was inevitable and wrote him at Charlottesville in February to be ready for the call.[12] Carrington left college to join the army. In the fall of 1917 he was invited by General Walter Gordon to be his aide.[13] His tour of duty took him overseas, where he saw action in France and was gassed in the summer of 1918. Stettinius visited his son in the hospital near Chaumont in September.[14]

The Stettinius family was not given to display or self-advertisement, but occasional references to them appeared in the society columns as Edward Stettinius became more and more of a public figure. They subscribed to the Metropolitan Opera for the season of 1917–1918 and occupied parterre box No. 22 on odd Monday evenings.[15] A feature story in the *New York World* for January 28, 1918, told about Mrs. Stettinius's war work with the Red Cross and the National League for Woman's Services and described her daughter Isabel's Canteen. The *New York Herald* of February 13 reported on Isabel's activities on the team of Mrs. Cornelius N. Bliss, Jr., in the Association for Improving the Condition of the Poor. Later in the same week, on February 17, a photograph of Isabel appeared in the *Philadelphia Public Ledger* with the caption, "Recently Introduced to Society." The *New York Sun* noted on June 18 that Mr. and Mrs. Stettinius and their daughter (it would have been Isabel; Betty was not old enough) attended the dinner given by the Japanese ambassador for the Italian ambassador the night before.

This was a period in American social history when resort hotels enjoyed great popularity. In the summer of 1918, after Stettinius had gone to Paris, Mrs. Stettinius and the girls went to one of the family's favorite summer resorts, The Greenbrier, at White Sulphur Springs, West Virginia. *Town Topics* reported on August 15: "The Greenbrier County Horse Show was the smartest in several seasons.

[11] PM 4, ERS to WCS, Oct. 15, 1915.
[12] RS 675 (2), ERS to WCS, Feb. 10, 1917.
[13] RS 675 (2), ERS to WCS, Nov. 7, 1917.
[14] Scrapbook II, Smith to ERS, Jr., April 22, 1933.
[15] RS 312, ERS to F. Dodd, Secretary, Metropolitan Opera and Real Estate Company, Sept. 27, 1917. The subscription price for opening night and eleven subsequent evenings was $3,575.

. . . Mrs. Edward Stettinius, with Betty and Isabel, were among the box-holders. Bell and Betty also rode in the ring and their equestrianship elicited the plaudits of onlookers. . . . White Sulphur is among the gayest of spas this summer."

Not all of the accounts were so agreeable. The spiteful little gossip-sheet *Club Fellow* had written up the same social whirl with a malicious twist on July 24:

> Mrs. Edward Stettinius . . . arrived recently at the White Sulphur Springs, and has installed herself, presumably for the Summer, in a cottage there. I do not know what were Judith's beginnings—save that she hails vaguely "from the South"—but now, because of Edward's position, she may be regarded as a personage, and I consider that considerable entertaining is due from her. And the White Sulphur is dull. No use denying that fact, although there was an attempt at liveliness during the tennis tournament which resulted in featuring various "leading New York women" who never were heard of before that event.

Club Fellow seems to have been particularly vindictive toward Mrs. Stettinius. Eight years later, in the issue of September 22, 1926, it noted that "Mrs. Stettinius and Cousin Mary—out from Richmond for the autumn foliage change—will be able to impress western and northern outlanders with the importance of the Old Dominion Carringtons, and make them feel uncouth and lowbrow when in their immediate vicinity."

Stettinius was abroad on war work during 1917 and 1918. In 1919 he returned to Europe, primarily on business for the Morgan firm. It was decided that Mrs. Stettinius and the two girls would join him there in the spring of 1919. Shortly before sailing, Mrs. Stettinius announced Isabel's engagement to Major John B. Marsh, who in civilian life was a lawyer. Stettinius was taken by surprise, for while he had been favorably impressed by the young man, with characteristic caution and fatherly concern he had asked Martin Egan, one of the younger executives at the Morgan firm, to look into the suitor's background, and the announcement preceded the report! Happily, the young man came through the Egan inquiry with flying colors.[16]

Isabel Stettinius and John Bigelow Marsh were married the following November, after Stettinius's return to the United States. The father of the bride wrote to his relative, Lucy Lee Brownlee, about the occasion:

> The wedding came off last week and everyone says it was a very successful and beautiful affair. Certainly the church was very attractive and

---

[16] RS 162, ERS to Egan, May 6, 1919.

the ceremony very impressive. The reception at the house was a jam of
the worst kind although everybody seemed to enjoy it. We all thought
and talked of you on the day of the wedding and wished that you had
been with us. You had so much to do with my youngsters in their baby-
hood and childhood that I feel that, after a fashion, they belong to you
and that on such an occasion as a wedding you should be with us.[17]

To John P. Grier he wrote the same day to thank him for putting
him up for The Links, to which he had just been elected. He
added: "Of course I missed you at the wedding, but congratulate
you on having escaped. There was a terrific crush—just the kind of
an affair that you would not have liked.[18]

A year later he received a note of congratulations from Thomas
Lamont on the birth of his first grandchild, Isabel Stettinius Marsh,
born October 24, 1920, in New York City.[19]

When the war was over Carrington returned to the University
of Virginia and after a year transferred to the Law School, as
undergraduates could do in those days, but did not graduate.[20]
Carrington left the University of Virginia to go into business in
Baltimore. He entered the Bartlett Hayward Corporation and ultimately became an upper-level executive in the firm's subsidiary,
the American Hammered Piston Ring Company.

Carrington became engaged to marry Miss Achsah Petre of
Baltimore. The wedding took place in Baltimore on March 30,
1921.[21]

Edward R. Stettinius, Jr., was a child when the family moved to
New York. Like his brother Carrington, he was later sent to
Pomfret School in Connecticut.[22] The elder Stettinius, so sensitive
and gifted in human relationships with all kinds of people, did not
understand his younger son. Adolescence is not much fun for anybody, and when one has a famous father and a brother going off to
war and being a hero, life can be very difficult. The father was
greatly disturbed because the son was moody, talked about going
into the ministry, and was doing indifferently in his studies. He
took the boy out of Pomfret and sent him to the Lake Placid
School.[23]

[17] RS 274, ERS to Brownlee, Nov. 22, 1919.
[18] RS 266, ERS to Grier, Nov. 22, 1919.
[19] RS 200, Lamont to ERS, Nov. 4, 1920.
[20] *Corks and Curls*, the University of Virginia yearbook, XXXII (1919), 72;
XXXIII (1920), 81. (For the citations here and in notes 26 and 27 I am in-
debted to William D. Barnard, who kindly allowed me to consult his paper
prepared for a seminar in American history at the University of Virginia.)
[21] *New York Times*, March 31, 1921.
[22] RS 676 (2), ERS to William B. Olmsted, April 28, 1916.
[23] RS 676 (2), ERS to John M. Hopkins, Sept. 26, 1917.

It was the father's wish that his son go to Yale, Princeton, or Harvard, not to his brother's college the University of Virginia. But he was prepared to abandon that hope if some college whose entrance examinations Edward could pass offered a business course.[24] Edward did enter the University of Virginia. His father wrote him letters so moralizing in tone as to put any young man's back up. One regrettable specimen is dated January 24, 1921:

> I agree with you fully that the development of character is just as important as the acquisition of knowledge and I hope that you will bear in mind that some of the elements that go to make up the well-rounded character are determination and perseverance. These qualities can be easily developed and require neither the assistance or guidance of professors. Take for instance the simple question of penmanship. Are you quite sure that you are showing either determination or perseverance in that direction? If you were to spend thirty minutes a day in practice, it would not be many months before you would have greatly improved your penmanship, but to spend thirty minutes every day, whatever the conditions might be, in practice, means both determination and perseverance. Why don't you demonstrate what you can do in this direction?[25]

The father need not have worried quite so much. While Edward was never a student, he became very active in the life of the university and received considerable recognition from his fellow students. The college annual of his fourth year, 1924, lists a long string of extracurricular activities and honors, including the presidency of the student body of the academic department or undergraduate college.[26] Edward Stettinius, Jr., did not finish his college course, but he became interested in a career in industry through the influence of Alfred Sloan, president of General Motors, and his assistant John Lee Pratt.[27]

Stettinius continued to keep Lucy Lee Brownlee abreast of family news. He wrote on April 28, 1921, a month after Carrington's wedding:

> The children are all fine. Carrington's wedding went off in great shape and he and his bride are as happy as can be. She is a delightful girl and we have come to love her sincerely . . . Carrington will of course continue to make his home in Baltimore where he is connected with the Bartlett Hayward Company and is doing very fine work.

[24] RS 676 (2), ERS to ERS, Jr., Jan. 24, 1919.
[25] RS 676 (1), ERS to ERS, Jr., Jan. 24, 1921.
[26] *Corks and Curls*, XXXVII (1924), 80.
[27] Thomas Moody Campbell, "Stettinius at the United Nations" (Ph.D. diss., University of Virginia, 1964), pp. 11-12.

Isabel is a perfect joy to all of us. The young granddaughter is beginning to show signs of intelligence and I have no doubt will, in time, be a source of such pleasure to me as she has been to her Mother and Grandmother since her arrival.

Edward is doing splendidly at the University of Virginia and is making substantial headway in his studies as well as in the activities of college life. He was elected recently a member of one of the select secret societies and during the probationary period was compelled, for several days, to dress like a convict and keep himself in evidence on the campus and on the streets of the town, all of which afforded him as well as his fellows much satisfaction.

Betty is growing entirely too rapidly to suit me. She always was a little tyrant, but now she rules me and, to a lesser degree, the family with a rod of iron. I suppose that, some of these days, she too will marry some little blatherskite and leave us and I certainly look forward to that day with dread.[28]

Stettinius did not live to see his daughter Elizabeth married. She was married on June 16, 1928, to Juan T. Trippe.[29] There is every reason to believe that the father would have approved of the "blatherskite" when he did come along, and not merely because this man turned out to be one of the most imaginative and effective business executives of his generation as the builder of Pan American World Airways.

Meanwhile, the New York establishment was becoming too large for Mrs. Stettinius to direct unaided. Her health was never very robust and the details of housekeeping and entertaining were more and more demanding. The solution was to engage Miss Celestine W. How as secretary, with responsibility for managing the family's domestic arrangements, hiring and paying the staff, and approving bills and forwarding them to John J. Bennett, Stettinius's private secretary down at the Morgan office, or his assistant Frank Ryall, for payment.[30]

An important member of the Stettinius household was Peter O'Neill. Peter had originally come to Staten Island as a butler in January 1916. Later he became Stettinius's valet. In July 1920 he reluctantly left because he wanted a change from domestic service.[31] In six months' time both master and man discovered that they couldn't get along without each other. Stettinius wired Peter in

[28] RS 274, ERS to Brownlee, April 28, 1921.
[29] *Who's Who in America*, XXXVI (1970–71), 2304.
[30] R.S. 497, How correspondence, Jan. 14, 1920–March 12, 1923.
[31] RS 734, 1021 Park Avenue—Personnel—Peter O'Neill file, ERS letter of recommendation, "To whom it may concern," Aug. 3, 1920.

Boston on February 10, 1921, "Would like to have you come at once." Peter's reply of the same day was, "Glad to accept your offer." [32] Both men were in poor health in 1924 when Stettinius wrote to Peter on February 19 urging him to remain in Atlantic City until he had quite recovered from surgery. [33]

The automobiles that carried Stettinius from 1021 Park Avenue to 23 Wall Street in 1921 were a Cadillac limousine and a Pierce-Arrow limousine, both driven by John J. McGowan. The following year the Pierce-Arrow was turned in on a second Cadillac. [34]

In the basement of 1021 Park Avenue, under the spiral stairway, was a cylindrical area. It was divided into two rooms. One housed the machinery for the elevator; the other was the wine cellar. An inventory of wines and spirits dated March 17, 1922, lists the contents of the cellar. Among the items were 336 bottles of gin, 40 bottles of Haig & Haig Scotch whiskey, 60 bottles of champagne, 196 sauterne, 88 claret, 114 vermouth, 32 port, and 79 sherry—53 Amontillado and 26 Park & Tilford topaz. [35] This list is useful not so much because of what it reveals about Stettinius's taste in liquor, but because it suggests the scale of entertaining at 1021 Park Avenue. Stettinius himself was most abstemious except for cigars.

The climax of this social activity was the ball held on Friday evening, February 9, 1923. [36] This affair was one of the high points of the New York social season. It received generous coverage in the *New York Times* the following day:

Miss Stettinius Greeted at Dance

Her Mother Entertains About 300 Guests at Her Home in Park Avenue

Bridge and Dinner Parties

Among Other Hostesses of the Day Are Mrs. Gawtry and Mrs. Morris

Mrs. Edward R. Stettinius entertained last evening with a dance at her residence, 1021 Park Avenue, for her debutante daughter, Miss Betty Stettinius, a number of dinners preceding it. There were about 300 guests, who were received by Mrs. Stettinius and Miss Stettinius, assisted by Mrs. John B. Marsh, another daughter of the hostess, and by Mrs. William Carrington Stettinius, her daughter-in-law.

Two Japanese dancers from the Royal Theatre in Tokio danced in

---

[32] RS 734, ERS to O'Neill, Feb. 10, 1921; O'Neill to ERS, Feb. 10, 1921.

[33] RS 734, ERS to O'Neill, Feb. 19, 1924.

[34] RS 451, Automobiles file, John J. Bennett to A. B. Ashforth, Feb. 1921; McGowan to Bennett, Sept. 21, 1921; Ashforth, Inc. to ERS, "Attention Mr. Ryall," May 24, 1922.

[35] RS 726, Inventory, March 17, 1922.

[36] RS 693, list of persons invited to the dance.

native costumes to Japanese music by Japanese musicians, who played on the samisen and koto.

Mrs. Lewis B. Gawtry gave a dinner for Miss Beatrice Gawtry and Miss Stettinius. The other guests included the Misses Olive Van Rensselaer Gawtry, Isabelle Kemp, Dorothy Stevens, Barbara Brown, Matilda Ellsworth, Sophie Duer; also Alfred Ely Jr., John Kean, John Davis, Henry Coster, Varick Frissell, Phillips Robinson, Arthur Fisk, Jr. and Van Rensselaer Halsey.

Mrs. Lewis Gouverneur Morris also entertained at her home with a small dinner for Miss Adele Reynal. The other guests were the Misses Carola Kip, Cathleen Vanderbilt, Julia Brokaw; also John Duer, Murray Hoffman, W. T. Adee, Eugene Reynal and W. E. Shepperd Jr.

Others who entertained at dinner, their guests going on to the dance, were Mrs. John Sloane Manson, whose dinner was for Miss Margaret Sloane Manson, and Mrs. N. Thayer Robb, who entertained for her daughter Miss Cornelia Robb.[37]

One of the penalties of being in the public eye and socially prominent was the constant nuisance of being defrauded in small ways. Especially annoying was the habit of petty crooks to charge purchases to Stettinius's accounts at shops. In the spring of 1922 someone walked into Benson & Hedges, the tobacconists at 435 Fifth Avenue, and charged a pouch and tobacco, total bill $15.50. Stettinius was outraged. A few months later the same thing happened at Brooks Brothers, the clothing store. This time the imposter charged a chauffeur's cap and a pair of leggings.[38]

Men who knew Stettinius in his youth in St. Louis remembered his enthusiasm for card-playing. The stag party with cards remained a source of pleasure and relaxation to him. His letters on the subject of cards were invariably whimsically worded but the words "cards," "bridge," or "poker" were never mentioned. In acknowledging the receipt of a cheque for substantial winnings he wrote to a loser: "Many thanks for your letter of the 30th enclosing check in my favor in the sum of $1555. representing the amount contributed by you, Mr. Peabody and others to the special fund which was raised for the benefit of Mr. Gibson and myself. I appreciate sincerely the courtesy and liberality of the little group of which you were the representative."[39] In proposing a friendly game to a crony of his he wrote, "I was about to send out invitations to the faithful to join me in an evening of meditation and prayer at my home on

[37] *New York Times*, Feb. 10, 1923.
[38] RS 406, ERS to Benson & Hedges, June 29, 1922; Brooks Brothers to ERS, Sept. 21, 1922.
[39] RS 601, ERS to Preston Dave, Aug. 2, 1920.

Friday, August 4." [40] Copies of this invitation went out to Messrs. P. A. S. Franklin, James Brown, Andrew Fletcher, Anson Burchard, Henry Sanderson, and Joseph W. Harriman. The following week he expressed similar sentiments: "I am asking a few of the faithful to join me in a 'Service of Hope' at my house on Friday evening, August 11." [41]

Ten twenty-one Park Avenue continued to be the town house of the Stettinius family for a few years after Stettinius's death in 1925. It was sold in the summer of 1928 to Anthony Campagna, a building contractor. Campagna tore the building down and replaced it with a fourteen-story cooperative apartment house during the period when Park Avenue was dominated by rows of monolithic brick apartment buildings, later to be replaced themselves by a double row of glass and steel boxes. [42]

[40] RS 792, ERS to F. P. Moore, July 25, 1922.
[41] RS 792, ERS to Moore, Aug. 3, 1922.
[42] *New York Sun*, Aug. 4, 1928; *New York Times*, March 3, 1929.

X. J. P. Morgan & Co.: Stettinius's Postwar European Mission and the Foreign Commerce Corporation

THE most significant thing about the decision that Stettinius remain in Europe until the fall of 1919 was that it placed him in his rightful position as a fully accepted peacetime partner of J. P. Morgan & Co. Heretofore his role had been that of a pinch hitter in a baseball game, a specialist brought in for a specific emergency. Now, although a few items of business remained to be attended to, the war emergency was over, and he had an important job to do within the firm. He was a regular member of the team.

Morgan, Harjes & Co.

We saw that the third of the four business matters that kept Stettinius in Europe after the war was the concern of the partners of J. P. Morgan & Co. about their Paris firm, Morgan, Harjes & Co. To Martin Egan, Stettinius described the malaise that afflicted Morgan, Harjes in the spring of 1919:

Business in the Paris house is dragging along in a most distressingly languid fashion. If we are to take the same leadership in international finance as we have in American finance, and as of course we must, the Paris house will, in my opinion, have to be completely reorganized, and fresh and very vigorous rich blood will have to be injected into it. I may be able to do some little good by "sitting in and looking wise" in the next four or five months and in handling some specific propositions that may from time to time come up, but as I look at it, the situation will never be put in satisfactory shape until we shall have permanently, at the head of the Paris house, a real leader who can with dignity and ability properly represent J. P. Morgan & Company in international negotiations.[1]

The 1919 mission to Paris was not a success. Early in June 1919 Stettinius had discussed confidently with J. P. Morgan the problems of what to do "in considering men for the reorganized Firm here," [2]

[1] RS 162, ERS to Egan, May 6, 1919.
[2] RS 256, ERS to Morgan, June 4, 1919.

as though the change were just about to take place and new em-
ployees would shortly be needed. But in September he reported to
Martin Egan with far less assurance. The fact was that the heads of
Morgan, Harjes resented what they regarded as Stettinius's snoop-
ing around their office, and even J. P. Morgan disagreed with his
views on the relationship between the New York and Paris houses.
In Paris, Stettinius's reorganization plan met with passive resistance.
He wrote Egan: "The situation with respect to Morgan, Harjes
& Company is unchanged. Herman returned four days ago from a
two weeks' stay at Bourbon-les-Bains and has not yet taken up
seriously the question of reorganizing the House although I think he
is now more than ever impressed with the importance of doing
something. I hope sincerely that something will be done and am
sorry that my idea of developing the House appeared to be too
ambitious." [3]

Not much was said at the time about the failure of the mission
but Stettinius referred to it sadly two years later in a letter to
Nelson Dean Jay, who had recently joined Morgan, Harjes:

I have no thought whatever of going abroad this year. Indeed, even if
there were work to do over there, I must say frankly that I would be
reluctant to undertake it. I have the very uncomfortable feeling that
both Herman [Harjes] and Jack [Carter] are not very kindly disposed
toward me and that they assume I have been more critical of them than
I have been in point of fact. In view of the position I have taken from
the very outset, and maintained consistently all the way through, that
they should be fully protected and recognized in whatever might be
done, I am, of course, a little hurt by what I conceive to be their attitude
toward me and naturally, under these conditions, I have not the slightest
desire to go abroad and was very happy indeed when it finally developed
that George [Whitney] was selected to make the trip.

I am over-joyed to note that you are happy in your work and en-
vironment. I believe, and have always believed, that there is a great
future in Morgan, Harjes & Co. and that you could, and would, play an
important part in developing that business. I have also believed, and still
believe, that you should be supported in the fullest possible way and
that some one member of the Firm here should be charged with the
responsibility of keeping in touch and working with you in connection with the various problems that arise. Here is where Jack Morgan
and I apparently do not agree, but this is another story and there is no
use wasting your time or mine thinking or writing about it. [4]

[3] RS 162, ERS to Egan, Sept. 20, 1919.
[4] RS 206, ERS to Jay, Aug. 29, 1921.

But, as we shall soon see, Stettinius's energies were diverted—perhaps fortunately—from the objective of working out a plan for revitalizing the Paris house.

In the midst of this tense situation, Stettinius was decorated by the French government with the order of the Legion of Honor with the rank of commander.[5]

European Business Prospects

The fourth and last of Stettinius's reasons for returning to Europe early in 1919 was to explore business possibilities abroad for J. P. Morgan & Co.

In the spring of 1919 the firm, and particularly Henry Davison, became increasingly interested in the problems of international trade. Davison, who had been the head of the American Red Cross throughout the entire period of United States participation in the war, was in a position to see at first hand Europe's needs for post-war reconstruction. It was obvious that great quantities of materials of all sorts would have to be imported from the United States to rebuild the war-torn countries and their economies. The question was how to meet this need for American goods. This involved finding out what the specific requirements would be and how to pay for the necessary goods. To Stettinius in Paris went the job of trying to find out what was needed, while Davison in New York worked out a financial plan.

A logical place to begin to explore the commercial and financial possibilities for the firm was the office of the Export Department, where a small staff continued to perform a number of leftover tasks. Stettinius asked Thomas J. White of the vestigial organization to make a study of American machine-tool exports to France. White found that the best American toolmakers already had exclusive distributing arrangements with French agents. Stettinius quickly saw that the machine-tool exporting idea was not a good one.[6] There was always a faint possibility, mentioned from time to time, that the contemplated postwar venture of the Morgan firm into foreign commerce might be carried out through the Export Department itself. Stettinius was not enthusiastic. He expressed the opinion to White "that there is little if any probability that we will receive

[5] *New York Times,* June 28, 1919.
[6] RS 217, White to ERS, April 3, 1919; ERS to White, May 7, 1919.

further orders or inquiries. It may be that a business in the Export Department could be built up, but that would involve an organization here [in London, where he was awaiting the arrival of Mrs. Stettinius and their daughters on the *Aquitania* at Liverpool on May 10] as well as an organization in America, and I do not believe that the prospects of developing a profitable business are sufficient to warrant our going to the expense." He wrote again three weeks later: "I do not think there is much probability that we will act as general purchasing agents for concerns either in England or France. If we should make an arrangement later on by which we may resume activities in the Export Department, it will, I hope, be under conditions where we will have complete control of anything we may handle." [7]

But Stettinius continued the inquiries about potentially advantageous foreign business.[8] He described his mission and his analysis of the trade situation:

The situation over here could not be more interesting, or, as a matter of fact, more difficult. I have been working, for the last sixty or ninety days, in an effort to round up the European situation and to determine what their requirements are in the way of materials and credit to be obtained in America during the next year,—all with the idea that some plan of financing America's exports on long terms could be worked out by private capital with some kind of governmental support and cooperation. My job has been almost an impossible one. Nobody seems to know just exactly what they do want, nor is any country prepared, up to the present time, except possibly Italy, to state clearly the security they are prepared to give. All of these countries, however, will have to be financed and given long terms of credit on everything they buy during the next year at least, but judging from reports I have received from the other side, there is little disposition there, on the part of exporters or banks themselves, to give any unusual terms. The only alternative, of course, is for the United States Government to take on the burden and carry it either alone or to support private capital. I am now awaiting developments on the other side, having myself gone as far as I can go.[9]

In writing to Grayson Murphy of the Guaranty Trust Company, Stettinius gave a more detailed breakdown of the conditions in several European countries relative to American purchases. The French were disorganized and at odds with themselves in various government departments. He found that "the Czechs seem . . . to be the best bet among the newly-formed countries." The Yugo-

[7] RS 217, ERS to White, May 7, 1919; ERS to White, May 27, 1919.
[8] RS 256, ERS to J. P. Morgan, June 4, 1919.
[9] RS 513, ERS to Henry Lockhart, July 26, 1919.

slavians "do not know exactly what they want, but nevertheless are very insistent that they get it." The Poles wanted a financial adviser. "At first I thought it would be a good plan to send one to them, but I have finally come to the conclusion that if anyone should go at all, he should go as a director and not as an adviser."

English bankers and importers did not think it necessary to make any special arrangements for buying in the United States. But Stettinius felt it of great importance for everyone and for world peace that Britain and the United States "establish the closest possible business relations and partnerships." [10]

He was surprised that no one was considering Germany in all this economic talk. He predicted that Germany would soon pull herself together economically and be doing business with all of the new nations.

Stettinius had strong convictions about the importance of the task at hand and his connection with it, however discouraging the immediate outlook. He wrote to Charles Day, a civil engineer:

The future of all these countries, however, depends on America and on the extent to which America, in some way or another, will or can finance, on long terms of credit, essential foodstuffs and raw materials. That some way will be found to meet the situation I have not a particle of doubt, but it will be a difficult process and needs the support of every right thinking American, and an appreciation, on the part of Americans, of the necessity of their dealing fairly with themselves as well as with Europe. The period through which we are now passing is merely the final period of the War, and our assistance is just as necessary now as it was before the Armistice.

He was optimistic about the production outlook in Great Britain: "I feel much more sanguine about Great Britain than you do. They are a pretty intelligent people, these Britishers (and even the Scotch are some times fairly keen) and I do not believe it is going to take very long to make all classes realize that the salvation and very life of the working man, as well as of the capitalist, lies in increased production."

It is interesting to find him just as wrong fifty years later as he was when he expressed that view. The narrow, shortsighted refusal of the British worker to produce to capacity lest he enrich his employers in the process continues to be a blight on British economic life and to have a depressing effect on labor's standard of living.

He was even more optimistic about the labor situation in France.

[10] RS 243, ERS to Murphy, July 20, 1919.

He continued: "There is a small and very noisy radical element among the French labor leaders, but the real influence is exerted by a very intelligent group, some of whom I have met. They are far from being radical, and, as a matter of fact, are not in the slightest degree in sympathy with the radical element in England. If the influence of this group extends, as I am assured it will, I believe you will be astonished at the development here."

Turning to the United States, Stettinius considered an aspect of the labor picture which was highly controversial at the time. Organized labor with Samuel Gompers as its spokesman had recently come out for legislation to stop immigration from abroad. Stettinius saw things from the employer's side: "If the flow of emigration from Europe to the United States should cease, and if industry should be active in the United States, we will necessarily experience greater difficulties in dealing with labor problems than would otherwise prove to be the case." [11]

Gompers and Stettinius saw eye to eye on cause and effect; they differed as to the desirability of the effect.

The Davison Proposals

While Stettinius was making his survey of the European economic prospects, Davison came up with two plans for financing American exports. The first was to form a debenture corporation which would raise capital by selling debentures—interest-bearing obligations similar to bonds—backed by the credit of the governments of the countries involved. The other idea was to set up an export and trading corporation or group of regional corporations to engage actively in foreign trade. Davison grew almost lyrical about the possibilities of such an organization in cabling the proposal to Stettinius on August 5. He had discussed it with the partners and all had "practically reached conclusion that there lies great opportunity for J. P. Morgan & Co. to enter into the merchandizing business really getting back to the old banker and merchant business." [12]

Stettinius thought about the matter for a week before commenting. When he cabled back on August 12 he raised some very serious issues: "Greatly interested your consideration formation Trading Department or Corporation but to us here it seems dif-

[11] RS 157, ERS to Day, Aug. 2, 1919.
[12] RS 248, Davison to ERS, Aug. 5, 1919.

ficult to form even tentative plan until it has been definitely determined in what manner Europe's essential requirements of foodstuffs and materials for next 12 months can be financed and to what extent if at all, U.S. Government directly or indirectly, will assist European situation."

As for the question of the form of organization, he was quite clear. He added: "While sympathizing fully in perfectly natural desire that operation, if it were undertaken, should be conducted as a branch of J. P. Morgan & Co., believe this would be difficult unless activities were limited." [13]

Personal Interlude

While he was involved in these exchanges about his Paris mission for J. P. Morgan & Co., Stettinius took time from the business routine to attend to the social amenities. On July 19, 1919, he wrote to Winston Churchill, then Secretary of State for War, to thank him for his help to the American forces in Europe and to express his pleasure on learning that the United States had given Churchill the Distinguished Service Medal. Churchill replied on July 25, thanking Stettinius and asking him to drop in to see him at his office.[14]

That very week word came that Prohibition had become law in the United States. Stettinius wrote a mock letter of condolence to Martin Egan at the Morgan office on the sense of bereavement he must feel now that liquor was no longer available.[15]

During this period Stettinius became very well acquainted with Jean Monnet of the French banking and brandy-distilling family. This is the same Jean Monnet who became one of the leading statesmen of Europe during World War II and its aftermath. There had been business conversations between Stettinius and the people at Morgan, Harjes on the one hand and the Veuve Rogée (Monnet) Cognac and the Société Vinicole J. G. Monnet & Cie. on the other. These negotiations came to nothing, but the friendship with Monnet continued.[16]

One evening Monnet and Stettinius went out on the town together. The Frenchman introduced the American to a fancy Paris

[13] RS 248, ERS to Davison, Aug. 12, 1919.
[14] RS 141, ERS to Churchill, July 19, 1919; Churchill to ERS, July 25, 1919.
[15] RS 162, ERS to Egan, Aug. 18, 1919.
[16] RS 361, Monnet correspondence.

restaurant, and when Stettinius returned home he was deathly ill. He wrote a poem about the disaster and dedicated it to his host:

Sept. 20, 1919

To J— — Monnet.
There was a young man named Monnet
Who thought he was awfully funny;
He took me to Escargots,
And gave me six cargoes
of Terribly poisonous snails.
They bit me,—they stung me,—
They hurt me,—they flung me
into horribly griping pains,
But now they're abating,
I am laying in waiting
To slaughter that man Monnet.
E.R.S.[17]

Mission to Brussels

Meanwhile, the Morgan firm was beginning a program of postwar reconstruction financing. Stettinius went to Brussels to represent the firm in discussions with the Belgian government about a loan. One result of the mission was that J. P. Morgan & Co. was designated primary financial agent for the Belgian Treasury in the United States.[18] Stettinius found the discussions stimulating, and he took some satisfaction in outmaneuvering the Guaranty Trust Company's representatives, who were in Belgium on the same errand but managed to achieve only a junior status. He wrote to Egan, "I enjoyed greatly the Belgian negotiation and hope that the experience of the Guaranty Trust Company in that quarter has convinced them, as well as other institutions, that they simply cannot handle large government obligations without our aid and leadership." [19]

While the loan was ultimately floated, the prospects for a Belgian loan did not look favorable at the beginning of 1920. Stettinius explained the situation to Leon deWaele, a Belgian friend:

[17] RS 361, ERS to Monnet, Sept. 20, 1919. M. Monnet wrote to the author on March 8, 1972: "What you report concerning me is generally true, except that I do not remember the episode Mr. Stettinius has related and about which he wrote a poem."
[18] *New York Times*, Sept. 18, 1919.
[19] RS 162, ERS to Egan, Sept. 20, 1919.

I have been "sitting in" at all of the meetings of the Belgian Group during the past two or three weeks and spent yesterday morning with one of the representatives of the Guaranty Trust Company, Arthur Anderson and our lawyers in going over the contract referring to the loan which is about to be issued. I hope sincerely that the operation, small as it is, will prove successful. It must be disappointing to you, just as it has been to us here, that we have been unable to do more for Belgium. I hope that neither the officials of the Government nor yourself will for a moment think that this is because of any lack of interest on the part of the Guaranty Trust Company or ourselves. The position here regarding foreign loans of all kinds could not be more discouraging. . . .[20]

Stettinius attributed the state of the foreign bond market to the United States income tax law, which made tax-exempt securities much more attractive to investors of means. This was also the period of the postwar economic slump, and the securities market in general was depressed.

Stettinius's own position was made more difficult by the attitude of the Belgian Treasury. He reported that the officials were "insisting that there was more than a moral obligation upon J. P. Morgan & Company and the Guaranty Trust Company to advance whatever funds the Belgian Government might require." He added, "Of course this is altogether impossible and cannot be considered much as we would all like to assist Belgium in these troublesome times."[21]

The Foreign Commerce Corporation

The discussions and correspondence about the Davison proposals continued into the fall of 1919. As these proceeded, the idea of a debenture corporation was abandoned, while that of the trading corporation gained in favor. Finally, on January 1, 1920, the *Wall Street Journal* ran the following item:

Form Large Foreign Commerce Corporation
Morgan Firm Organizes Big Company to Engage in International Trade
—Grayson M. P. Murphy Will Head It

J. P. Morgan & Co. have formed a large corporation to engage in international trade. The new organization will be known as the Foreign Commerce Corporation of America and is chartered under the laws of New York. It has a nominal capital of 1,000 shares of no par value, all of which are owned by the firm of J. P. Morgan & Co.

[20] RS 460, ERS to deWaele, Jan. 2, 1920.
[21] RS 460, ERS to deWaele, Feb. 11, 1920.

The new company will be headed by Grayson M. P. Murphy, who will resign from the Guaranty Trust Co.

The incorporators are J. P. Morgan, H. P. Davison, T. W. Lamont, E. R. Stettinius and also Grayson M. P. Murphy, who will be president of the corporation.

The directors of the corporation will be members of the firm of J. P. Morgan & Co. and Mr. Murphy.

One of the members of the firm explained that the formation of the Foreign Commerce Corporation was designed to fit in with and to develop all lines of commerce between America and other parts of the world, particularly Europe. This member said: "It is evident that America must devise new ways and means for developing foreign trade. Old formulas will not work now and we must be awake and adopt new measures to keep abreast of the times. The Foreign Commerce Corporation is distinctly an American corporation to further American trade with foreign nations."

The *New York Tribune* added some details in its announcement, which also appeared on New Year's Day, 1920:

Although the business of the new corporation [the Foreign Commerce Corporation of America] will be trade, and not finance, it will extend credit to its customers, it is said. Whether this will be long time or not could not be definitely ascertained, but the assumption is that it will, because the incorporators are determined to meet the new facts of international commerce with novel methods and expedients. One of the reasons for the undertaking is the feeling that the old formulas of trade fail to meet the present situation, in which America's balance of trade with Europe is hopelessly against the Old World and is no longer offset by the payment of interest on debts held in Europe, by the extensive use of European-owned tonnage, by the spending of American tourists abroad, or by the other means by which exchange between the two continents were equalized substantially in the ante-bellum days.

As a practical matter, it is anticipated that the new corporation will promptly seek to step into the breach and forward the raw materials, machinery and manufactured goods that are so sorely needed in Poland, Czecho-Slovakia and the other distressed countries of Central Europe, which must have material things, but are for the moment without means of payment. The recent statement by Premier Clemenceau that Poland would be aided promptly was by some associated with the formation of the new Morgan trading company.

But the corporation has wide powers and aspirations to become a vehicle for the development of American trade with all parts of the world. It was indicated that it will try to put into practice those new maxims which leading bankers have been preaching in the matter of building up a permanent foreign trade in recent months. In dealing with the countries of Middle Europe, which are bordering on despair and,

according to some observers, Bolshevism, it is likely that the new corporation will encourage simple barter—the exchange of goods for goods,
eliminating temporarily all the intricacies of foreign exchange.

Grayson Murphy, the president of the newly organized Foreign
Commerce Corporation, had recommended himself to the attention
of the Stettinius group the previous summer and indicated that he
might be willing to leave a post of some responsibility with the
Guaranty Trust Company for a venture into the foreign trade field.
Stettinius had responded with some gratification.[22]

The Foreign Commerce Corporation was a failure; not a spectac-
ular disaster, but a quietly unsuccessful venture. The year 1920 was
its only period of active operation, and this was a year of world-
wide economic depression. The corporation was Davison's grand
design, but Stettinius was the partner most closely associated with
the scheme. Ironically, he had been lukewarm about it from the
very beginning. But he did feel strongly the need for American
exports to be financed and distributed, and he was deeply devoted
to Davison, whose health had already begun to fail by 1920. It is
not easy to assess Stettinius's precise role in the affairs of the corporation because his role was not, in fact, precise. J. P. Morgan &
Co. was a loosely and informally organized partnership at the top
level, and while responsibility for a given undertaking tended to be
concentrated in the hands of a single partner, he did not have
absolute control. The actual management of the concern was given
over to the president, Grayson Murphy.

Stettinius favored an extremely cautious and conservative approach from the outset. In responding to a congratulatory letter
from Polish Minister Casimir Lubomirski on his part as an incor-
porator, Stettinius wrote: "I think you should understand that we
expect to move with great deliberation and that it is not our purpose to undertake large operations until we shall have had full
opportunity to study the situation carefully in all its phases and
also to build up an organization so that whatever business we
undertake can be carried out successfully." [23]

At the end of January, Stettinius wrote to Jean Monnet that
Murphy was coming to Paris "to look over the situation and to
consider arrangements by which the business of the Corporation
can be established and developed." [24]

[22] RS 243, ERS to Murphy, July 20, 1919.
[23] RS 436, Lubomirski to ERS, Jan. 17, 1920; ERS to Lubomirski, Jan. 19,
1920.
[24] RS 361, ERS to Monnet, Jan. 31, 1920.

The corporation was prepared to be flexible in its trading. It was ready either to act as agent and buy and sell commodities on commission or to buy and sell on its own account. A single example will illustrate the kind of transaction contemplated. In late March and early April 1920 there was a flurry of interest in Roumanian trade. Grayson Murphy cabled from the Paris office of the corporation at Morgan, Harjes to Carl Taylor, who had opened the New York office at 15 Broad Street, around the corner from Morgan's:

Following transaction proposed for immediate acceptance. We to sell to Mines de Bor, important French Company, and transport to Gallatz, Roumanian port on Danube, 15,000 tons Metallurgic Coke in monthly deliveries of 3,000 tons, completed by October 15th, 10% each shipment can be anthracite at our option, we to transport from Gallatz to New York and sell for account of French Company about 2200 tons of electrolytic copper. Coke to be used for copper smelting and should be in large lumps. No element of barter or credit involved. Coke will be paid for in dollars in New York against shipping documents. Our company to act either, first—on commission for each sale, or second—on straight sale of coke and commission for copper.

To make up return cargo in addition to copper, we can probably secure oak and pine lumber, dried fruit, and rape seed and sell these products in New York City for account of Gallatz exporters at very low price, by reason of exchange.

French Company is one controlled by Mirabaud Bank Group, strong people with whom I desire to make permanent connection.

Wire whether coke and shipping obtainable, and price of coke for deliveries indicated F.O.B. New York and C.I.F. Gallatz. This business would probably lead to large future transactions, and I urgently request you do all possible to secure favorable quotations and give prompt answer.

Steamers not over twenty foot draft and 3,000 tons carrying capacity. Round trip estimated roughly two months, so several steamers necessary. If shipping unobtainable in America, cable me in London and I will endeavor to arrange there.

Address answer this cable to Paris.[25]

Taylor in New York ascertained that coke and shipping facilities were available, consulted Stettinius as to the commission to be charged,[26] and cabled back that the office was ready to "act in the matter purely as buying agents in bringing parties together" and the commission "should be not less than two and one half percent on cost of coke FOB vessel and some smaller percentage on all

[25] RS 545, Murphy to Foreign Commerce Corporation, New York. Cable received March 29, 1920.

[26] RS 545, Taylor to ERS, April 1, 1920.

charges including ocean freight." Two days later, after looking into the market situation in the United States, Taylor cabled again, "Will be pleased act as agent on sale Roumanian products here charging one and half percent commission on gross sales copper and two and half on gross sale other products mentioned. . . ." [27]

Other corporations were added to the original Foreign Commerce Corporation of America. The Foreign Commerce Corporation of France was set up despite Stettinius's grave misgivings. In recounting a later conversation on the subject, he wrote: "I told him, at the same time, that I thought a mistake had been made in forming the Foreign Commerce Corporation of France, that at the time it was formed I did not see any occasion for its existence and that I thought it extremely doubtful that the Company would ever develop any serious or interesting business. It seemed to me that, nevertheless, arrangements should be made to handle any correspondence and to answer such inquiries as would probably result from the activity of the Foreign Commerce Corporation of America during the preceding year." [28]

Soon the F.C.C. of North Africa and the Foreign Commerce Corporation of Holland followed. The original investment in the Dutch corporation was $469,504.60, or 1,500,000 florins. [29]

The corporation's principal method of doing business was to furnish capital to existing companies either in the form of secured loans or by the purchase of stock. Sometimes the corporation would provide the money entirely itself; at other times it would enter joint ventures with banks. The North African branch, the Société pour le commerce extérieur de l'Afrique du Nord, was involved in enterprises with the Banque de l'Algérie, [30] and the Dutch branch entered joint operations with the Rotterdamsche Bank. [31] The Foreign Commerce Corporation of Holland and the Rotterdamsche Bank went into the Amsterdam Batavia Trading Company together and participated jointly in the establishment, on September 28, 1920, of the Bank voor Indie. [32]

In the United States, the corporation went into the coal export-

[27] RS 545, Taylor to Murphy at Morgan, Harjes, Paris, April 2, 1920, and April 4, 1920.

[28] RS 273, ERS to Nelson Dean Jay, June 24, 1921.

[29] RS 462, F. Carrington Weems, "Memorandum Regarding the Foreign Commerce Corporation's Holding in the Bank voor Indie," Jan. 10, 1924.

[30] RS 224, Major Varaigne to ERS, Oct. 28, 1920.

[31] RS 462, Lamont to ERS, May 15, 1921.

[32] RS 462, Lamont to ERS, May 15, 1921; Weems, "Memorandum Regarding the Bank voor Indie," Jan. 10, 1924.

ing business by acquiring an interest in the Tuttle Corporation.[33] The Tuttle firm and the Foreign Commerce Corporation became involved in dealings with the British coal importing and distributing company of Stephenson Clarke & Co. toward the end of 1920. Very little coal business was transacted in 1921, however, because of the business slump in Europe and the maritime strike in the United States.[34]

In London the Foreign Commerce Corporation became involved with Yule, Catto & Co., the Morgan firm's managing agents for rubber companies in the Straits Settlement.[35]

But the Foreign Commerce Corporation did not prosper. President Grayson Murphy became disaffected. Business was slack. He did not receive much encouragement from the Morgan home office. In late January 1921 he resigned. He announced his resignation to the London associates of the corporation with the following cablegram:

Situation here now is and I believe for some time to come will be unfavorable for development international trade. Accordingly I believe and have so advised my associates that in my opinion wisest policy for Foreign Commerce Corp. of America to pursue is to practically mark time until conditions here and abroad improve and lines of development can be more clearly seen. For these reasons and in view of my past experience I have concluded that instead of continuing as President of Foreign Commerce Corp. of America I can render more useful service by forming my own firm to deal with the organization and re-organization of industrial companies and to assist in handling troubled situations. Accordingly I announce very regretfully my retirement as President of the Foreign Commerce Corp. of America with which however I will still be connected as director. E. R. Stettinius will succeed me as President. G.M.P. MURPHY.[36]

Stettinius followed this up with a postscript to Stephenson Clarke & Co. endorsing Murphy's recommendations: "Supplementing G. M. P. Murphy's cable, while we regret his resignation we are in full accord as to the policy which Foreign Commerce Corporation of America should pursue as expressed in his cable. You will, of course, understand however that the Company will continue

[33] RS 273, ERS to Jay, July 20, 1921.
[34] RS 80, C. E. Tuttle, "Report of Operations of Tuttle Corporation," received by ERS on Aug. 30, 1921.
[35] RS 200, ERS to Lamont, Aug. 17, 1920; RS 79, ERS to Charles D. Norton, First National Bank of New York, Feb. 7, 1922.
[36] RS 243, Murphy to Sir Thomas S. Catto and to Stephenson Clarke & Co., Jan. 28, 1921.

develop its Coal business along lines that may seem wise and I hope in such a way as will permit of a good trade being established with or through you. Regards Kent, Hindley, Miral. E. R. STETTINIUS." [37]

At the same time, Carl Taylor, the number two man in the organization, was invited to go into the law office of F. W. M. Cutcheon.[38] He accepted and began his new duties on April 1, 1921, but agreed to stay on as vice-president of the Foreign Commerce Corporation. Stettinius was sympathetic to Murphy's position, but felt that he had let down his associates in resigning so suddenly. He thought that Taylor, on the other hand, had acted with greater consideration.[39] Still, there were no hard feelings, and the directors of the corporation voted to continue Murphy's salary of $100,000 a year through June 30, 1921.[40]

Liquidating the Foreign Commerce Corporation

Stettinius was left with the Foreign Commerce Corporation. He immediately began to wind up the affairs of the company. His procedure was to slow down the activities of the several component corporations and seek to extricate them from their financial involvements, meanwhile keeping alive the corporate entities against a possible, if improbable, future resuscitation. He wrote to Davison, who was lying ill at his Magnolia Plantation in Georgia, and gave him a somewhat tempered account of events: "We are giving as close attention as possible to the affairs of the Foreign Commerce Corporation and are nursing and developing the coal business although we are, at the same time, cutting off all needless expenses and letting out men who have no particular talent or experience in trading in general or in any particular commodity. The machine is not being scrapped but will be kept in operation although at low speed and can be speeded up later to such extent and in such directions as may seem wise."

He went on to discuss the prevailing state of business. The depression was still on, but there were faint suggestions of improved conditions: "There has been an improvement in trade during the last week or two, but not by any means to as great an extent as was anticipated six weeks or two months ago. . . . On the whole, it seems to me that while the process of liquidation and readjust-

[37] RS 243, ERS to Stephenson Clarke & Co., Jan. 28, 1921.
[38] RS 154, ERS to Davison, Jan. 31, 1921, and March 26, 1921.
[39] RS 154, ERS to Davison, Jan. 31, 1921.
[40] RS 243, ERS to Murphy, Feb. 14, 1921.

ment has been completed in some lines, it is not by any means completed in all and that, necessarily, a considerable time will elapse before the situation, as a whole, can be considered even moderately satisfactory." [41]

Stettinius visited Davison in Georgia some time later, and in his bread-and-butter letter remarked about the Foreign Commerce Corporation: "We are clearing up as rapidly as possible some situations which merely involve expense without any reasonable hope of profit." [42]

The difficulties—personal, financial, and moral—relating to the liquidation of the Foreign Commerce Corporation were enormous. The decision to curtail the activities of the Foreign Commerce Corporation of France brought up the question of what to do about J. Darrigan, a Frenchman who had entered the company with high enthusiasm, feeling that his career was now established. He seems to have married on the basis of his prospects and expressed a special closeness to Stettinius because his own wedding took place the day before that of the older Stettinius son, William Carrington.[43] Stettinius wrote to Nelson Dean Jay in Paris that some arrangement should be made to keep Darrigan at Morgan, Harjes.[44]

The following month, Stettinius wrote again to Jay and gave him the latest news about the liquidation:

So far as the Foreign Commerce Corporation of America is concerned, we have made even further curtailments, having only recently concluded to dispose of our interest in The Tuttle Corporation through which we have done some coal export business. The business was sound, clean and profitable, but as we came to look into the matter it was made quite clear that we could not hope to develop the business along satisfactory lines unless we engaged in actual mining operations in the United States on a fairly substantial scale. This would have been objectionable from a great many standpoints and accordingly, in justice to Tuttle, we suggested our retirement from his Corporation in order that he might develop it as he might wish.

We are still hoping that we may be able to extricate ourselves from the situation in Holland which is decidedly embarrassing. Up to the present time, McKnight has not been able actually to dispose of our shares in either the Amsterdam Batavia Trading Co. or the Bank voor Indie. VanTienhoven apparently is not showing a very co-operative

[41] RS 154, ERS to Davison, Jan. 31, 1921.
[42] RS 154, ERS to Davison, March 26, 1921.
[43] RS 273, Darrigan to ERS, June 14, 1921.
[44] RS 273, ERS to Jay, June 24, 1921.

spirit; Kroller, on the other hand, appears more disposed to work out some scheme by which we can withdraw.[45]

The officers of the Rotterdamsche Bank had looked forward to a continuing relationship with the Morgan subsidiary and particularly to trading with Germany, so they were deeply disturbed by the sudden decision to dissolve the Foreign Commerce Corporation.[46] Ultimately the Dutch branch was liquidated on January 9, 1922, and $243,697.49 (649,700 florins) realized, with stock in the Bank voor Indie carried on the books at $225,807.11 retained in a pooling agreement with the Rotterdamsche Bank and Wm. H. Muller and Company, drawn up to continue through 1925.[47]

The residual business of the Foreign Commerce Corporation dragged on for several years. On January 11, 1924, Stettinius estimated that a fair value of the Morgan interest in the corporation would be $334,000.[48] The largest asset was the Bank voor Indie stock. The second largest was the C. E. Tuttle note for approximately $150,000. The note had as collateral shares of stock in the Paragon-Elkhorn Collieries Company in Dunleary, Kentucky.[49] Stettinius tried unsuccessfully to sell the mine to the Chesapeake & Ohio Railway Company in February 1924 to satisfy the debt.[50] A settlement was made between the Foreign Commerce Corporation and C. E. Tuttle by September 1924.[51]

At the end of 1924 Stettinius summarized the position of the Foreign Commerce Corporation:

The assets of the Foreign Commerce Corporation, as of Dec. 31st, 1924 are as follows:

Cash with J. P. Morgan & Co.	$107,298.10
Investment, Bank voor Indie stock	225,807.11
Total	$333,105.21

The debit balance against the Foreign Commerce Corporation stock and loan account on the books of J. P. Morgan & Co. is $342,976.98, as evidenced by memo attached hereto. I suggest it be written down to $330,000 as of Dec. 31st, 1924, that the Foreign Commerce Corporation

[45] RS 273, ERS to Jay, July 20, 1921.
[46] RS 462, Lamont to ERS, May 15, 1921.
[47] RS 462, Weems, "Memorandum Regarding the Bank voor Indie," Jan. 10, 1924.
[48] RS 462, memorandum, ERS to E. C. Bacon, Jan. 11, 1924.
[49] RS 462, Foreign Commerce Corporation of America balance sheet, Jan. 1, 1924.
[50] RS 462, ERS to Arthur M. Anderson, Feb. 14, 1924.
[51] RS 80, memorandum, Weems to ERS, Sept. 2, 1924.

pay $100,000 in cash to apply against the account, carrying the balance at $230,000 pending the sale of the shares of the Bank voor Indie and the dissolution of the Foreign Commerce Corporation.[52]

Stettinius wrote an obituary for the Foreign Commerce Corporation in September 1924 in his reply to a man inquiring about the possibility of a job with a Morgan-connected foreign trade company:

I do not think there is any likelihood at all of our taking up again the organization of a Company to engage in international trade. As a result of our investigations and studies during the year 1920 and since then, I am convinced that it would be a decided mistake for a banking house to attempt to engage in lines of trade in which technical knowledge and years of experience are important if not essential. The plans that we worked out in the Fall of 1919, and the character of business we had in mind at that time to undertake, seemed to be abundantly warranted by the conditions then obtaining but, as you will recall, there was little done in the way of actual trading and such connections as we established, and such small investments as we made, did not by any means prove satisfactory in the long run.[53]

[52] RS 859, memorandum, ERS to Junius Morgan, Dec. 30, 1924.
[53] RS 516, ERS to Harold J. Dreher, Sept. 2, 1924.

XI.   *J. P. Morgan & Co.:*
General Motors Corporation

Far larger than the affairs of the Foreign Commerce Corporation were the financial problems of General Motors, which occupied Stettinius during the same period.

During wartime the manufacture of consumer goods for the civilian population is naturally curtailed, so that when the war is over there is a great pent-up demand for those items. This was true after both World War I and World War II, and both times the demand was particularly strong for automobiles. General Motors took advantage of this situation and experienced enormous prosperity in 1919, with net earnings of $60,000,000.[1] Since the management apparently believed that this boom would last indefinitely, they went ahead with an ambitious expansion program. Alfred P. Sloan, Jr., who was to become president of General Motors, describes the situation in his autobiography, *My Years with General Motors*: "Late in March 1920 the Executive Committee approved for the corporation as a whole an optimistic production schedule of 876,000 cars, trucks, and tractors for the year beginning in August, 1920. In March and April, Mr. Raskob, as chairman of the Finance Committee, began making arrangements for the sale of $64 million worth of common stock to provide money for continuing capital expenditures aggregating about $100 million. The du Ponts, J. P. Morgan and Company, and some British interests participated in this effort, and representatives of the new interests came on the board."[2]

The company sold 3,219,856 shares of common stock at $20 a share. The new directors who were added to the board at the time of this sale were Edward R. Stettinius, George F. Baker, Jr., of the First National Bank (New York), Seward Prosser of the Bankers Trust Company, Owen D. Young of General Electric, William H. Woodin of American Car & Foundry, and Clarence M. Wooley of American Radiator.

The summer of 1920 was a busy time for Stettinius. While the

---

[1] Arthur Pound, *The Turning Wheel* (Garden City, N.Y., 1934), p. 183.
[2] *My Years with General Motors* (Garden City, N.Y., 1964), p. 30.

General Motors matter was in progress, J. P. Morgan & Co. undertook to float a $100,000,000 loan for the French government, and Stettinius wrote to Dean Jay in Paris on August 19: "Mr. Morgan . . . felt that I had better look after Parmentier [of the French finance ministry] and take general charge of matters pertaining to French financing."[3] The negotiations proceeded rapidly during the next fortnight, and on September 3 the loan agreement was signed.[4]

In the midst of all this activity, Stettinius was operated on for appendicitis.[5] While he was at White Sulphur Springs recuperating, a bomb was set off on September 17 in front of the Morgan office at 23 Wall Street. The explosion took place at the noon rush hour and caused several deaths. Two employees of J. P. Morgan & Co. were among those killed. Stettinius wrote to Dwight Morrow about the tragedy: "I have had Joyce and Donohue very much on my mind and would be very glad if you would tell me what, if anything, was done for their families."[6]

Signs of an economic slump began to appear while Stettinius was ill, but he was able to recommend a slowdown at General Motors without sounding alarmed. He wrote to Thomas Lamont: "The General Motors Corporation requires a little watching during the next month or two, and while basically the Company appears to be all right, there is decided need for retrenchment in expenditures and curtailment of production. I think continued pressure will have to be applied in order to keep the Company working in accord with this policy and thereby greatly reduce, if not pay off, its banking indebtedness which is uncomfortably large in these times."[7]

While general business conditions deteriorated, the automobile industry suffered more acutely than most other activities. Alfred Sloan reports, "In September the bottom dropped out of the automobile market."[8]

While the market was declining, it was discovered that William C. Durant, the president of the company, had been buying General Motors stock and borrowing the money to buy it with, in turn putting up General Motors stock he already held as collateral for the loans. As the value of the pledged stock declined still farther, Durant's creditors were forced to the brink of having to sell the shares, and it was realized that this would cause a violently

[3] RS 206, ERS to Jay, Aug. 19, 1920.
[4] Nicolson, *Dwight Morrow*, p. 178.
[5] RS 298, ERS to H. B. Lusch, Oct. 12, 1920.
[6] RS 345, ERS to Morrow, Sept. 29, 1920.
[7] RS 200, ERS to Lamont, Aug. 17, 1920.   [8] Sloan, *My Years*, p. 31.

accelerated decline which could lead to a panic and collapse of the whole stock market. Something had to be done to bail out Durant.

The du Ponts, already large stockholders of General Motors, came to the rescue with the help of J. P. Morgan & Co. Stettinius gives an account of the rescue operation and his part in it in a letter of November 1920 to Davison:

it was found that Durant owed about $27,000,000 to brokers and banks. His assets consisted wholly of approximately 2,700,000 shares of General Motors stock. The duPonts, who had learned of the situation only a day or two before and who had insisted that Durant should advise us fully of his position, agreed finally to buy all or at least the greater part of Durant's holdings at 9½ a share, on the conditions that Durant would receive a portion of any profits that might be realized in the sale of the stock above cost. Durant accepted this proposition and the duPont Securities Company was formed with a capital consisting of $7,000,000 preferred stock and 100,000 shares of common stock no par value. The duPonts and the Chevrolet Company took the entire issue of preferred stock and also 40,000 shares of common stock. A like amount of common stock was set aside for Durant and the remainder, namely 20,000 shares, was reserved for us as managers of a Syndicate to purchase $20,000,000 one year 8% notes of the duPont Securities Company, secured by General Motors stock at $5 per share, the duPonts and the Chevrolet Company turning over to the duPont Securities Company sufficient additional stock to make up the total of 4,000,000 shares. The notes were distributed among eight banks, we taking $2,500,000. During the past week, we have placed $1,200,000 of the notes with some outside institutions and it has not yet been determined whether these will come out of our own allotment or whether it will be for account of the Group. This briefly is a statement of the details of the financial set-up in connection with the purchase of a portion of Durant's interest in General Motors. He was permitted to retain about 150,000 shares of stock on which he had negotiated loans at about $10 per share from individuals and I understand that members of his family have approximately a like amount. He is said to have large amounts owing him by individuals to whom he loaned stock and Raskob informed me a day or two ago that he would probably have in the neighborhood of $8,000,000 to $10,000,000 in the final round-up. This may or may not prove to be the case.

It is of course perfectly obvious that Durant has lied continuously and persistently to all of us here and to all of his associates. He has apparently been trading heavily in the stock of the Company for years and continued to do so after we came into the situation, notwithstanding his repeated assurances to me that he had no interest whatever in the market. There was at first a disposition on Pierre duPont's part to deal rather leniently with Durant and at our meeting last Sunday he suggested that Durant might take the Chairmanship of the Board. None of us agreed to that suggestion of course, and we all insisted that Durant would have to be eliminated from the situation. Since Sunday last, Pierre duPont has had a series of conferences with Durant and last Wednesday it was definitely agreed that Durant would retire as President, and yesterday Pierre duPont told us that he would agree to take the presidency. We all feel that this is the best arrangement that can be made, for while Pierre duPont is not fitted in all respects to hold the position permanently, he is certainly the one man in sight who is able to assume immediate direction of the Company's affairs and whip the organization into shape. I have not had an opportunity of talking to him since Wednesday, but I understand that he proposes to work along the line of building up the organization and of taking on additional men whenever the right kind of men can be found and of breaking in an understudy who can succeed him later on.

As far as duPonts are concerned, their attitude has been fine throughout and Dwight [Morrow] and Tom Cochran, who were in the situation from the outset, were as much impressed as I am with Pierre's fairness and desire to do the right thing. We questioned Pierre closely last Sunday about his own affairs and the affairs of the duPont Company and both Dwight and I were satisfied with his emphatic statement that neither the duPont Company nor any of his associates had speculated in the stock or were carrying any stock on margin or on loans.

In regard to our own position, we still hold intact the shares which were bought by our original group and which average about 14.40 a share after considering stock, cash dividends and interest. The stock bought by the Pool to which I have referred above, was turned over, at cost, to the duPont Securities Company and the Syndicate will be dissolved. Whatever operations may be undertaken in the market in the future in the way of buying or selling stock will be for the account of the duPont Securities Company. Both Pierre and Raskob have had in mind that it would be possible to sell a large amount of stock on the market for the account of the duPont Securities Company and that by this means funds would be provided for the payment of the $20,000,000 of notes of the duPont Securities Company, maturing in one year. I doubt whether this can be accomplished; certainly it will be impossible unless there is a very great improvement in the automobile industry in the course of the next three or four months, but even under these conditions I seriously question whether the market will absorb this amount of stock together with other stock which will have to be liquidated sooner or later. Accordingly, I have urged Pierre and Raskob to begin to consider immediately the question of some form of permanent financing by which this entire situation can be cleaned up. In the meantime, we have sold about 60,000 shares of stock for the account of the duPont Securities Company and are holding the proceeds together with about $1,500,000 for the purpose of protecting the market.

With regard to the condition of the Company itself, the reports that have been submitted to me since my return are quite encouraging.

Seward [Prosser] has been keeping in close touch with the situation through Shibley and is very much encouraged if indeed he is not optimistic. It is claimed that the Company's net earnings even now are running about $3,000,000 per month. While sales of some cars have almost completely stopped, the Company is still doing a very satisfactory business with the Cadillac and Buick. On the other hand, the inventory is being reduced very slowly and even under favorable conditions, indebtedness to banks will, in my opinion, be in the neighborhood of $50,000,000 on January 1st. Whether the present rate of earnings will be maintained or increased, or whether they will disappear altogether is a question that, of course, depends upon general business conditions as well as upon the condition of the automobile trade. The liquidation of commodities and labor that is taking place is proceeding so rapidly and is so drastic, and there has already been such a tremendous improvement in the labor situation that it may be that the depression will be comparatively brief and that we may have a substantial improvement in trade in the spring. On the other hand, it seems to me not at all improbable that we may have pretty hard times through the Spring and Summer and that nothing in the way of a general improvement will develop until Fall.

Of course, I have felt very badly in consequence of the developments in connection with Durant and while I most certainly do not wish to pass on to anyone else the responsibility which is mine, I nevertheless cannot comprehend how it has been possible for the entire duPont crowd to have been in such complete ignorance, as they undoubtedly were, of Durant's position.[9]

On this final point, it is amusing to find the du Ponts raising a similar question about the Morgans. Pierre du Pont wrote to his brother Irenée on November 26, 1920: "Both Wm. Raskob and I have felt that Morgan & Company have been ignorant of the extent of Mr. Durant's operations since they became purchasers of General Motors Common stock. Morgan & Company have had every opportunity to question Mr. Durant on the subject and I have not felt it my duty to pry into Durant's affairs." [10]

Durant resigned as president of General Motors on November 30, 1920, and was replaced by Pierre du Pont.

The directors who were brought into the company from the financial community in July 1920 were in an uncomfortable situation from the outset. As early as November 1920 Stettinius wrote Davison that George Baker was restive: "I think he has confidence in the Company but feels that we should all either increase our interest in and control over the affairs of the Company or should withdraw altogether."

[9] RS 154, ERS to Davison, Nov. 27, 1920.   [10] Sloan, *My Years*, p. 32.

Stettinius was able to take a more relaxed position, and while he was no happier than the others, he was prepared to live with the situation rather than engage in a running battle with the duPonts or invest heavily in an automobile company during a business slump. He continued:

I am not prepared at this time to say that I agree with him. Certainly we cannot withdraw from the situation at this time in justice either to the banks who hold the Company's paper or the paper of the duPont Securities Company or in justice to the duPonts. On the other hand, I do not believe that the business outlook is sufficiently clear to justify our increasing our holdings at this time. Moreover, I question the wisdom of our taking on our backs the responsibility which we would assume if we were to insist, as against the duPonts, upon the selection of the chief executives of the Company. I think that we should work along quietly and patiently and watch developments in the Company as well as in the general trade and we can take such action six months or even a year hence as may be considered wise in view of the conditions obtaining at this time.[11]

Stettinius was a member of the General Motors Finance Committee from July 1920 until his death in 1925. The minutes of the committee do not show the parts taken by individual members in the deliberations and decisions of the group, but we do know how strongly Stettinius felt about the responsibilities of membership. He held austere views on the obligation of a director to the corporation not to use his influential position for the advantage of his friends. This comes out in a letter to Thomas Nelson Perkins of the law firm Ropes, Gray of Boston:

Tom Lamont told me the other day that Otis Cutler had spoken to him about the Fisk Rubber Co. and asked whether I could not help them to get some of the General Motors business. I replied that I believed that the door was wide open and that it was up to the Fisk Rubber Co. to make a proposition that would be advantageous and attractive to the General Motors Corporation. Some time ago, an official of another rubber company in which we are interested asked me to use my good offices with the General Motors Corporation in his behalf and I gave him the same advice.

I do not believe that a week passes that I am not asked by some one to help in an effort to get some business from the General Motors Corporation. My reply has invariably been to make the right prices and terms. This is not very helpful; it is, however, the only position I can properly take as a Director of the General Motors Corporation and as one who has consistently and persistently urged that the corporation should make

[11] RS 154, ERS to Davison, Nov. 27, 1920.

its purchases without favor or discrimination and that it should not, under any circumstances, give preference to companies in which its directors or managers might happen to have an interest.[12]

In General Motors affairs, as in everything else he undertook, Stettinius applied himself with all his force. He wrote to Davison in March 1921: "For the past three weeks I have been working morning, noon, and night and Sundays in an effort to work out a scheme for financing the duPont Securities Company and Chevrolet Company. . . ."[13]

During Stettinius's period of active membership, the finance committee reorganized the internal operations of the company in three principal areas: the handling of appropriations, inventory valuation, and divisional reporting.[14] In the committee Stettinius consistently advocated a conservative financial policy for General Motors. He wrote to his fellow director Seward Prosser on July 25, 1922: "We had a very interesting meeting the other day of the Finance Committee of the General Motors Corporation at which we were asked to consider a programme involving expenditure of the modest sum of approximately $20,000,000 for additions and improvements. I was unladylike enough to inquire as to what additional funds, in the form of working capital, would be needed in the event that the $20,000,000 were made available. That had the effect of casting gloom over the entire meeting and a motion was passed referring the entire matter back to the Executive Committee and the Finance Department for further study."[15]

He wrote to Prosser again on the same subject on August 9, 1922:

Since I wrote you a week or so ago, we have had another meeting of the Finance Committee of the General Motors Corporation and again took up the question of appropriations. On this occasion, however, we were asked to consider only appropriations relating to the Chevrolet Division and the Fisher Body Corporation. The Operating Department were strong in recommending that the Chevrolet capacity be increased to 2,000 cars per day including 500 copper-cooled [16] cars. The total amount involved was about $5,000,000 and involved assembly plants in Buffalo and Cincinnati.

I took the position that we were justified in spending a reasonable

[12] RS 761, ERS to Perkins, Feb. 10, 1922.
[13] RS 154, ERS to Davison, March 26, 1921.
[14] Maurice Wyss, Director of Communications, Public Relations Staff, General Motors Corporation, to the author, March 26, 1970.
[15] RS 102, ERS to Prosser, July 25, 1922.
[16] The experimental air-cooled engines, called "copper-cooled," proved unsatisfactory, and the Chevrolets fitted with them were recalled (Sloan, *My Years*, p. 87).

amount of money for handling efficiently and satisfactorily a volume of business equal to that done in June, but I objected to any appropriation that involved a substantial increase in working capital due to a large increase in volume. I pointed out that the Company was in a strong position today and that we could not adopt a policy which would call for a large amount of money that was not in sight.

The question was raised as to the possibility of forming a syndicate to advance the price of the outstanding preferred and debenture stock with a view of selling a new issue of $50,000,000 of 7% preferred stock some time within the next six months. I stated that we were unwilling to commit ourselves to such an operation and that, while it was barely possible we might take a different view of the matter six months hence, we did not regard with favor a proposition that would involve our assuming responsibility for the entire $100,000,000 of preferred and debenture stock now outstanding in addition to $50,000,000 it was proposed to issue. I stated that a note issue could undoubtedly be negotiated, but I did not consider it wise, from the standpoint of the Corporation, to put out a note issue at this time.

Pierre [du Pont]'s attitude was all that I could have asked it to be. He showed no disposition to force through his proposal notwithstanding the fact that it was made quite plain that the Operating Staff were exerting a great deal of pressure upon him. Finally it was agreed that the Company should go ahead and spend whatever amount might be required up to about $5,000,000 for additions and improvements on the condition, however, that this did not involve any increase in working capital.[17]

The company had a deficit of $38,680,770 in 1921, but in 1922 earned a net return of $54,474,493. Dividends continued to be paid through 1921 at the rate of one dollar a share, but a quarterly dividend was not declared on February 1, 1922 "as a matter of precaution." The dividends for the next three quarters were suspended, too, but a special fifty-cent dividend was declared in December.[18] Stettinius defended the suspending of dividends in a conciliatory letter to an irate stockholder who had written to J. P. Morgan: "The Board of Directors of the General Motors Corporation believed that, in suspending dividends on the common stock, they were acting in the best interests of the shareholders of the Corporation. As you know, the automobile business has been very bad during the past year and a half and the Company will be required to make very heavy charges against surplus account both in consequence of the reduction in the volume of business as well as in connection with depreciation in the inventory values." [19]

[17] RS 102, ERS to Prosser, Aug. 9, 1922.
[18] Pound, *The Turning Wheel*, p. 203.
[19] RS 550, ERS to Miss M. G. Bryson, Jan. 14, 1922.

Dividend policy was an issue on which the bankers on the General Motors board were in sharp disagreement with the du Ponts. The du Ponts wanted to distribute earnings to the stockholders, while Seward Prosser, George Baker, and Stettinius favored a more cautious policy until the company was on a sounder financial footing. The du Ponts were able to have dividends declared in February [20] and November 1923 [21] by what the bankers regarded as steam-roller tactics. These events were reported to Stettinius, who was in poor health and unable to attend the meetings. Stettinius commented on the November episode: "I was astonished to learn that Pierre du Pont had proposed an extra dividend of 30 cents per share and that he had 'sprung' it at the eleventh hour." [22]

He came to accept this struggle over dividend policy as a fact of life at General Motors. Early in 1924 he wrote: "The tendency of the du Ponts is to increase the dividend rate or pay extra dividends whenever there appears to be the slightest excuse for doing so. It may be that, some of these days, something will be done in this direction which will affect the market price of the stock, although I cannot conceive that they would be so unwise as to do anything in the immediate future in view of the large borrowings of the Acceptance Corporation which now amount to $72,000,000 and to the further fact that the Company itself has gone into the banks." [23]

The matter of dividends came up again in 1925. Alfred Sloan, who had succeeded Pierre du Pont as president of General Motors in 1923, reported to Stettinius that the dividend had been increased.[24] Stettinius, predictably, was not pleased with this gambling on future profitability. He replied from Atlantic City just before leaving for his long vacation in Augusta, Georgia:

I note with interest what you have to say in regard to the recent action of the Corporation in raising the dividend rate. I am sorry that I am not in agreement with you and your associates as to the advisability of hav-

[20] RS 245, Morrow to ERS, Feb. 21, 1923; RS 550, Prosser, memorandum for a telephone call to ERS at Augusta, Ga., Feb. 15, 1923.
[21] RS 550, Baker to ERS, Nov. 9, 1923.
[22] RS 550, ERS to Baker, Nov. 23, 1923. Pierre du Pont's biographers do not discuss this difference in viewpoint over dividend distribution policy. They do say that in the more prosperous period which followed, du Pont and the finance committee distributed big dividends, all the while "retaining earnings for expansion and replacement" (Alfred Dupont Chandler, Jr., and Stephen Salsbury, *Pierre S. du Pont and the Making of the Modern Corporation* [New York, 1971], p. 573).
[23] RS 143, ERS, "Memorandum for Mr. Wigren," Jan. 16, 1924.
[24] RS 550, Sloan to ERS, Feb. 13, 1925.

ing taken this step at this time. I think the effect market-wise and in-
vestment-wise would have been much better if action had been delayed
until the anticipated profits for at least some portion of the year had
been actually realized. As the matter stands, the dividend seems to me
to have been clearly paid out of surplus. On this point, I do not suppose
there is any disagreement. The question of dividends seems to come up
regularly every year just about this time and I find myself wondering
what new proposition will be presented a year from now. I have no
doubt, however, that the Company will fully earn its dividend this year
with a comfortable margin in excess of dividend requirements.[25]

Dwight Morrow, in a letter of February 1923 to Stettinius, was
inclined to give him great credit for his part in the recovery of
General Motors. He wrote: "The fine work you have done in the
Company in the last two years is showing itself in the financial
position and the earnings of the Company today, and if, when you
get back, you want to get off the Board, there is absolutely no reason why you should not do so." [26]

There is no question but that Stettinius's restraining hand and
financial acumen were very helpful to the company's recovery.
But the role of the bankers on the governing boards was by the
very nature of their position more that of watchdogs than of inno-
vators. The fragmentary records of Stettinius's connection with
General Motors put him primarily in that role.

Stettinius's attendance at General Motors meetings became less
regular after his 1923 illness and his participation in the company's
decisions tapered off, though he continued to be interested in the
corporation's affairs.

[25] RS 550, ERS to Sloan, Feb. 26, 1925.
[26] RS 245, Morrow to ERS, Feb. 21, 1923.

XII. *J. P. Morgan & Co.:*
The Guaranty Trust Company

E DWARD STETTINIUS was an important figure in the rescue of the Guaranty Trust Company from very serious financial embarrassment in the latter half of 1921. The Guaranty had engaged in an aggressive policy of expansion in the immediate postwar period. Times were good, optimism was widespread, and even members of the banking community were occasionally carried away and led into making imprudent loans.

Britain had been the world's banker before the war, and American bankers saw a shift in the financial center of gravity to New York. The Mercantile Bank of the Americas, with its extensive connections in Central and South America, China, and Japan, appeared an attractive investment for a group of leading American banks. The principal shareholders were the Guaranty Trust Company with 40 percent, Brown Brothers with 10 percent, and J. & W. Seligman and Company, with an undisclosed smaller percentage.[1] Other stockholders included the Columbia Trust Company, the Continental & Commercial Trust & Savings Bank of Chicago, the Hibernia Bank & Trust Co. of New Orleans, the Anglo and London-Paris National Bank of San Francisco, the Guaranty Trust Company of Cleveland, and the National Shawmut Bank of Boston. An important individual stockholder was Adolph Stahl of Schwartz & Co. of Guatemala.[2]

The Mercantile Bank of the Americas was organized on August 10, 1915, under the laws of Connecticut. It was given, among other powers, the authority to carry on banking, trade in commodities, and own and invest in the securities of other corporations.[3] Its expansion was very rapid, and it organized, acquired, or controlled a number of subsidiary banking and mercantile corporations and either directly or through them did business in the United States, Cuba, Venezuela, Columbia, Peru, Ecuador, Brazil, Argentina, Costa Rica, and the Orient. It had branches in New Orleans,

---

[1] *Wall Street Journal*, Aug. 10, 1922.   [2] *Buffalo Express*, Aug. 13, 1921.

[3] Material here and below, except as noted, is based on memoranda in the files of counsel for Guaranty Trust Company of New York, made available to the author with the permission of the client.

Paris, Hamburg, and in Spain. The Mercantile Bank extended loans and advances and accepted drafts drawn on it by other institutions.

The postwar boom in commodities in 1919 and 1920 was in full swing and the bank extended large credits, particularly to sugar producers in Cuba. The subsidiary and affiliated banks financed by the Mercantile Bank of the Americas financed, in turn, local trading companies. Too often these lower-echelon banks lent more heavily than was prudent. In the fall of 1920 and spring of 1921 world prices of the products financed by the Mercantile Bank and its affiliates fell sharply. The effect of the price decline hit sugar hard. It became virtually impossible to renew credits, but at the same time the borrowers' inability to liquidate commodities to pay off the credits made the renewals necessary. As the situation worsened, it became clear that drastic steps would be necessary to keep the Mercantile Bank and its subsidiaries from defaulting on their obligations. These amounted to $45,000,000 maturing between June 1, 1921, and the end of the year. Failure of the bank to pay maturing obligations could have gravely affected the American investing banks and caused a crisis.

The first phase of the rescue effort was called the Financing Plan of May 31, 1921. Under this arrangement the Mercantile Bank raised $20,000,000 from its stockholders through the sale of additional stock and notes, and a banking syndicate was formed to extend a further $35,000,000 in credits to the bank.[4] By August 1921 slightly more than half of the $35,000,000 promised by the seventeen participating New York banks had been advanced. But it was now obvious that the money available from the syndicate and from liquid receivables of the Mercantile Bank was not going to provide for all the liabilities.

It was at this critical point that J. P. Morgan & Co. stepped in, initiating the second phase of the rescue operation. Under the revised plan, which went into effect on August 8, 1921, the syndicate was enlarged to include those creditors of the Mercantile Bank who were willing to pool their claims with those of the syndicate, and the Syndicate Committee was given greater freedom in making loans to the Mercantile Bank and in making such loans without collateral. J. P. Morgan himself postponed his planned departure for Europe and on August 12 issued a statement designed to stop the flood of rumors about the Mercantile Bank. He mentioned the funds already made available and concluded, "it was considered

---

[4] The original members of the syndicate and the extent of their participation are listed in Appendix D, below.

desirable to provide further facilities which might possibly be required for the effective working out of the bank's affairs. These facilities have now been arranged and cause for anxiety is, in our opinion, eliminated." [5] The *Wall Street Journal* noted cryptically four years later, "As to the amount of the 'further facilities' no authoritative statement has ever been made." [6]

The man in charge of the revised plan was Stettinius, representing the Morgan firm, although Gates W. McGarrah was chairman of the syndicate committee. Public statements about the Mercantile Bank of the Americas were made by Stettinius, who was named to the Syndicate Committee on August 22, when the original three-man group was enlarged. On August 23, 1921, Stettinius announced: "The committee representing the syndicate formed in connection with the Mercantile Bank of the Americas, Inc., has been increased to five and consists of the following: Gates W. McGarrah, chairman of the Mechanics & Metals National Bank, W. C. Potter, chairman of the Guaranty Trust Co. of New York, Walter E. Frew, president of the Corn Exchange Bank, W. V. King, president of the Columbia Trust Co., Edward R. Stettinius of J. P. Morgan & Co." [7]

The *New York Bulletin of Commerce* reported the same day: "This committee it is understood has complete charge of the operations and policies of the Mercantile Bank, directing the liquidation of its holdings and any new undertakings upon which it may venture. The control of the funds contributed by the stockholding institutions and houses and of the credits supplied by the syndicate is also reported to be in its hands."

The Guaranty Trust Company of New York was the largest stockholder in the Mercantile Bank of the Americas and the largest participant in the financing of the bank and its subsidiaries. As of early August 1921 the Mercantile Bank and its subsidiaries owed the Guaranty Trust Company $16,000,000. In addition, the Guaranty held securities or obligations of the bank and its subsidiaries in the amount of $17,000,000, so the total involvement of the Guaranty Trust Company was $33,000,000. [8] The actual loans and other transactions by the Guaranty had been made by that company's officers with subsequent ratification by the directors. The lawyers for the Guaranty told the directors that while they had acted in good faith in approving loans to the Mercantile Bank and its subsidiaries,

[5] *New York Times*, Aug. 13, 1921.   [6] *Wall Street Journal*, July 30, 1925.
[7] *Wall Street Journal*, Aug. 23, 1921.
[8] Memorandum prepared Dec. 14, 1925, by Stetson, Jennings & Russell, counsel for Guaranty Trust Company, "Re: Mercantile Bank of the Americas, Inc.," pp. 11–13.

it might be claimed, if the Mercantile Bank failed, that the loans to that bank and its subsidiaries could be regarded as loans to a single institution and therefore excessive under the banking laws. If this were the case the directors might be held liable for approving such loans or for not having secured their liquidation. The directors were interested in correcting this situation, and a means for doing so was adopted.

The syndicate committee was faced in early August 1921 with the general problem of raising more money to keep the Mercantile Bank of the Americas afloat until its assets could be made available, as well as with the specific problem of how to get the highly vulnerable Guaranty Trust Company out of its predicament. Two alternative plans were suggested, both by Morgan partners.[9] Of the two, Stettinius's plan was chosen in preference to George Whitney's. The principal feature of the Stettinius plan was the organization of a new corporation—sometimes referred to in the correspondence as "the Stettinius corporation"—to buy up certain obligations held by the Guaranty Trust Company. The new company, Imports Advancement Corporation, was organized on August 16, 1921. Some of the directors of the Guaranty Trust Company, acting as individuals through a committee, bought $10,000,000 worth of the corporation's common stock. On September 9, the corporation bought at par from the Guaranty $16,000,000 in claims and obligations against the Mercantile Bank. The corporation raised additional money to acquire these last by borrowing $8,000,000 on a one-year 6 percent note from J. P. Morgan & Co. Some of the guarantors of the note were directors of the Guaranty Trust Company.[10]

Thomas Lamont telegraphed Stettinius at White Sulphur Springs on September 9, the very day the agreements were completed, and gave him credit for the success of the negotiations: "Reference to Bill Potter matter loan went through today so that sixteen out of the eighteen million dollars is now taken out the other five represented by preferred stock will be taken out Monday and the two remaining to complete the twenty-three at earliest possible moment stop So you see matter has been substantially completed Congratulations and hearty thanks again All well Love Tom."[11]

---

[9] Information on these plans is from memoranda in the files of counsel for Guaranty Trust Company.

[10] Memorandum, "Re: Mercantile Bank of the Americas, Inc.," p. 14. A list of guarantors and amounts is given in Appendix E.

[11] RS 200, Lamont to ERS, Sept. 9, 1921. (William Potter was to succeed Charles Sabin as president of the Guaranty Trust Company.)

By December, Stettinius could write reassuringly to vanTienhoven of the Rotterdamsche Bank, his associate in the Foreign Commerce Corporation. The Dutch banker had been uneasy about the situation at Guaranty. Stettinius wrote:

I am glad that you have written so frankly about the Guaranty Trust Company and that you have given me an opportunity of removing the doubt which you apparently entertain respecting the strength of that institution.

At the outset, permit me to state that you need have no fear whatever as to the soundness of the Guaranty Trust Company and the goodness of any obligation it may assume. There was, unfortunately, much discussion last spring and summer about the affairs of the Guaranty Trust Company, due largely, if not entirely, to the difficulties of the Mercantile Bank of the Americas, in the shares of which it was interested and the paper of which it held in a large amount. The difficulties of the Mercantile Bank of the Americas were due, as you are probably aware, to the abrupt decline in prices of commodities and merchandise. These difficulties were aggravated by the fact that the Bank, instead of confining itself to banking, had engaged on a very large scale in trading through subsidiary corporations. No one can appreciate better than you, because of your close contact with South America and the Far East, the unprecedentedly adverse conditions which confronted banks and trading companies engaged in South America and Cuban trade. And as the Guaranty Trust Company had been most active in extending its foreign business, it is not at all strange that queries should have been raised as to the amount of its losses when the extent of the demoralization in South America and Cuba became manifest; nor is it remarkable that, as usual in such cases, its losses were greatly exaggerated. Without attempting to describe the various measures that were taken to deal with the situation, I will say briefly that the Guaranty Trust Company was relieved, without loss, of all of the acceptances and loans to the Mercantile Bank of the Americas and its subsidiaries which it was carrying in July; and subsequently it charged off, or established reserves considered ample to provide for, possible losses in this and other directions. At the same time, measures were taken looking toward caring for the requirements of the Mercantile Bank of the Americas, and the question is now being studied of reorganizing the institution and some of the subsidiaries with a view of continuing the development of business along conservative lines in countries where the outlook is favorable.[12]

Imports Advancement Corporation raised additional money and bought from the Guaranty Trust Company some $4,500,000 worth of deferred notes of Textile Securities Company and $500,000 worth of unsecured three-year notes of the Mercantile Bank of

---

[12] RS 159, quoted in ERS to Potter, Jan. 11, 1922.

the Americas. By the end of 1921 Imports Advancement Corporation had received $10,275,000 from the sale of its capital stock.[13]

The lawyers of the Guaranty Trust Company summarized the situation this way: "The effect of the organization and operations of Imports Advancement Corporation was to relieve the Guaranty Trust Company of approximately $16,000,000 of loans and advances to the Mercantile Bank and subsidiaries, of its investment of $4,496,150. in Textile notes and of $2,433,480. in three year deferred Mercantile Bank notes and reduce its existing investment to an indirect investment through ownership of $4,000,000 of that Corporation's common stock and its $1,000,000 promissory note,— a total of $5,000,000 which was clearly within the Guaranty Trust Company's legal limits." [14]

Faced with a question of legal liability under the banking laws, certain directors of the Guaranty Trust Company participated actively in putting up money to relieve the bank of its embarrassment. Stettinius's prodding undoubtedly helped bring this about. Stettinius believed strongly in the responsibility of the directors of a company to direct. He wrote Nelson Dean Jay of Morgan, Harjes: "I may be a little old-fashioned, but I have a very strong feeling that men, in going on boards, assume a very real responsibility to the stockholders and creditors of the Corporation and I do not think that this responsibility can be discharged unless a man gives considerable time and atttention to the business so as to be competent to form an intelligent judgment of the various propositions that are presented from time to time." [15]

In the same vein, Stettinius afterwards told Lewis E. Pierson, chairman of the board of the Irving Trust Company (on which board Stettinius had sat from May 7, 1912, to September 7, 1915), apropos of the Guaranty Trust Company's troubles, "that he had come to the conclusion that this country would sometime see the day when organizations would avoid large directorates composed of men whose attendance and attention to their responsibilities were perfunctory, and instead would substitute smaller boards of directors composed of men of experience and ability who would give sufficient time to the corporation's matters to properly discharge their directorate responsibilities and be able to assist the active management in developing the company's business—and further that these directors would be properly paid for their services." [16]

[13] Memorandum, "Re: Mercantile Bank of the Americas, Inc.," p. 15.
[14] *Ibid.*, p. 23.   [15] RS 206, ERS to Jay, June 8, 1921.
[16] Scrapbook II, "Lewis E. Pierson's Recollections," Pierson to ERS, Jr., Aug. 27, 1937.

This was an issue on which Stettinius was entirely consistent. In resigning from the board of Pierson's own Irving National Bank in 1915 when the pressure of war purchasing at Morgan's took all his energies, he wrote: "I am not willing to serve as a Director of an institution unless I actually do some work for the institution and am of some help to its management. I have been of no help whatever to the Irving National Bank during the last seven or eight months, and I cannot see that there is any prospect of the situation changing in the near future. Under the circumstances, therefore, I am compelled to ask, in justice to myself as well as to the Bank, that my resignation as Director, member of the Executive Committee, etc., be accepted." [17]

C. J. Fay applies these views to Stettinius's actions in the Guaranty Trust situation: "Mr. Stettinius was always insistent on placing responsibility where it rested. This was shown by the firmness with which he dealt with the Guaranty Trust situation in 1921, when he placed the responsibility with the directors, resulting in a very substantial assessment at that time, pro rata to their length of service and to their private means." [18]

Naturally, a new flock of rumors spread up and down Wall Street, and we find that incorrigible gossip Clarence W. Barron broadcasting misinformation. In an item date-lined Washington, D.C., November 30, 1921, he writes: "P. A. O'Farrell [former Montana copper man and politician, later with Canadian Pacific Railway] tells me that the Guaranty Trust losses were $43,000,000; that Harry Payne Whitney was called upon to put up $6,000,000 and Thomas F. Ryan $9,000,000. The Morgan people put up the cash but the other people had to put up the security." [19]

The figures are absurd, but the fact remains that directors did put up money to help rescue the bank.

The directors of the Guaranty Trust Company elected Stettinius a director of that bank at their meeting of October 5, 1921. He was immediately appointed to the executive committee.[20] Charles H. Sabin, president of the bank, wired him on October 6, "Am delighted to welcome you on our board." [21]

On May 1, 1922, the long-awaited general audit of the Mercantile Bank of the Americas by Price Waterhouse & Co. was completed.

---

[17] RS 284, ERS to Pierson, Aug. 21, 1915.

[18] Scrapbook II, Fay, "Recollections," Dec. 22, 1936.

[19] Clarence W. Barron, *They Told Barron* (New York and London, 1930), p. 25.

[20] Scrapbook II, excerpts from minutes of Guaranty Trust Company, Oct. 5, 1921.

[21] RS 159, Sabin to ERS, Oct. 6, 1921.

It showed the conditions of the bank and its affiliates as of September 3, 1921. This report estimated that senior participants in the syndicate would recover 70 percent of their principal; subordinate creditors and stockholders would get nothing. Participants in Imports Advancement Corporation would recover about $11,200,000 of the $16,000,000 they had put up on their interest in the syndicate represented by participation certificates, but nothing on their stock or other obligations held.[22]

Since the bank syndicate was due to expire on June 15, 1922, Stettinius's committee circularized the members, urging that it be extended. The letter read: "The Banking Syndicate formed to make advances for the benefit of the Mercantile Bank of the Americas, Inc., and its subsidiaries, expires on June 15, 1922. It is quite obvious that the Mercantile Bank of the Americas cannot pay off any substantial part of its obligations prior to that date. The opinion of the Syndicate Managers is that it will be for the benefit of all parties in this situation to have the Syndicate extended for a further period. . . ." [23]

The next important development following the extension of the syndicate was to set up a new operating bank and convert the old Mercantile Bank of the Americas into a holding company. The *Commercial & Financial Chronicle* reported the event on August 12, 1922:

Organization of Bank of Central and South America to Carry on Business of Mercantile Bank of the Americas

In making known the organization of the Bank of Central and South America to conduct the business heretofore handled by the Mercantile Bank of the Americas, E. R. Stettinius, of J. P. Morgan & Co., issued a statement on Aug. 10, saying:

"In working out the affairs of the Mercantile Bank of the Americas, Inc., in connection with which a banking committee was formed last year, there has just been organized the Bank of Central & South America, with a capital of $5,000,000 and a surplus of $2,500,000 to carry on in New York the banking business formerly handled by the Mercantile Bank of the Americas. The name of the new bank accurately describes the field in which its principal operations will be conducted. It will take over the shares formerly held by the Mercantile Bank of the Americas in five affiliated institutions in Colombia, Peru, Costa Rica, Venezuela and Nicaragua, and its own shares in turn will be held for the time being

[22] Memorandum, "Re: Mercantile Bank of the Americas, Inc.," p. 22.
[23] RS 444, "Extension of Syndicate from June 15, 1922, to June 15, 1924" file, Mercantile Bank Creditors Committee to James Brown, President, Mercantile Bank of the Americas, Inc., May 22, 1922.

by the Mercantile Bank of the Americas, which last-named corporation will cease to function as a banking institution.

"While the board of directors of the new institution has not yet been definitely named, it will consist of men approved by the banking committee formed last year, which consists of Walter E. Frew, W. V. King, Gates W. McGarrah, W. C. Potter and E. R. Stettinius.

"The commercial activities of the Mercantile Bank of the Americas and its subsidiary institutions which were primarily responsible for the shrinkage in value of the bank's assets last year had been terminated and the new institution will operate solely along banking lines."

The Bank of Central and South America was incorporated under the laws of Connecticut on Aug. 5.[24]

A week later, Stettinius wrote to Thomas Cochran, a fellow partner at Morgan: "The reorganization of the Mercantile Bank is going along leisurely, the Bank of Central and South America having been formed last week. Matters of organization, however, are held in abeyance owing to the continued absence from the City of our hard working Chairman, the Hon. Gates W. McGarrah." [25]

Then, as is so typical of Stettinius and of the Morgan partners in their relations with each other, he shifted abruptly from important financial matters to intimate personal ones. He expressed satsifaction on learning that Cochran's sister seemed to have recovered from an illness. The satisfaction was premature. She suffered from cancer. A year and a half later we find Stettinius moving heaven and earth to get a newly-developed X-ray tube for radiation therapy for her. He was on the board of General Electric, but despite the efforts of officials from the president on down, the firm could neither supply nor locate a tube. He turned to Walter Cary, one of the vice-presidents of Westinghouse, and Westinghouse undertook to manufacture one immediately.[26]

While he was engaged in organizing the Bank of Central and South America, Stettinius continued to be concerned about the banks that had rallied round and put up money to keep the Mercantile Bank of the Americas from going down and dragging the Guaranty Trust Company with it, with potentially disastrous results for the entire banking and financial community. He came up with the idea of the Syndicate Participation Corporation, a securities trading company to be organized for the benefit of the syndicate members. This was ostensibly a plan put forward by the Guaranty Trust Company, but it was a Stettinius invention and

[24] *Commercial & Financial Chronicle*, Aug. 12, 1922, p. 708.
[25] RS 143, ERS to Cochran, Aug. 16, 1922.
[26] RS 143, ERS to Cochran, Jan. 17, 1924.

was referred to by his partner Thomas Cochran as "your child." [27]

The invitation to join the Syndicate Participation Corporation was sent to members of the syndicate in the summer of 1922. A draft prepared by Stettinius is dated July 17. It summarizes the main events to date and gives an admirable review of the whole complex situation before presenting the new proposal:

July 17th 1922.

To _____

About a year ago, the affairs of the Mercantile Bank of the Americas, Inc. were in such condition that a large amount of money was needed by it in order to prevent its suspension. Owing to financial conditions then existing, the failure of this Bank would have far-reaching effects of a serious nature. The requirements of the Mercantile Bank were so large that it was impossible for those interested in it to furnish, without aid, the necessary assistance. In view of this critical situation, the Guaranty Trust Company, in connection with others, felt justified in calling to the Mercantile Bank's assistance a number of institutions and private bankers who, with the Trust Company, formed a Syndicate which, from time to time during the past year, has advanced to the Mercantile Bank the sum of $18,130,000. This Syndicate was later enlarged to include creditors of the Mercantile Bank who pooled with the Syndicate claims in the aggregate amount of approximately $22,991,000, with all relative collateral, in exchange for Syndicate participation certificates in an equivalent amount. Against these cash advances and pooled claims the Syndicate holds assets consisting almost entirely of obligations of the Mercantile Bank, secured by obligations of banking subsidiaries of the Mercantile Bank and otherwise. A recent audit by Messrs. Price, Waterhouse & Co., however, foreshadows a loss of approximately thirty per cent. to Syndicate members whose participations are in the preferred position.

In view of the Guaranty Trust Company's interest in the Mercantile Bank and of the circumstances under which the Syndicate was formed, the Trust Company has felt much concerned that members of the original Syndicate, who advanced cash in aid of the Mercantile Bank's situation against participations in a preferred position, should be called upon to face any loss by reason of their generous and timely support. In order to give these institutions an opportunity to reduce their probable loss, the Trust Company proposes the following plan:

A business corporation will be formed under the laws of the State of New York with power to deal in stocks, bonds and other securities, and to become a member of Syndicates or of buying and selling groups interested in the marketing of securities of various kinds. The Trust Company will endeavor from time to time to assist this corporation to obtain such business and interests in the purchase and sale of securities for

[27] RS 143, Cochran to ERS, March 6, 1923.

public marketing as may be feasible and will try to make similar arrangements with others and also with banks and bankers originally interested in the Mercantile Bank. It is believed that the business thus acquired by the new corporation will be profitable.

In order to carry out this plan and furnish the new corporation with capital, it is proposed that the new corporation will purchase from the members of the original Mercantile Bank Syndicate whose participations are in a preferred position a 30% interest in their participations (which interest shall be deferred to the 70% retained by such Syndicate members) and also a 50% interest in the 10% cash dividend about to be paid them by the Mercantile Bank Syndicate. For this 30% interest in the Syndicate participations and for the 5% cash dividend the corporation will issue its five-year debentures. The corporation will have a small amount of no par value stock which will be issued to the Syndicate participants who may avail themselves of this plan, in the proportion of their holdings of Syndicate participations. This stock will be subject to a five-year voting trust in the usual form, which will also provide that, when the debentures have been paid off, the voting trustees will take steps to dissolve the corporation. The exact amount of stock of the corporation and of the debentures to be issued can only be determined when we are informed as to the number of those among the original Syndicate participants who wish to take part in the plan. Will you kindly answer promptly whether or not you desire to be included?

Very truly yours,

GUARANTY TRUST COMPANY [28]

By _____

Stettinius wrote Seward Prosser of the Bankers Trust Company before the public announcement and gave a hint of what was planned: "I am glad to report that the Guaranty Trust Company is completing the organization of the corporation about which I spoke to you and I hope it will be launched in the near future although I do not expect it will do much, if anything, for some time. Brown Bros. and Seligman have both agreed to go along and to throw some profitable business to the new company so that I am very much in hopes that it will prove to be the means by which the losses of the 'Rescue Party' will be greatly reduced." [29]

All of the original outside syndicate members except the National Bank of Commerce agreed to join the Syndicate Participation Corporation.[30] The Corporation began operations on about September 15, 1922.[31] Officers were Gates W. McGarrah, president;

[28] RS 444, Legal Box No. 5.

[29] RS 102, ERS to Prosser, Aug. 9, 1922.

[30] RS 820, [Arthur M. Anderson], "Memorandum for Mr. Stettinius," Dec. 20, 1924.

[31] RS 820, Harold Stanley to ERS, Sept. 25, 1923.

Albert A. Tilney, vice-president; and B. Atterbury, secretary-treasurer.[32]

On December 17, 1924, Harold Stanley of the Guaranty Trust Company stated in a memorandum that earnings of the Syndicate Participation Corporation to date amounted to $725,582.59.[33]

The remainder of the story of the Guaranty Trust Company and the Mercantile Bank of the Americas is one of the slow accumulation and distribution of moneys to lenders. The $8,000,000 loan to Imports Advancement Corporation from J. P. Morgan & Co. was extended several times, and by the end of 1923 was down to $4,000,000, thus relieving the Class "B" guarantors of liability.[34] By September 3, 1924, the loan had been reduced to $2,500,000, and there were additional funds on hand with which the Syndicate Committee intended to reduce it to $1,700,000 within thirty days.[35]

Eventually, on July 30, 1925, the following announcement appeared on the financial pages:

Banks in the syndicate that came to the assistance of the old Mercantile Bank of the Americas about four years ago have received word that they may expect final payment of the amount advanced by them within the next few days. Under the reorganization plan certain of the slow loans of the concern were placed in the hands of a liquidating committee which from time to time has been making payments to the banks in question as assets were realized upon. Recent payments had reduced the balance of advances to a relatively small amount. Forthcoming settlement payment, therefore, will remove the last traces of the Mercantile Bank's affair from the books of the syndicate banks. Total amount advanced by the group of banks was understood to be in the neighborhood of $35,000,000.[36]

The rescue did not end too badly for the rescuers. In December 1925 the bank's attorneys could say: "In the actual liquidation the Price, Waterhouse & Co. estimates have been exceeded and dividends paid to senior participants in the Syndicate aggregating 72½% of the principal amount of their participations, and it is now estimated that such participants will realize about 80% of principal." [37]

The Guaranty Trust Company recovered its position in the financial community, but this did not happen overnight. In January

[32] RS 820, Atterbury to Anderson, Sept. 3, 1924.
[33] RS 820, quoted in [Anderson], "Memorandum for Mr. Stettinius," Dec. 20, 1924.
[34] RS 236, Anderson, "Memorandum for Mr. Stettinius," Jan. 3, 1924.
[35] RS 236, ERS to Thomas F. Ryan, Sept. 3, 1924.
[36] *Wall Street Journal*, July 30, 1925.
[37] Memorandum, "Re:Mercantile Bank of the Americas, Inc.," pp. 22–23.

1923 Stettinius wrote to Charles Whigham at Morgan, Grenfell & Co., the London house of J. P. Morgan & Co., and asked him to put in a good word for the Guaranty Trust Company with the Imperial Tobacco Company, which had taken its money out of the Guaranty in 1921 when there were disturbing rumors about its solvency. He summarized the condition of the bank:

While I think you were advised of the steps that were taken a year and a half ago to strengthen the Trust Company and relieve it of losses arising from the Mercantile Bank of the Americas situation, I am not sure that you are aware of the progress that the Company has made during the past year and of its greatly improved position inherently, as well as in the financial community in this country. I enclose copy of the Trust Company's last report, which shows a thoroughly satisfactory position. Its earnings were most satisfactory during 1922, having amounted to approximately $11,000,000., but practically all of this, less dividends, was applied in establishing reserves on doubtful items and contingencies and in otherwise improving the position of various accounts.

The Company is in fine shape; it has successfully weathered a most terrific storm; it has reorganized its various departments, improved its personnel and generally is entitled to and I think has fairly won the confidence of its customers and of the community at large. I believe you need have no hesitation whatever in speaking most favorably of the Company in the event any inquiries are made of you by the Imperial Tobacco Company or otherwise, and I hope that if the occasion arises you will do what you can to help.[38]

Stettinius in his role as the doctor of sick companies had saved the patient, and now he was ill himself. He left New York for a long vacation in Georgia and was granted a leave of absence from the board of directors of the Guaranty Trust Company at the meeting of February 7, 1923.[39] He was granted another leave on September 11, 1924.[40]

A postscript to this story is that the Bank of Central and South America was bought by the Royal Bank of Canada in February 1925.[41]

[38] RS 159, ERS to Whigham, Jan. 5, 1923.

[39] RS 159, M. T. Murray, Jr., Secretary, Guaranty Trust Company, to ERS, Feb. 9, 1923.

[40] RS 159, Murray to ERS, Sept. 12, 1924.

[41] *Wall Street Journal*, July 30, 1925.

XIII. *Miscellaneous Business Concerns after World War I*

While the Foreign Commerce Corporation and General Motors and Guaranty Trust affairs were in progress, Stettinius was interested in a number of other enterprises which he did not always control. Some of these were matters of Morgan business, others were private ventures in which he participated as a director or simply an investor. The natural result of his less active part in these undertakings is that he has left us relatively little material about them. What remains is often so fragmentary as to make difficult a clear over-all view of the enterprises or his contribution to them. We have assembled from these pieces an outline that attempts to clarify a highly complex series of events.

International General Electric Company

The International General Electric Company was incorporated under the laws of New York on January 13, 1919. It was an independent corporation formed by the General Electric Company to take over all foreign investments and manufacturing and sales organizations of that concern. I.G.E. was both an export trading company and a holding company. It was organized on a geographical basis into three main departments: the Department of the Americas, the Department of the Far East, and the Department of Europe. At the close of 1919, it held stock as a holding company in twelve electrical companies with a total book value of approximately $14,600,000. The companies were Mexican General Electric Company, General Electric Company of Cuba S.A., General Electric S.A. (Brazil), General Electric S.A. (Argentina), South African General Electric Co., Ltd., China General Edison Co., Inc., Shibaura Engineering Works (Japan), Tokyo Electric Company, Australian General Electric Co., Ltd., British Thomson-Houston Company, Ltd., Cie. Française Thomson-Houston, and Franco Tosi Company (Italy).[1]

The president of the new company was Gerard Swope, former

[1] International General Electric Company, *First Annual Report* (Dec. 31, 1919).

vice-president of American Telephone & Telegraph's manufacturing subsidiary, Western Electric Company.[2] Swope's first appointee to the board of directors was E. R. Stettinius.[3] In 1920 Stettinius accepted the invitation to serve on the executive committee of the company.[4] Stettinius remained on the board for the rest of his life. Stettinius and Gerard Swope were warm friends, but both tended to be formal in social relationships. When Stettinius was recovering from a serious illness in the spring of 1923, Swope sent him a radio set—an uncommon luxury in those days—and had it installed in his Locust Valley house.[5] But it was not until more than a year later that they came to be on a first-name basis. Stettinius proposed it, and Swope wrote on July 14, 1924: "Dear *Ed:* You see I am accepting the very kind invitation you extended to me the last time we were together, and this is evidence of how much I appreciate your permission to address you on such a friendly basis." [6]

Stettinius replied just as stiffly, "My dear Gerard, In evidence of the pleasure I derive from your adoption of my suggestion, I address you as you addressed me." [7]

In 1922 Swope was elected president of the parent General Electric Company, but stayed on as chairman of the board of International.[8]

Anson W. Burchard succeeded Swope as head of International General Electric. Relations between Burchard and Stettinius had their ups and downs. In the course of their correspondence Stettinius addressed the other as Anson or Mr. Burchard, depending on the state of their amity at the moment.[9] On August 3, 1922, Stettinius invited him in the friendliest way to his house to play cards.[10] A little over two months later he telegraphed him less graciously: "Have communicated terms your astounding proposition Doctor Humphreys and informed him I could not see my way clear contribute Stevens under the circumstances You are a piker as well as a welcher." [11]

[2] John Winthrop Hammond, *Men and Volts; The Story of General Electric* (New York, Philadelphia, and London, n.d. [ca. 1941]), p. 381.

[3] Scrapbook II, Swope to ERS, Jr., June 21, 1933.

[4] RS 232, Swope to ERS, April 17, 1920; ERS to Swope, April 28, 1920.

[5] RS 254, John J. Bennett to Swope, April 28, 1923.

[6] RS 254, Swope to ERS, July 14, 1924.

[7] RS 254, ERS to Swope, July 17, 1924.

[8] *Who Was Who in America*, III (1960), 838–39.

[9] RS 723, ERS to Burchard, Aug. 21, 1922, "Dear Anson"; ERS to Burchard, Dec. 21, 1922, "Dear Mr. Burchard"; RS 232, ERS to Burchard, July 17, 1924, "Dear Mr. Burchard"; ERS to Burchard, Dec. 8, 1924, "Dear Anson."

[10] RS 792, ERS to F. P. Moore, Aug. 3, 1922.

[11] RS 723, quoted by Burchard to ERS, Oct. 28, 1922.

The reference was to the fiftieth-year fund drive of Stevens Institute of Technology in Hoboken, New Jersey, with which Burchard was associated. The previous year Stevens had offered the honorary degree of Doctor of Engineering to Stettinius. Stettinius was humorously skeptical of President Humphreys' motive in offering this award and wrote to E. H. Wells of Babcock & Wilcox beforehand and asked him to find out what it was all about: "I have not the faintest idea what I have done to be entitled to the degree of Doctor of Engineering. Do you know what it means, and do you know who ever received the degree heretofore and who will probably receive it in June? Far be it from me to attribute any but the loftiest of motives to my friend the Doctor, but I have wondered whether the conferring of this degree has anything to do with the Endowment Fund which I understand Stevens is endeavoring to raise?"[12]

Stettinius reluctantly accepted the degree, and from this we learn what size of man he was. In asking President Humphreys to order him academic regalia, he gave his measurements: "my height being about 5 feet 10½ inches, weight 165 pounds, and cap size No. 7." He added as a precaution, "I presume that it will not be necessary for me to make an address of any kind, but I will be glad to be reassured on this point."[13]

The commencement exercises were held at the Castle Point campus on June 21, 1921. The speaker of the day was Charles M. Schwab, the steel man, and other recipients of honorary degrees included Rear Admiral W. S. Sims of the U.S. Navy and Frank Julian Sprague, the electrical engineer who was perhaps the one person most responsible for the trolley-car era.[14] In subsequent correspondence, President Humphreys addressed him as "Dr. Stettinius."[15]

Stettinius's appraisal of the motive behind the degree was realistic, of course, and the request for money followed as expected. After the stormy exchange with Burchard, Stettinius sent a cheque for $5,000 for the Stevens Institute of Technology Endowment Fund.[16]

Stettinius and Burchard lie buried not far apart in Locust Valley Cemetery.

Stettinius did not attend directors' meetings faithfully after his health began to fail, but he was very useful to International General

[12] RS 723, ERS to Wells, May 19, 1921.
[13] RS 723, ERS to Alexander C. Humphreys, May 19, 1921.
[14] *New York Times*, June 22, 1921.
[15] RS 723, Humphreys to ERS, Nov. 18, 1922.
[16] RS 723, ERS to Burchard, Dec. 21, 1922.

Electric in their financing. In the spring of 1921 he was the go-between in the negotiation of a loan made by Morgan, Harjes & Co. to the French Thomson-Houston Company.[17] He also smoothed the path for negotiations that fall betwen Swope and the Morgan firm for the issue of British Thomson-Houston 7 percent forty-year mortgage debenture stock in the amount of a million and a half pounds sterling. The issue was taken by Morgan, Grenfell & Co. and was opened and fully subscribed for on November 21, 1921.[18]

Stettinius was helpful in interpreting the views of the International General Electric officers to the Morgan partners. On one issue, for example, the two groups were poles apart. There was talk of a merger between the British Thomson-Houston Company, Ltd., and the British-based General Electric Co., Ltd. The Morgan firm opposed the merger violently because of the lesser "standing" of the latter concern. This was entirely a matter of prestige, almost of the social position of the respective managements.[19] It was Stettinius who quietly pointed out that while British Thomson-Houston might operate on a loftier plane, General Electric Ltd., was the more profitable concern.[20] The facts of the situation were brutally set forth in a letter from Charles Coffin, the grand old man of General Electric, who wrote from retirement to H. C. Levis, the dignified head of British Thomson-Houston, so admired by the Morgans: "It has been a matter of frequent comment among our directors that upon the basis of our present dividends it is a very burdensome charge to carry investments paying so small a return as has been the case with the B. T. H. Company, covering a period of twenty years."[21]

Stettinius also advised International General Electric in its dealings with the Tata Iron Works of Calcutta. In the fall of 1922 he warned Anson Burchard to be wary of accepting debentures in part payment for electrical apparatus sold to an Indian electric company partly owned by the Tata Iron Works unless he was assured beyond question that the debentures could be sold.[22] Two years later he suggested that a plan to settle part of the indebtedness

[17] RS 232, ERS to P. M. Haight, Treasurer, International General Electric Company.
[18] RS 232, ERS to Charles F. Whigham, Nov. 14, 1921; minutes, 26th meeting of the board of directors, International General Electric Company, Dec. 2, 1921.
[19] RS 232, cablegram, Morgan, Grenfell & Co. to ERS, Nov. 7, 1921.
[20] RS 232, ERS to Morgan, Grenfell & Co., Nov. 10, 1921; ERS to Whigham, Nov. 14, 1921.
[21] RS 232, Coffin to Levis, Jan. 16, 1922.
[22] RS 232, ERS to Burchard, Nov. 17, 1922.

of Tata by the purchase and resale of pig iron be extended to cover the whole amount owed by Tata.[23]

Texas Gulf Sulphur Company

Stettinius represented J. P. Morgan & Co. briefly in the affairs of the Texas Gulf Sulphur Company because the firm was a major stockholder. His role was to take part in the policy decisions of the company during the early 1920's.

Texas Gulf Sulphur came into existence by accident. Men who were prospecting for oil in Matagorda County, some eighty miles southwest of Houston, found the Bill Hill Dome sulphur deposit. In 1916 Bernard M. Baruch, who had watched the early struggles of the Gulf Sulphur Company, believed the time was ripe for developing the sulphur industry and interested J. P. Morgan & Co. and William Boyce Thompson, the mining man, in buying up the company. The entrance of the United States into World War I interrupted the progress of the new concern. Baruch and Seeley W. Mudd, president of the company, both went into war work, and Thompson's chief engineer, Walter H. Aldridge, became president.

In 1918 the corporate name was changed to Texas Gulf Sulphur. The capitalization at this time was $3,000,000. Immediately following the war, a new stock issue was sold and the capitalization raised to $6,350,000. The company was now in production, but the war-stimulated demand for sulphuric acid, the principal final product of sulphur, had declined, and the company found itself in a weak position.[24] At this time a plan was prepared by Judge Edwin B. Parker, late of the Liquidation Commission, to reorganize the company. Stettinius appears, by his insistence on almost unanimous approval of the plan, to have had doubts about it.[25] Apparently support for the plan was insufficient, because the reorganization did not take place and the proposed debentures were not issued.[26]

When Seeley Mudd's son, Harvey S. Mudd, went to France in

[23] RS 232, Burchard to ERS, July 15, 1924; ERS to Burchard, July 17, 1924.
[24] Harry C. Echols, "Texas Gulf Story, Part I," *The Golden Triangle*, VII, 9–16, (April 1968); Texas Gulf Sulphur Company, *Annual Report* (1959), pp. 7–8.
[25] RS 466, Aldridge to Harvey Mudd, March 16, 1920.
[26] Moody's *Manual of Investments and Security Rating Service, Industrial Securities* (New York, 1925), p. 695 (hereafter cited, with year of publication, as *Moody's Industrials*); telephone conversation with Mr. David Crawford, Secretary, Texas Gulf Sulphur Company, May 19, 1971.

the summer of 1920 to continue negotiations toward the establishment of a French subsidiary, Stettinius directed him to Nelson Dean
Jay of Morgan, Harjes. Stettinius wrote to Jay and asked him to
help Mudd in every way possible.[27] The French project was
abandoned, however, when the younger Mudd discovered that it
would cost too much to refine sulphur in France because of the
high price of coal.[28]

Beginning in 1921 the company's business improved greatly, and
in that year Texas Gulf Sulphur was listed on the New York Stock
Exchange and earned $3.07 per $10-par-value share. An initial
dividend of fifty cents and fifty cents extra per share was paid on
December 15, 1921.[29] This burst of prosperity caused the company
to launch a vigorous program of enlarging sulphur reserves by
exploration and land-buying. In the enthusiastic campaign to buy
sulphur properties, Stettinius advocated a conservative course. He
wanted the company to get its money's worth.

One of the important acquisitions considered by the Texas
Gulf Sulphur Company in late 1921 and early 1922 was the Hoskins
Mound sulphur deposit owned by the Texas Company. The stakes
were considerable. Gulf's total sulphur reserves were estimated on
December 2, 1921, to be 11,000,000 gross tons, and the Hoskins
Mound deposit was estimated at 6,000,000 gross tons.[30] Negotiations
hinged on the percentage of Gulf stock which would be given to
the Texas Company in return for this large deposit. The Texas
Company wanted up to 29 percent but appeared agreeable to 20
percent. In reporting on the whole matter to Bernard Baruch,
Stettinius favored a much lower figure: "After listening to the
arguments advanced by [Walter H.] Aldridge and by [Edwin B.]
Parker and Herman [Baruch], it seemed to me that the Texas Gulf
Sulphur Co. would not be warranted in making a trade that would
call for much if any more than a 10% interest to the Texas Company. I certainly would not favor a trade on a basis of a 20%
interest even if I were certain that the Texas Company would immediately build a plant and start a company in competition with
the Texas Gulf Sulphur Co."[31]

But all the discussion turned out to have been waste motion. The

[27] RS 466, ERS to Jay, July 2, 1920.
[28] RS 466, memorandum by A. N. Arragon of Morgan, Harjes, "Texas Gulf
Sulphur Co.," Aug. 10, 1920.
[29] *Moody's Industrials* (1925), p. 695.
[30] RS 466, "Memorandum concerning Texas Gulf Sulphur Company and
Hoskins Mound sulphur deposit owned by the Texas Company."
[31] RS 466, ERS to Baruch, Jan. 28, 1922.

Texas Company entered into a deal with the Freeport sulphur firm for the sulphur in Hoskins Mound.[32]

From the correspondence we get the impression that Stettinius's advice was taken very seriously, but his connection with the company was an informal one. The official agent of J. P. Morgan & Co. was George Whitney, who became a director of the company toward the end of Stettinius's association with Texas Gulf Sulphur.[33]

Commercial Solvents Corporation

During World War I the chemist Chaim Weizmann developed in Britain a process for making explosives which led a grateful government to press for the creation of the state of Israel in accordance with his Zionist aims. During the same period he invented a process for the manufacture of butyl alcohol. Exclusive licensees in the United States for this butanol process were the Commercial Solvents Corporation, incorporated on December 19, 1919.[34]

Stettinius was one of five major subscribers to the Commercial Solvents Corporation stock syndicate, each of whom agreed to participate to the amount of $170,000.[35] In this venture he was associated with his friend Henry Lockhart, Jr., of the Goodrich Lockhart Company and with John M. Goetchius, president of General Syndicate, Inc. Goetchius had been a colleague in Washington during the war, and he and Stettinius had kept up their friendship.

David M. Goodrich and W. D. Ticknor of the Goodrich Lockhart Company were the syndicate managers,[36] and, prodded by Henry Lockhart, they turned to Stettinius for advice and help when the corporation was in trouble. Commercial Solvents was in difficulties from the outset, so Stettinius had a number of occasions to be helpful. In March 1920 they wondered whether they ought to spend $350,000 for a by-products plant to make use of waste materials at the Terre Haute, Indiana, plant. Stettinius advised against it.[37]

In 1921 Stettinius negotiated with Fin Sparre of E. I. du Pont

[32] RS 466, Aldridge to ERS, March 25, 1922.

[33] *Moody's Industrials* (1926), p. 130.   [34] *Ibid.*, pp. 500–501.

[35] RS 689, W. D. Ticknor, Vice-President, Goodrich Lockhart Company, to ERS, June 23, 1921.

[36] RS 689, statement of ERS account, June 30, 1921.

[37] RS 689, Ticknor to ERS, March 24, 1920, with penciled note by ERS dated March 25.

de Nemours for the sale of the corporation. He was not able to convince Commercial Solvents that they would do well to meet the du Pont terms, however, so the deal fell through. It was later apparent that Stettinius was considerably nettled by the failure of his plan.[38]

One of the problems facing the company early in 1922 was its debt of $1,000,000 to the National City Bank. The syndicate managers proposed to pay off the debt by the sale of bonds, but Stettinius argued in favor of selling stock instead.[39] The following year the corporation issued $1,000,000 in 8 percent cumulative preferred stock.[40]

In April 1922 Stettinius, still critical of the way the company was being run, wrote to Goetchius, "What would you think of our forming a small group to take over all of the interests of the members of the Syndicate, reorganizing the Company and running it in proper shape?" [41] But nothing came of the idea.

Production troubles went hand in hand with financial troubles. From the summer of 1922 until November 1923 there were technical difficulties at the plant in Terre Haute.[42] In April 1923 the directors authorized the raising of $1,000,000 from the company's customers to build a new plant, because, as Goetchius wrote Stettinius, "It was felt that manufacturing difficulties current in the present plant would be obviated in the new plant." [43]

Stettinius's position relative to Commercial Solvents was ambivalent at this time. He sold his stock in the company and he wrote to Goetchius: "In your meeting with the Commercial Solvents people this morning, I hope that you will make clear that while I was interested in the Company at one time, I have practically no interest in it at the present time; that some years ago I made an effort to induce the people in control to sell out to the duPont Company and make some kind of a deal with them and that when they declined to do so I really gave the matter no further concern at all." [44]

But he followed every move of the company and received de-

---

[38] RS 293, ERS to Sparre, March 22, 1921; RS 689, memorandum, ERS to Goetchius, Oct. 10, 1923.

[39] RS 689, ERS to Lockhart, Jan. 27, 1922.

[40] *Moody's Industrials* (1926), p. 501.

[41] RS 689, memorandum, ERS to Goetchius, April 28, 1922.

[42] RS 689, memorandum, Goetchius to ERS, October 10, 1923; Goetchius to ERS, Jan. 2, 1924.

[43] RS 689, Goetchius to ERS, April 18, 1923.

[44] RS 689, memorandum, ERS to Goetchius, Oct. 10, 1923.

tailed reports from Goetchius on all of its activities. Presumably he still had in the back of his mind his plan for taking over the shares of the company.

The fear that gripped the stockholders and syndicate managers was that the company's customers would become so exasperated with the slow and erratic deliveries of butyl alcohol, acetone, ethyl alcohol, and other vital raw materials for their industries—plastics, synthetics, and paint, among others—that they would build their own plants and drive the company out of business. The customers were large concerns and could easily have done just that. They included duPont, Eastman Kodak, Hercules Powder, Maas & Waldstein, and Egyptian Lacquer.[45] The solution to the problem was to put a man from a customer's plant in charge of production.[46] This worked so well that early in 1924 Goetchius was able to report booming production, rising returns, and general satisfaction.[47] Stettinius expressed himself as being "delighted to hear that the Company has turned the corner and that its prospects of making money are so good." [48]

The correspondence with Goetchius continued. From time to time he wrote to Stettinius and offered him a "piece" of some syndicate or concern. In July 1922 Goetchius wrote that he had "reserved" for Stettinius a $5,000 interest in the San Miguel Tlaxpampa Mine, one of the holdings of General Syndicate, Inc. before its liquidation.[49] Another time he wanted to let him in on the Deepwater Coal and Iron Corporation.[50] Stettinius's reply to this last offer explains the composition of his investment portfolio at his death, the concentration in a few selected securities: "I have not a particle of doubt that an investment in the securities of this Corporation would, bearing as it does your recommendation, prove profitable, but at the present time I am very diligently working along the lines of contraction and liquidation rather than expansion. I do not want to go into any new operations of any kind at the present time however attractive they may appear to be." [51]

It was Goetchius who arranged for James F. Mimnaugh's move from assistant to J. J. Bennett, Stettinius's secretary, to secretary and man of affairs (at a 50 percent increase in pay) for Goetchius's brother-in-law, William Fahnestock of the securities house Fahne-

[45] RS 689, memorandum, Goetchius to ERS, Oct. 10, 1923.
[46] *Ibid.*   [47] RS 689, Goetchius to ERS, Jan. 2, 1924.
[48] RS 689, ERS to Lockhart, Jan. 16, 1924.
[49] RS 784, memorandum, Goetchius to ERS, July 13, 1922.
[50] RS 784, Goetchius to ERS, May 23, 1924.
[51] RS 784, ERS to Goetchius, May 26, 1924.

stock & Co. Stettinius's illness and prolonged absence from 23 Wall Street had left Mimnaugh with little to do.[52]

The Bartlett Hayward Corporation

In March 1920 Stettinius wrote to his old friend Harry Lusch of Chicago as follows:

I have recently gone into a small operation which seems to me to have a good deal of merit and if you care to come along, I will be glad to have you join on the same basis, of course, as I am going in myself. The operation to which I refer contemplates the purchase of $1,300,000 of the 8% preferred cumulative stock of the Bartlett Hayward Corporation at par. I enclose memorandum, balance sheet, etc., which you may wish to look over. I know the people connected with the enterprise and have the utmost confidence in their integrity and ability and believe that the investment is not only safe, but that there is a possibility of making, in the course of four or five years, a very nice profit over the 8% dividends.[53]

The Bartlett Hayward Company was an old and substantial Baltimore company that had been engaged in manufacturing metal products since 1830. Their foundry made stoves, then branched out into heating plants and structural and ornamental cast iron, including building façades. From castings they went into machinery, specializing in gas plants and sugar refineries. The company was among the first to manufacture munitions for the British Army through contracts negotiated by Stettinius's Export Department. They later made munitions for the United States forces. After the war, the company diversified by buying a controlling interest in several companies engaged in manufacturing special lines of products. On December 31, 1919, they bought the entire capital stock of the American Hammered Piston Ring Company,[54] and the following May they acquired 75 percent of the stock of George Oldham and Company, manufacturers of pneumatic tools in Philadelphia.

The shares of the Bartlett Hayward Company, the operating company, were bought up by the Bartlett Hayward Corporation,

[52] RS 784, Goetchius to ERS, April 29, 1925. Mimnaugh was still looking after the private financial interests of the Fahnestock family at the time of my conversation with him on April 22, 1968.

[53] RS 515, ERS to Lusch, March 2, 1920.

[54] We noted in Chapter IX that Stettinius's elder son, William Carrington Stettinius, went to work for Bartlett Hayward and became an officer of the piston-ring subsidiary.

the holding company, in April 1916.[55] Stettinius negotiated a financial reorganization of the company through an amendment to its
certificate of incorporation dated March 10, 1920, with the result
that its capital now consisted of $1,500,000 preferred cumulative 8
percent convertible stock and $3,000,000 common stock. Stettinius
agreed to buy 13,000 shares of the preferred at $100 a share, or a
total of $1,300,000 worth of stock.[56] Stettinius wrote to a number of
his friends and associates along the lines of the letter to H. B. Lusch
already quoted. The result was that within a fortnight the 13,000
shares were distributed as follows:

E. R. Stettinius	2000	$200,000
H. P. Davison	1750	175,000
T. W. Lamont	1000	100,000
W. H. Porter	500	50,000
William Ewing	900	90,000
George Whitney	500	50,000
Carl Taylor	250	25,000
John F. Bowie	250	25,000
Charles Day	150	15,000
C. D. Norton	2250	225,000
Henry Lockhart, Jr.	2000	200,000
E. H. Wells	1000	100,000
George H. Gard[i]ner	200	25,000
H. B. Lusch	250	25,000
	13,000	$1,300,000 [57]

Lockhart subsequently sold his 2,000 shares back to Stettinius,
who resold them to other associates.[58]

The company prospered, and Stettinius was able to report to his
friends the following year: "The profits of The Bartlett Hayward
Corporation and its subsidiaries for the four months ending April
30th, 1921, were $208,261.24 or at the rate of say $600,000 a year,
which is five times the amount required for the dividend on the
preferred stock, some of which you hold. The position of the Company appears to me to be quite satisfactory and I believe that the
officials of the Company have put it in the best possible shape to
withstand the depression in general business through which we are
now passing." [59]

[55] RS 298, "Memorandum on the Bartlett Hayward Co.," Feb. 10, 1920.
[56] RS 298, Agreement between Howard Bruce and ERS, March 10, 1920.
[57] PS 27, Bartlett Hayward file, "Memorandum re Distribution of Bartlett
Hayward Corporation 8% Preferred, Cumulative, Convertible Stock. Par
Value $100," March 11, 1920.
[58] PS 27, Bartlett Hayward file, ERS to F.W.M. Cutcheon, July 26, 1921.
[59] RS 298, ERS to William Ewing, May 27, 1921.

In the spring of 1925 Howard Bruce, who had been president of the company for some years, carried on negotiations with the McClintic-Marshall Construction Company for the sale of Bartlett Hayward.[60] The transaction went through. The final figure agreed upon as the value of the net tangible assets of the company was $9,800,000. In accordance with the original agreement, the preferred stockholders were invited to turn in their shares before April 15, 1925, to receive $125 a share plus accrued dividends.[61] And thus Stettinius's prediction of 1920 was borne out. The investors did in fact make, "in the course of four or five years, a very nice profit over the 8% dividends."

Goodyear Tire & Rubber Company

The Goodyear Company very nearly became a casualty of the 1920–1921 economic depression. It found itself overextended in the fall of 1920. It had large inventories of rubber, cotton, and tires on hand and was further committed to increase that inventory at war-inflated commodity prices. Sales fell off in the slump. Then, just as a committee was arranging for a substantial credit and refinancing, it was found that the company's indebtedness was greater than originally believed, so the bankers backed off. There was considerable alarm lest a Goodyear receivership cause a chain reaction leading to other failures across the country. So another creditors' committee was created, with Myron C. Taylor as chairman.[62]

A number of banking houses were invited to help to head off the collapse of the Goodyear Company. J. P. Morgan & Co. was one of several invited to participate. Robert Swaine of the Cravath firm, lawyers for the Goodyear Company, was critical of Stettinius and the Morgan firm for not taking the lead in the campaign to save the company.[63] The fact is that Stettinius was very active in the discussions. He made the Morgan position clear from the outset: "We ourselves have no interest as creditor or otherwise in the Goodyear situation, but, nevertheless, we have kept in touch with the various committees representing the creditors and stockholders of the company and have discussed and advised with them regarding the plans of reorganization, etc." [64]

[60] RS 298, Bruce to ERS, March 3, 1925.
[61] RS 298, Bruce to ERS, April 4, 1925.
[62] RS 644, ERS to Danforth Geer, Feb. 7, 1921.
[63] Robert T. Swaine, *The Cravath Firm*, 2 vols. (New York, privately printed, 1948), II, 273.
[64] RS 664, ERS to Geer, Feb. 7, 1921.

The Cravath firm prevailed upon Clarence Dillon of Dillon, Read & Co., to take the chief responsibility for the rescue. Dillon's proposed reorganization plan of January 14, 1921, was the basis of the plan actually followed to save the company.[65]

Stettinius was prepared to be helpful in any way possible. He wired the president of the Illinois Trust & Savings Bank that J. P. Morgan & Co., "have expressed willingness take participation in syndicate which under certain conditions Dillon, Read & Co. have indicated willingness to form to underwrite issue of first mortgage bonds." [66] On the other hand, to avoid causing Dillon any embarrassment, he assured him that if Dillon, Read & Co. preferred to leave them out, it would be entirely agreeable to the Morgans.[67]

Once the reorganization plan had been set up there was the problem of securing approval from the various parties at interest. Stettinius's old company Babcock & Wilcox, to whose board he had been reelected after a long absence, was among the creditors who had refused to accept securities in payment of the debt to them. So at the suggestion of Joseph M. Hartfield of White & Case, Stettinius was asked to use his influence to get the treasurer of Babcock & Wilcox to change his mind.[68]

By coincidence Stettinius had had an absurd exchange with Hartfield just the preceding October. Hartfield, who was quite a practical joker, sent him a bill for the 10,000 francs he would have won from him at "Matador" if they had played that game together while crossing on the *Aquitania* in the first week of October. He also billed him for the 100 francs he had probably won on a crossing on the *France* a year earlier, or at least would have won if the score card had not been lost! Stettinius, John J. Watson of the International Agricultural Corporation, and Hartfield made quite a game of this nonsense.[69] Stettinius's genuine regard for Hartfield is shown in his reply to a dinner invitation from him late in 1921: "I am delighted to accept your invitation, not only because of my admiration for Judge Mayer [70] but also because of my affection for you and the pleasure that I always derive from your company." [71]

[65] Swaine, *The Cravath Firm*, II, 273.

[66] RS 644, ERS to J. J. Mitchell, Jan. 17, 1921.

[67] RS 644, ERS to Dillon, April 6, 1921.

[68] RS 644, H. M. Young to ERS, Feb. 24, 1921.

[69] RS 413, bill, Hartfield to ERS, Oct. 18, 1920; ERS to Watson, Oct. 27, 1920; Watson to ERS, Nov. 5, 1920.

[70] Judge Julius M. Mayer of the U.S. Circuit Court of Appeals will appear again in connection with the reorganization of the Interborough Rapid Transit Company.

[71] RS 178, ERS to Hartfield.

Stettinius wrote to J. G. Ward of Babcock & Wilcox to say he hoped that Ward would reconsider his decision as a Goodyear creditor, observing that "the plan cannot succeed without the cordial support of the merchandise as well as the bank creditors." [72] It was most appropriate that Stettinius was asked to exert gentle pressure on Babcock & Wilcox, because his chief usefulness to that company upon returning to the board of directors after the war was his strategic position to exert influence in its behalf. He did not go back to making or selling boilers. Scarcely a month before writing to Babcock & Wilcox on behalf of Goodyear he had written on their behalf to Everett B. Sweezy of the First National Bank, a member of the Finance Committee of the Pennsylvania Company, which controlled the Cheswick Power Company, to ask that the boiler company's $400,000 machinery contract with Cheswick not be cancelled without adequate compensation. [73] A month later he wrote to George F. Baker, Jr., to ask him to help Babcock & Wilcox to get a $200,000 contract from United Electric Light & Power, an Edison company. [74] Baker did exert himself in response to this appeal, and his associate at Edison wrote back wryly, "I think . . . that you could help by getting them to modify their price, as I am afraid that they do not yet know that the war is over." [75]

The following year, Stettinius inadvertently uncovered a lack of enthusiasm toward Babcock & Wilcox—though not toward their high-quality boilers—at the Day & Zimmermann engineering firm in Philadelphia, when he wrote his good friend Charles Day suggesting that the firm specify Babcock & Wilcox boilers. Babcock & Wilcox told Stettinius: "Day & Zimmermann's leanings have always been toward Edge Moor boilers. We have done practically no business with them other than B&W 8532 in 1915 for the Erie County Electric Co., where we were able to club them into buying our boilers by reason of the fact that the American Brake Shoe & Foundry Co. shell machine plant at Erie was to purchase current from the Erie County Electric Co." [76]

John E. Zimmermann corroborated this with an observation similar to that of George Baker's friend at Edison: "It is true that we have done very little business with Babcock & Wilcox Company

[72] RS 644, ERS to Ward, March 7, 1921.
[73] RS 336, ERS to Sweezy, Feb. 9, 1921; Sweezy to ERS, Feb. 10, 1921; ERS to Sweezy, Feb. 11, 1921.
[74] RS 336, E. H. Wells to ERS, April 1, 1921; ERS to Baker, April 1, 1921.
[75] RS 336, N. F. Brady to Baker, April 5, 1921.
[76] RS 336, Babock & Wilcox memorandum on Day & Zimmermann, Inc., May 18, 1922, forwarded by ERS to Day with covering letter same date.

because we have always found their prices considerably higher than those of other reputable boiler makers, such as Edge Moor." [77]

Stettinius would not use his position as a director to throw business to friends in other companies,[78] but he actively solicited business from his friends on behalf of companies of which he was a director.

Returning to the difficulties of the Goodyear Tire & Rubber Company: by the end of April 1921 more than 90 percent of the Goodyear creditors had agreed to the readjustment plan and the outlook was very favorable indeed. This plan rescued the company from certain failure, but litigation dragged on for six years before the situation was finally cleared up.[79] It is true that Stettinius "thought it was not the kind of situation in which Morgan's should take the lead," [80] but his helpfulness in the Goodyear crisis was recognized by two individuals deeply concerned with the favorable outcome. On April 21, 1921, Myron C. Taylor of the creditors' committee telegraphed Stettinius: "Desire to thank you for the great assistance you gave us in a very trying dangerous situation." [81] The same day Clarence Dillon, author of the readjustment plan and the person responsible for issuing the new Goodyear bonds, wired almost the same message: "I wish to express my appreciation of the great help I received in a very trying situation from your council and advise [*sic*]." [82]

The conflicting reactions of Stettinius and his younger partner Thomas Cochran to the news of the successful reorganization of the Goodyear company illustrates the looseness of the Morgan organization. While the partners were generally aware of what the others were doing, they were not fully conversant with the details. Cochran wrote, "You will have seen by the papers that the Goodyear plan has finally been consummated. We are not in the Syndicate. Dillon did not ask us." [83] Stettinius replied, quietly setting the record straight:

In regard to the Goodyear Company, I must say that I have derived a good deal of satisfaction in consequence of the successful reorganization

---

[77] RS 336, Day & Zimmermann, Inc., interoffice memorandum, Zimmermann to Day, May 19, 1922.

[78] We have seen, for example, that he refused to intercede for the Fisk Rubber Company when he was a director of General Motors (Chapter XI, above).

[79] Swaine, *The Cravath Firm*, II, 278–81.   [80] *Ibid.*, II, 273.

[81] RS 644, Taylor to ERS, April 21, 1921.

[82] RS 644, Dillon to ERS, April 21, 1921.

[83] RS 143, Cochran to ERS, April 23, 1921.

of the Company. It would certainly have gone into the hands of a receiver if we had not stepped in at the psychological moment, and while
we can all derive some satisfaction from the consciousness that we were
of help, we cannot, I am sorry to say, measure, in dollars and cents, the
value of the work. Dillon was very fine about the underwriting and
gave us every opportunity, up to the last minute, to go in and of course
had we done so we would have made a very nice little profit on our
participation. He is down here and I have seen quite a little of him during the past few days.[84]

Cuba: Public and Private Financing

Government Loans

J. P. Morgan & Co. was interested in financing the government
and some private businesses in Cuba during World War I and its
aftermath. In 1914 the firm floated a $10,000,000 loan for the Cuban
government (to the astonished chagrin of Speyer and Company,
who thought they had the inside track).[85]

The Cuban political and economic situation during the period
that followed the first loan is well summarized in the "Memorandum
on Cuba" circulated at J. P. Morgan & Co. and dated February 8,
1923. In large measure it was an expression of the economic developments which we have already considered in connection with the
Guaranty Trust Company's relations with the Mercantile Bank of
the Americas.

Cuba during the war enjoyed unusual prosperity, due to the heavy demand for sugar; a prosperity mainly limited to the people and shared in
by the Government only in part, since although the revenues leaped to
unforeseen heights, the extravagance and corruption of the administration resulted in the enrichment of the politicians and the impoverishment
of the Government.

Sugar collapsed in 1920 and bank failures ensued. Heavy losses followed with forced liquidation, a moratorium and serious loss of revenues
to the Government and financial chaos.

The extravagance and corruption rife under Menocal created a floating debt of uncertain size, with unpaid claims, unpaid wages, salaries,
etc., and when the Banco Nacional failed, there resulted a heavy loss to
the Government, which had large sums on deposit there, and the whole

---

[84] RS 143, ERS to Cochran, April 25, 1921.
[85] Russell H. Fitzgibbon, *Cuba and the United States, 1900–1935* (New
York, 1964), pp. 232–33.

financial machinery of the Government broke down since the Bank was the paymaster for national finances.

General Crowder was sent to Cuba in the Winter of 1921, as the personal representative of the President of the United States. He made a careful, thorough study and analysis of the political and economic situation. This culminated in the Spring of 1922 in the delivery to President Zayas, who took office in April 1921, of the last of a series of important memoranda. By reason of the pressure exerted by the Department of State (U.S.) and General Crowder these were finally accepted by Zayas and put into effect.

As a result the budget was balanced at about 56 million, the lottery was reformed and the worst of the graft cut out, a commission was created to audit and pass for payment the many uncertain claims against the Republic, additional revenues were provided for by the creation under American expert supervision of the 1% Sales Tax and finally in June 1922, the first cabinet of President Zayas, incompetent and in part corrupt resigned and a new cabinet satisfactory to General Crowder was installed. Financial operations were arbitrarily cut off as of July 1, 1922, and revenues received after that date were devoted to the payment of obligations coming due thereafter and all claims and obligations due before July 1, 1922, were unpaid. They were either to be marked off if improper or were later to be paid off out of the proceeds of the projected Government loan or out of surplus revenues expected in future when the Sales Tax should become effective.[86]

Following the election of Alfredo Zayas to the presidency, but before his reforms had been put into effect, Stettinius wrote to Raleigh Hansl, the Morgan firm's man on the ground:

We have given a great deal of consideration to the problems confronting Cuba and are sincerely anxious to assist in every way in our power. The more fully we have gone into the matter, however, the more serious it appears.

As you are probably aware, we negotiated last Fall with the Cuban Government for a loan in this market, having been requested by the State Department to go into the matter. Our negotiations came to naught. Recently, however, because of the many reports that we received of the distressing situation in Cuba, we called upon the State Department and expressed our willingness to consider a loan if it were desired. We discussed the matter at some length with Under-Secretary Fletcher and also Mr. Sumner Welles, and also have exchanged several letters with them. We have had in mind that it might be possible, later on, to float a loan of not to exceed $50,000,000 if offered on sufficiently attractive terms. It would, of course, be necessary to show that this loan, together with the proceeds of an internal loan, which we understand is

---

[86] RS 743, "V. M.," "Memorandum on Cuba," Feb. 8, 1923.

being discussed, would suffice to meet the necessities of the Cuban Government Treasury and to facilitate the movement of sugar and, to some extent at least, relieve the sugar situation. It would also be necessary, of course, to give adequate guarantees with respect to revenues and expenditures. Obviously, however, we cannot formulate a plan for dealing with the situation until we have received and examined reports concerning the present financial position of the Government, its income, expenditures, current deficit, etc., etc.[87]

A week later Stettinius wrote to Hansl again to say that the United States Department of State did not think that the time was ripe for a loan.[88]

In October 1921 J. P. Morgan & Co., represented by Dwight Morrow, negotiated a stopgap loan with President Zayas in the amount of $5,000,000.[89] The purpose of the loan was "to provide service for the external debts then threatening default, to take care of the most pressing necessities of the Government and to give a breathing space during which it was hoped that the promised reforms might become effective." [90] The loan was participated in by a syndicate of American banks including the Morgan firm; Kuhn, Loeb & Co.; the National City Company; the Guaranty Trust Company; the Bankers Trust Company; Harris, Forbes & Co. of Chicago; Dillon, Read & Co.; and J. & W. Seligman. So matters rested until the following year.

In the summer of 1922 the loan question was taken up again. Before the conversations about the actual loan could begin, Cuba had to put her political and financial house in order under the guidance of General Enoch Crowder and it was necessary for the Cuban legislature to approve the loan. The United States State Department had ultimately to approve the loan. Stettinius described the flurry of activity to Thomas Lamont, who was vacationing at North Haven on Vinalhaven Island, Maine:

Discussions have been quite active during the past week in regard to the proposed Cuban loan. Following the receipt of letters from Crowder, we instructed [Raleigh] Hansl, who happened to be in Havana, to get in touch with Crowder and discuss the proposed loan statute. The private wire of the Royal Bank of Canada, between here and Havana, has been kept pretty hot with the exchange of cables and we are sending this afternoon a long message to Hansl embodying suggestions which have been made by George [Whitney], [Arthur] Ander-

[87] RS 444, ERS to Hansl, July 7, 1921.
[88] RS 227, ERS to Hansl, July 15, 1921.
[89] Fitzgibbon, *Cuba and the United States*, p. 235.
[90] RS 743, "Memorandum on Cuba," Feb. 8, 1923.

son and [G. H.] Gardiner. Of course all of this is preliminary and no action will or can be taken in regard to negotiating for a loan until the loan statute has been passed by Congress which will probably not be for several weeks.[91]

In the fall, Morrow went to Havana to carry on the negotiations over the terms of the $50,000,000 loan.[92]

The key figure in the Cuban financial picture was General Crowder, a dedicated public servant in a very delicate and anomalous position, with financially irresponsible Cuban politicians attacking him from one direction and jealous army officers trying to force him into early retirement from another. He confided his worries to Stettinius while the loan was being negotiated[93] and received a strong vote of confidence in reply.[94] Stettinius's optimism about the public recognition that Crowder should look forward to was subsequently justified, and Crowder was appointed United States Ambassador to Cuba.

On January 12, 1923, the Morgan firm was the high bidder for the $50,000,000 bond issue, and the same group of banks that had underwritten the 1921 loan participated in the new loan under Morgan auspices.[95] The writer of the Morgan memorandum saw mixed results from the loan. He thought that the Cuban economy would be stimulated but political corruption encouraged, since there would now be no financial incentive for reform.[96] He was particularly pessimistic about the future role of the Morgan firm, now that the Cuban government had got the money it wanted.

Private Concerns

The Trust Company of Cuba

In 1920 J. P. Morgan & Co. had an arrangement in force with the Trust Company of Cuba under which they entered into a series of joint loan transactions. When the financial crisis precipitated by the fall in world sugar prices took place, the borrowers of those loans were unable to repay them in full—an already familiar story.[97] The

[91] RS 200, ERS to Lamont, Aug. 18, 1922.
[92] Nicolson, *Dwight Morrow*, p. 265.
[93] RS 697, Crowder to ERS, Nov. 25, 1922.
[94] RS 697, ERS to Crowder, Dec. 8, 1922.
[95] Fitzgibbon, *Cuba and the United States*, p. 236; RS 743, "Memorandum on Cuba," Feb. 8, 1923.
[96] RS 743, "Memorandum on Cuba," Feb. 8, 1923.
[97] RS 743, memorandum, Hansl to ERS, Nov. 17, 1921.

Trust Company of Cuba also had incurred obligations to the Royal Bank of Canada and the Chase National Bank of New York.[98]

Stettinius undertook to recover as much as he could of the money lent by the Morgan Company, a task which involved negotiating with the Trust Company—especially its manager, Norman H. Davis—and with officers of the major creditor institution, the Royal Bank of Canada. In the course of these discussions, a number of individuals suggested that Stettinius take on the monumental task of stabilizing the entire sugar business. He was not optimistic about this. He wrote Emory W. Clark of the First and Old Detroit National Bank in October 1921: "I doubt whether it would be possible. The various parties interested in the sugar business are in my opinion not yet ready to coöperate and to make the concessions without which no plan of stabilization can be successful. I am afraid that our friends in the sugar business will have to learn by bitter experience. So far as Cuba is concerned, it seems to me that we shall have to go through some stormy weather before we can hope for anything like smooth sailing." [99]

Norman Davis of the Trust Company of Cuba seems to have realized that the affairs of the company called for greater gifts than he possessed, so he arranged for the Royal Bank of Canada to send down their man Joseph R. Bruce to take charge of the company.[100] One of the economy measures of the Royal Bank managers was to reduce the payroll from $150,000 a year to $39,250 by December 1922.[101] By the end of 1922 the condition of the Trust Company had greatly improved under Canadian management.[102]

On December 18, 1922, the Royal Bank of Canada estimated the J. P. Morgan & Co. interests in joint loans to be as follows:

Cia. Azucarera Caobillas	$218,377.38
Isidro Garcia	237,046.43
J. I. Lezama	319,894.59
L. R. Munoz y Cia	504,067.76
Zarraga y Cia	300,114.69 [103]

Three days later, after a conversation with S. R. Noble of the Royal Bank of Canada, Stettinius told Hansl that the Morgan claim against the Trust Company of Cuba would be paid in full with in-

[98] RS 227, cablegram, Hansl to ERS, April 13, 1922.
[99] RS 227, ERS to Clark, Oct. 24, 1921.
[100] RS 227, ERS to Hansl, July 15, 1921.
[101] RS 227, S[olomon] R. Noble to ERS, Dec. 18, 1922.
[102] RS 227, C. E. Neill to ERS, Dec. 15, 1922.
[103] RS 227, Noble to ERS, Dec. 18, 1922.

terest, but that they would probably lose some money on the loans made on joint account. Stettinius privately felt that the maximum recovery on the joint loans would not exceed $500,000.[104] A month later Hansl reported that a plan was proposed to reorganize the Caobillas Company, the concern owing the least amount to the joint lenders.[105]

At the end of 1924 the Morgan firm still held claims on joint account with the Trust Company of Cuba amounting to somewhere between $1,750,000 and $2,000,000.[106]

Tarafa and Cintas

On February 9, 1922, Stettinius wrote to his younger son, Edward, Jr., at his fraternity house at the University of Virginia, "We leave Saturday by steamer for Nassau where we expect to spend about three or four weeks after which we will run over to Cuba, planning to return here about April 1st."[107] The trip was to combine business with a search for health in a warm climate for Mrs. Stettinius and their daughter Betty. They sailed for Nassau on February 11.[108] By the middle of March they had reached Havana, and the business part of the trip began.

During his fortnight in Cuba, Stettinius talked primarily with two Cuban businessmen. One was Colonel José Miguel Tarafa, who was a power in Cuban politics and business. The other was his son-in-law Oscar B. Cintas, an importer of heavy machinery, particularly railroad equipment. Tarafa and Cintas seem to have unrolled the red carpet for the American financier. When he got back to New York, Stettinius wrote to Tarafa thanking him several times for his "innumerable courtesies," including arrangements at Key West on the return journey and a supply of fresh fish and lobsters delivered to his private railroad car for the trip north.[109] Cintas arranged for a trip through the interior of Cuba by private railroad car, sometimes by special train, extending from a Thursday afternoon to Sunday afternoon with visits to Camagüey, Port Tarafa, Cunagua, Moron, and Ciego de Avila.[110]

One set of discussions involving both Tarafa and Cintas had to do with the contemplated purchase of the sugar-producing properties

[104] RS 227, ERS to Hansl, Dec. 21, 1922.
[105] RS 227, Hansl to ERS, Jan. 10, 1923.
[106] RS 227, memorandum, ERS to George Whitney, Dec. 29, 1924.
[107] RS 676, ERS to ERS, Jr., Feb. 9, 1922.
[108] RS 679, Nassau and Cuba in 1922 file.
[109] RS 781, ERS to Tarafa, April 7, 1922.
[110] RS 577, Cintas to ERS, March 20, 1922.

of Francisco J. de Sola. They talked about the possibility of an arrangement under which Tarafa, Cintas, Stettinius, and William Woodin of American Car & Foundry Company would take over certain properties, including Compania Azucarera Central Sixto.[111] Stettinius's interest in the deal diminished considerably by the time he returned to New York and thought at greater length about the problems of satisfying the de Sola creditors and floating a security issue on the property.[112] The de Sola project finally fell through when Tarafa reported unfavorably on his visit to inspect the property.[113]

The other principal topic of discussion was the Cuba Northern Railways. Stettinius was acting for J. P. Morgan & Co. in the Cuba Northern conversations, not as an individual. Colonel Tarafa dominated the railroad. He wanted "some new financing to take care of all the present outstanding bonds and provide for the construction of the Line to Santa Clara, the locomotive and car repair shops and increased warehouse facilities at our Terminal." [114] Stettinius was prepared to help Tarafa in any way possible, including making it easy for Redmond & Co. to market bonds for the railroad. He told Tarafa that before he could hope to sell any securities it would be necessary to have the company's books audited and its properties assessed by a competent firm of engineers.[115]

In the course of the correspondence that followed Stettinius's visit to Cuba and his inspection of the railroad, an odd misunderstanding occurred between him and his Cuban acquaintances. Cintas wrote with some heat to complain that Tarafa had told him that Stettinius had alleged that he, Cintas, had claimed to be able to force Tarafa to sell the Cuba Northern Railways at any time.[116] Stettinius's immediate reaction was to send a copy of Cintas's letter to Tarafa with a note asking "What is your young friend trying to get at?" and wondering what remark of his could have been so interpreted.[117] Tarafa had indeed understood Stettinius to say that Cintas had said he could force Tarafa to sell the railroad.[118]

Everything was finally straightened out; Cintas apologized for the offensiveness of his letter,[119] but there remained a lingering dis-

[111] RS 764, H. J. Steinbreder to ERS, April 4, 1922.

[112] RS 764, ERS to Tarafa, April 7, 1922; RS 764, ERS to Cintas, April 7, 1922.

[113] RS 781, Tarafa to ERS, April 18, 1922.   [114] *Ibid.*

[115] RS 781, ERS to Tarafa, April 11, 1922.

[116] RS 577, Cintas to ERS, Sept. 8, 1922.

[117] RS 577, ERS to Tarafa, Oct. 3, 1922.

[118] RS 577, ERS to Cintas, Oct. 9, 1922.

[119] RS 577, ERS to Cintas, Oct. 30, 1922.

trust. This comes out in a letter Stettinius wrote to his son Edward a little over a year later:

I received this morning in an envelope which I thought was addressed to me the enclosed letter from Oscar Cintas, which is intended for you.

How much have you seen Cintas during the last year or two, and have you run around with him at all? I am particularly anxious to know if you have seen much of him during the past year as it has some bearing upon my business relations with him and Tarafa. I will have a talk with you about Cintas when next we meet, but for the present let me express the hope that you will go a little slow and that you will not do anything to establish an intimacy with him. I wish that you would not, under any circumstance or condition, put yourself under the slightest obligation to him, and indeed the less you have to do with him the better it will suit me.[120]

The discussions about refinancing the Cuba Northern Railways continued into the fall, with Stettinius very carefully committing himself to nothing and playing down the possibility of any Morgan connection with the enterprise. Meanwhile, the rumor was abroad that the refinancing had been agreed to and that J. P. Morgan & Co. had either acquired or was planning to acquire a substantial interest in the railroad. S. R. Noble of the Royal Bank of Canada wrote to Stettinius and asked that the Trust Company of Cuba, which as we have seen was being operated by the Royal Bank, be appointed trustees for the bond issue.[121] Stettinius hastily explained that no definite agreement had been reached.[122]

On November 10, 1922, Tarafa sent Stettinius a memorandum summarizing the plans that they had discussed for refinancing the railroad. Stettinius wrote back to make some corrections and carefully added the disclaimer: "Both you and I understand, of course, that the sole purpose in preparing this memorandum was to set out, for possible use in the future, a statement of the plans that we discussed. You are under no commitment whatever to us to make any proposition along the lines set out in the memorandum or along any other lines; nor are we under any obligation to you to either directly or indirectly finance or reorganize the Cuba Northern Railways Co. on any basis,—both of us being without any commitment whatever one to the other."

He concluded: "You are now about to return to Cuba to take up with the representatives of the Cuban Government various matters

[120] RS 676, ERS to ERS, Jr., Jan. 3, 1924.
[121] RS 781, Noble to ERS, Oct. 27, 1922.
[122] RS 781, ERS to Noble, Oct. 30, 1922.

in connection with the relations between the Cuba Northern Railways Co. and the Cuban Government. I hope that you will be successful in effecting some adjustment that will be satisfactory to you as well as to the Cuban Government. If, after you have done so, you desire to discuss with us the reorganization of your property, we will be glad to answer the matter in the light of conditions then obtaining, and in any event, I will, of course, take pleasure in rendering every possible assistance." [123]

That same day Stettinius wrote another letter to Tarafa confirming the loan of $500,000 from J. P. Morgan & Co. to Tarafa personally, to run for four months at 6 percent per annum, secured by $1,000,000 in 6 percent first mortgage bonds of the Cuba Northern Railways Company and postdated November 22.[124]

The next day Stettinius wrote to General Crowder to corroborate Dwight Morrow's assurances that the Morgan firm was not planning to take over the Cuba Northern Railways Company as had been reported in the press. He summarized the negotiations to date:

Largely as a result of a personal acquaintance with Colonel Tarafa extending over several years, and of a trip that I made over the lines of the Cuba Northern Railways Co. last Spring, I have had a number of conferences with him during the last three or four months in regard to his Company and the possibility of assisting him, directly, or indirectly, in reorganizing it and in securing the capital required for the completion of the enterprise. However, as I became familiar with the position of the Company, and particularly with the nature of its arrangements, etc., with the Cuban Government, I came to the conclusion that it would be difficult for him to make an arrangement with any one to reorganize and finance the Company until its various contracts and agreements with the Cuban Government had been gone over and, to some extent at least, modified. I have, accordingly, advised him to return to Cuba and take up the entire matter with the representatives of the Cuban Government and your good self.

In the meantime, and in order to enable him to meet certain obligations, we have made him, individually, a loan as a purely banking matter without any commitment on his part or ours as to future financing for his Company or himself.

I am writing you in order to keep you advised of a matter which may be of interest to you in view of the possibility of your making a general study of the railroad situation in Cuba.[125]

---

[123] RS 781, ERS to Tarafa, Nov. 15, 1922.
[124] RS 781, ERS to Tarafa, Nov. 15, 1922.
[125] RS 781, ERS to Crowder, Nov. 16, 1922.

The following month Stettinius wrote to Tarafa and reported that he had discussed the proposed reorganization of the road with S. R. Noble of the Royal Bank of Canada, which had carried the company during the lean years and should be considered in any recapitalization plan. He closed by offering to resume discussions about reorganization with Tarafa whenever the latter wished after he had clarified and straightened out the existing agreements between the company and the government.[126]

The immediate and direct connection of Stettinius with the Cuba Northern Railways ended on this note of good will and a readiness to be helpful if needed. A postscript to these conversations about new money and reorganization falls into two parts. The railroad secured funds by the issue in March 1924 of 6½ percent equipment gold bonds totaling $1,680,000 offered by the National City Company. This offering was followed on August 1, 1926, by $400,000 in 5½ percent Series B bonds.[127]

The reorganization took the drastic form of a merger of the Cuba Northern Railways with the Cuba Railroad and a third line to form the Consolidated Railroads of Cuba. The new company was incorporated July 28, 1924, with an authorized capital of $40,000,000 6 percent cumulative preferred stock and $400,000 common stock. The Consolidated Railroads of Cuba corporation was controlled by the Cuba Company, which owned 94 percent of its common stock.[128] Directors of the Cuba Company were Herbert C. Lakin, president of the company, Edward J. Berwind, Howard Mansfield, William H. Woodin, W. V. Griffith, Elton Parks, Percy A. Rockefeller, Oscar B. Cintas, Henry W. Bull, C. E. Dunlap, Horatio S. Rubens, José M. Tarafa, and R. B. Van Horne.[129]

Even though the Morgan firm did not play a part in the consolidation, Stettinius had already used his good offices to help Tarafa's business reputation with the Cuba Company. Stettinius was very close to William H. Woodin, and his opinion would have carried great weight. In December 1922, when Tarafa feared a loss of face from his inability to raise money for the Cuba Northern, Stettinius wrote to him:

> Now in regard to the Cuba Company, you wrote me that the people connected with the Company might feel that you had acted lightly and that they would rejoice about your poor judgement if they learned

---

[126] RS 781, ERS to Tarafa, Dec. 22, 1922.
[127] *Moody's Manual of Investments and Security Rating Service, Railroad Securities* (New York, 1926), pp. 1761–62.
[128] *Ibid.*, p. 1760.   [129] *Ibid.*, p. 1756.

that you had not actually financed your property. I have taken pains to make clear to some of the parties interested in the Cuba Company that, after going over the entire situation, it seemed unwise to do any financing at this time. I stated that your operations during the coming six months would show up so much more handsomely than for corresponding periods of previous years that it seemed desirable, from every standpoint, to defer the issue of any securities until you could submit a statement of the results of the operations of your road for the first four or six months of the present grinding season. This statement was obviously received as a perfectly natural explanation and will, I am sure, serve to negative any such impressions as you fear might have been formed.[130]

General Electric Company

Stettinius was elected to the board of directors of the General Electric Company at the meeting of November 17, 1921.[131] This association with the parent company undoubtedly resulted from Stettinius's work on the board of International General Electric during the previous two years. He came to the board just at the end of the first period in the company's development and saw a new generation of executives take over the management.

The company had been formed in 1892 by the joining of the Edison General Electric Company of Schenectady, New York, with the Thomson-Houston Electric Company of Lynn, Massachusetts, and its international affiliate. In 1902 the Sprague Electric Company was acquired, and in the following year the Stanley Electric Manufacturing Company of Pittsfield, Massachusetts, was also absorbed.[132]

Charles A. Coffin of the Thomson-Houston company was the first president. After more than twenty years as president, he became chairman of the board in 1913 and was still in the chair at board meetings when Stettinius came on the board. Owen D. Young, vice-president and general counsel, followed Coffin as chairman, and Stettinius's friend Gerard Swope was elected president to succeed Edwin W. Rice, Jr., who had followed Coffin in 1913.

The General Electric Company management was quick to make use of Stettinius's many talents. They appointed him to the execu-

---

[130] RS 781, ERS to Tarafa, Dec. 22, 1922.
[131] Scrapbook II, minutes, 291st board meeting, General Electric Company, Nov. 17, 1921.
[132] *Moody's Industrials* (1925), pp. 1939-43.

tive committee immediately, along with his partner Dwight Morrow.[133] At the board meeting of June 23, 1922, Robert Treat Paine, II, moved that a committee of the board, to be called the general conference board, be appointed to "act in an advisory capacity to the General Officers on questions of policy affecting the affairs of the Company, and with power to make recommendations to the Board of Directors for action." Chairman of this advisory body was Charles Coffin. Stettinius was appointed a member. The others were Gordon Abbott, George P. Gardner, and Dwight Morrow.[134]

Stettinius was useful to the company in numerous ways. When Radio Corporation of America, the collaborative radio communication concern formed by General Electric in 1919, was looking for a president in 1922, Stettinius suggested to Owen D. Young that he consider General James G. Harbord, whom Stettinius had watched at work during the war. Harbord was made president of the company and Young wrote to Stettinius, "I am just tickled to pieces with Harbord and I am sure it will be a good thing for him and for us. Many thanks for all the help you gave me in that matter and my personal matters." [135]

Stettinius also served as a member of the salary and bonus committee of the company. As an outsider, he was able to bring a detachment to the problems of the committee that company officials would have found impossible, but he was sympathetic with the position of top management, which had to live with the people involved. A particularly sensitive area within the committee's purview was the distribution of bonuses among the higher executives of the company—Edwin W. Rice, the honorary chairman of the board; Owen D. Young, the chairman; Anson W. Burchard, the vice-chairman of the board; and Gerard Swope, the president of the company. In March 1923 Stettinius wrote to Young from Augusta, Georgia, about this:

But as to the allotments to yourself and Swope, I agree to the amounts proposed because I understand you consider that (to quote [Gordon] Abbott), "in view of the extreme delicacy of the situation regarding Burchard and Rice," it would be unwise to allot to you and Swope any more stock than that allotted to them; and as you are the head of the Company and responsible for its organization, I do not feel that I should insist at this time upon an arrangement that you think would be unwise. But I hope that you will agree some of these days that in the interest of good organization and of the Company itself, a line or lines

[133] Scrapbook II, minutes, 291st board meeting, Nov. 17, 1921.
[134] Scrapbook II, minutes, 300th board meeting, June 23, 1922.
[135] RS 750, R.C.A. file, Young to ERS, Oct. 25, 1922.

should be drawn between those really at the head and those who have been placed in conspicuous positions mainly in order to maintain harmony, and finally that the amount of the bonus should be fixed with direct reference to the value and importance of the services rendered during the preceding year and not in accordance with any arbitrary rule.

I am sure you will agree that the Salary Committee, in their desire and determination to deal fairly with some men, should not be forced to allot to others amounts larger than are reasonably due them.[136]

It is ironic to find Stettinius, the man who habitually overworked and drove himself unmercifully, taking a strong line with Young in the next paragraph on the subject of neglecting his health: "However, do show that you are at least fairly intelligent by taking care of yourself,—that's a duty you owe the Company, even if you are entirely indifferent to your obligations to your family."

The question of executive bonuses came up again in 1924, a year later. Stettinius restated his earlier position that bonuses should be awarded on the basis of value of services received by the company, not for sentimental reasons or merely to keep peace in the family.[137]

It is significant that whatever personal differences Stettinius might have had with Burchard in the past, he went out of his way to argue for generous treatment of him, on the basis of a prior agreement within the company, apparently in opposition to some sentiment on the board. This same fierce Roman virtue was apparent in the case of the Japanese loan of 1924, which came up a fortnight before the bonus letter just quoted. J. P. Morgan & Co. had brought out the $300,000,000 thirty-year 6½ percent external loan for the Imperial Japanese Government, and Dwight Morrow invited his colleagues on the executive committee of the General Electric Company to consider authorizing the company to participate in the loan, which was to help Japan to recover from the effects of the disastrous earthquake of 1923. The minutes of the meeting go on to record: "After extended discussion and upon motion, duly seconded, it was RESOLVED that, because of the commercial importance of conserving our large investments in Japan and developing and extending our export trade with Japanese customers, and because the rehabilitation of Japan, in the opinion of the Committe, should be furthered in every possible way, to this end a participation by the General Electric Company in the proposed loan up to a total subscription of $10,000,000 was referred with

---

[136] RS 750, General Electric file, ERS to Young, March 12, 1923.
[137] RS 750, General Electric file, ERS to Baker, Feb. 24, 1924.

power to Messrs. Burchard and Swope, *Messrs. Morrow and Stettinius not voting*" (italics added).[138]

Interborough Rapid Transit Company

In the spring of 1922 Stettinius became involved in the reorganization of the Interborough Rapid Transit Company and related holding companies.

The story of the surface, elevated, and subway railroad lines of
New York City and their financing is complicated beyond belief,
but J. P. Morgan & Co. was interested primarily in the Interborough
system, which started out to operate the Broadway subway line
financed by August Belmont & Co. in 1901. The Morgan firm was
responsible for the issue of $25,000,000 in three-year notes in 1908
and $10,000,000 in one-year notes in 1911.[139]

The bulk of the Interborough Rapid Transit Company shares had
been acquired by the Interborough-Metropolitan Company in 1906.
When this company was recapitalized in 1915 as the Interborough
Consolidated Corporation, it still had outstanding approximately
$68,000,000 of Interborough-Metropolitan 4½ percent collateral
trust bonds secured by the pledge of Interborough Rapid Transit
stock.[140] During the war period, the IRT paid out dividends on a
lavish scale: 20 percent in 1915, 1916, and 1917, and 17½ percent in
1918.[141] This met the interest on the Interborough-Metropolitan
bonds and paid 6 percent dividends on the Interborough Consolidated preferred stock. But the IRT was unable to maintain its dividend payments because of the wartime rise in costs and the political
sanctity of the five-cent fare.

Anticipating a default on the interest payments on the Interborough-Metropolitan, the bondholders formed a bondholders'
committee under the chairmanship of Grayson M.-P. Murphy, who
was later to become president of the Morgan firm's Foreign Commerce Corporation. The bondholders forced the Interborough Consolidated Corporation into a receivership in March 1919.

As the plight of the IRT, the operating company which was the
source of revenue, worsened, another committee was set up to keep
the IRT alive. J. P. Morgan was chairman of the new committee,

[138] Scrapbook II, minutes, 830th executive committee meeting, General Electric Company, Feb. 6, 1924.
[139] Swaine, *The Cravath Firm*, II, 68.   [140] *Ibid.*, II, 282.
[141] *Electric Railway Journal*, Sept. 10, 1921, p. 405.

which represented $38,000,000 in secured notes and almost $155,-
000,000 in first and refunding mortgage bonds. The IRT managed
to stay barely solvent from one quarter to the next by the greatest
effort until the spring of 1922.[142] It was finally realized that a volun-
tary reorganization was necessary, so a plan was put forward on
May 1, 1922.[143] It was in connection with this drastic reorganization
that Stettinius entered the picture as the representative of J. P.
Morgan & Co.

A major stumbling block to the acceptance of the reorganization
plan was the opposition of the stockholders of the Manhattan Railway Company, the elevated line, because under the plan that company would no longer receive a guaranteed 7 percent rental on its
property used by the Interborough. The holdouts were the officers
of the Equitable Life Assurance Society, one of the largest shareholders. The critical date was September 1, 1922, when the $38,000,-
000 in IRT notes was due to mature. If the reorganization plan were
not approved by that date the possibility was very great that J. P.
Morgan & Co. would be called upon to put up the $9,500,000 repre-
sented by the uncooperative stockholders' holdings. So Stettinius
was applying pressure to Paul D. Cravath, lawyer for the Interborough-Metropolitan bondholders and chief negotiator.[144]

Stettinius reported the progress of negotiations through the summer of 1922 in frequent letters to Thomas Lamont, on vacation at
North Haven, Maine. Stettinius wrote Lamont on August 18:

As we approach the 1st of September, meetings with [Paul D.]
Cravath, [James L.] Quackenbush[145] and others, in regard to the
Interborough situation, have become more frequent. Judge [Wil-
liam A.] Day, of the Equitable,[146] is still holding out, and as his holdings
represent about 3⅓% of the capital of the Manhattan and as he is said
to have quite a following, we told Cravath the day before yesterday
that we thought he should be asked to return to New York at once to
go over the situation and decide definitely as to whether he will or will
not deposit his stock. Meantime, some slight changes have been suggested by [George H.] Gardiner[147] and approved by Dwight [Morrow]
which may make his assent easier. I have asked [Alexander C.] Humphreys (one of Day's Finance Committee) to lunch with me Monday, and
as the old gentleman happens to want something from me at this time I
may be able to do a little missionary work with him particularly as he

---

[142] *Ibid.*, Jan. 3, 1920, p. 72.   [143] Swaine, *The Cravath Firm*, II, 281–86.
[144] RS 790, ERS to Lamont, Aug. 25, 1922.
[145] Attorney for the Interborough Rapid Transit Company.
[146] President of the Equitable Life Assurance Society.
[147] Attorney with Stetson, Jennings & Russell, counsel to the IRT committee.

himself has, within the past week or two, broken away from Day and deposited the shares which he controls.[148]

Stettinius added a paragraph which gives an amusing view of activities at the J. P. Morgan office: "So far as the banking business of the shop is concerned, there is little to report. We are running strong in cash and the boys are continuing their purchases of tax-exempt securities whenever possible. This morning, taking advantage of Jack [Morgan]'s absence from the City, we authorized the purchase of $1,000,000 State of Tennessee nine months' tax anticipation notes on about a 4% basis, George [Whitney] being very strong in his recommendations as to their goodness, etc."

He wrote Lamont again a week later: "There is nothing new here particularly, although discussions have been quite warm during the last day or two in regard to the Interboro situation. Cravath assures us that there will be some favorable developments in that quarter between now and next Tuesday, but we here knowing Cravath, all have our doubts." [149]

At the very last minute the requisite number of Manhattan shareholders deposited their stock and enabled the reorganization to begin. Thomas Lamont gave Stettinius credit for the outcome. He telegraphed on August 30, "Hearty congratulations on apparently favorable outcome of Interboro matter after your long and laborious negotiation." [150]

Stettinius replied with characteristic restraint: "While one very formidable hurdle has been jumped in the Interborough matter, I do not think that we can safely say the race is won. Additional deposits must be obtained of Manhattan stock as well as of 8% notes and the approval of the McAneny Commission must also be secured as to the proposed issues of 7% and 6% notes." [151]

The reorganization eventually went through. It was approved by all the parties at issue, representing various layers of security issues. Judge Julius M. Mayer of the U.S. Circuit Court of Appeals and the New York Transit Commission gave it their blessing and the IRT was saved from bankruptcy—for ten years. The company went into a receivership in August 1932, a victim of the hallowed five-cent fare, and was finally taken over by New York City.[152] (By 1973 the New York subway fare had risen to thirty-five cents and was in

---

[148] RS 200, ERS to Lamont, Aug. 18, 1922.
[149] RS 200, ERS to Lamont, Aug. 24, 1922.
[150] RS 200, Lamont to ERS, Aug. 30, 1922.
[151] RS 200, ERS to Lamont, Aug. 31, 1922.
[152] Swaine, *The Cravath Firm*, II, 285.

constant danger of rising further as the operating deficit became more and more of a drain on the tax revenues.)

Anglo-American Corporation of South Africa, Ltd.

The financial section of the *New York Times* noted on July 15, 1921, that Sir Ernest Oppenheimer, the South African mining magnate, chairman of the Anglo-American Corporation of South Africa, had recently been in New York to make preliminary arrangements for the listing of the company's stock on the New York Stock Exchange. The article went on to say that "A New York committee is to have charge of the listing." By the following March, the *Commercial & Financial Chronicle* was able to announce that E. R. Stettinius had become chairman of the New York committee, and no-par "American shares" of the company would be listed on the New York Curb Exchange against foreign shares of £1 par value deposited with the Guaranty Trust Company on the basis of one American share representing five foreign shares deposited.[153]

The Anglo-American Corporation of South Africa was organized in 1917 by Sir Ernest Oppenheimer.[154] It was interested in gold mines in the Rand and diamond mines in South-West Africa. Its holdings were primarily in companies of which it was the largest stockholder, either directly or through a subsidiary such as the Rand Selection Corporation, Ltd. In the production area it worked closely with Consolidated Mines Selection Co., Ltd. The gold mines were located in the far eastern Rand district and included Brakpan, Springs, West Springs, and Daggafontein Mines. The diamond holdings consisted of a substantial share of ownership of Consolidated Diamond Mines of Southwest Africa, Ltd., a company which owned virtually all of the diamond properties in South-West Africa. By the fall of 1921 the corporation had an authorized capital of £4,000,000 in shares of £1 each, of which 3,194,028 had been issued and paid for.

The American committee consisted of Edward R. Stettinius, chairman, Charles H. Sabin, W. L. Hannold, and William Boyce Thompson.[155] Stettinius, representing the Morgan firm, was active

---

[153] *Commercial & Financial Chronicle*, March 4, 1922, p. 951.

[154] *Who Was Who, 1951–1960* (London), p. 835.

[155] "The Anglo-American Corporation of South Africa: Its Organization, Resources, and Operations," *Engineering and Mining Journal*, Oct. 29, 1921, pp. 718–19.

in the organization of a syndicate to buy the shares of the company.[156]

The earnings record of the stock of Anglo-American Corporation of South Africa can be readily traced. The *Commercial & Financial Chronicle* reported on July 1, 1922: "the company earned £257,221 in 1921, which, when added to the undistributed profit of 1920 of £152,301 came to £409,522. After payment of dividends at 5% and miscellaneous expenses, there was an unappropriated profit of £177,953." [157]

Later in the year, the company entered into a provisional agreement with Consolidated Mines Selection Co. to take over the latter concern for a consideration and give its former shareholders—now substantial owners of Anglo-American—representation on the Anglo-American board of directors.[158] The result of this amalgamation was that no dividend was paid for the year ending December 31, 1922.[159] This suspended dividend was partly made up by a special dividend of 7½ percent per "Sterling share" payable on about March 1, 1923. American shares were to receive like dividends payable at the rate of exchange prevailing on the date of distribution.[160] This special dividend, disbursed to holders of "American shares" by the company's agents, the Guaranty Trust Company of New York, amounted to $1.76 a share.[161]

Stettinius was interviewed upon his return from Europe on the *Leviathan* toward the end of the year, and the *Wall Street Journal* of December 22, 1923, quoted him as most enthusiastic about the prospects for Anglo-American:

"Earnings of the Anglo American-South Africa Corp.," he said, "greatly exceed dividend requirements for 1923. The 10% dividend recently recommended will probably be declared after the first of the year.

"The corporation is very ably managed by men with long experience in South African affairs and it could not be in better hands. Prospects are excellent both for diamond and gold production. The diamond market is steadily rising, and the company should show a big increase from this source.

"On the whole I would say prospects for 1924 are at least as good and will probably be better than in 1923."

The formal declaration of the 10 percent dividend, payable on about March 20, 1924, was reported in the *Commercial & Financial Chronicle* of March 8, 1924.[162]

[156] RS 656, memorandum, ERS to Thomas Cochran, Dec. 30, 1924.
[157] *Commercial & Financial Chronicle*, July 1, 1922, p. 77.
[158] *Ibid.*, Dec. 9, 1922, p. 2583.   [159] *Ibid.*, Jan. 6, 1923, p. 80.
[160] *Ibid.*, Jan. 27, 1923, p. 413.   [161] *Ibid.*, March 10, 1923, p. 1054.
[162] *Ibid.*, March 8, 1924, p. 1138.

The Anglo-American Corporation of South Africa was a successful concern, and Stettinius's part in making it available to American investors in general and especially to participants of the syndicate was a minor coup on Wall Street.

One of the most interesting aspects of the Anglo-American venture was the kind of men Stettinius was brought into association with through this undertaking. The two most colorful were Sir Ernest Oppenheimer (1880–1957), perhaps the most important figure in South African mining history after Cecil Rhodes, and William Boyce Thompson (1869–1930), the American mining magnate.

The name Oppenheimer is virtually synonymous with leadership in the exploitation of South African diamond fields and gold mines, finance, manufacturing, and politics. He came originally from Friedberg, in Hesse, Germany, but moved to Kimberley at an early age. He was knighted in 1921.[163]

Thompson, known to business associates as "W. B.," was an old friend from the days of the reorganization of the International Agricultural Corporation, and we have already met him in that connection. He appears here as a participant in the Anglo-American syndicate.[164]

At the end of 1924 it was decided to dissolve the syndicate and distribute the proceeds among the participants.[165] It was proposed to set up a new pool to purchase stock in the deBeers Company, two-thirds for account of the Anglo-American Corporation and one-third for account of a pool in which the Oppenheimer would have a 50 percent interest, J. P. Morgan & Co., a 37½ percent interest, and the London partners of Morgan, Grenfell & Co., a 12½ percent interest.[166] There was general agreement that if W. B. Thompson wanted a "piece" of the investment he would be welcome to participate.[167]

Stettinius's continuing interest in South African mineral properties in the last year of his life is suggested by a brief notice in the March 21, 1925, issue of the trade journal *Automobile Topics:*

Stettinius in Platinum Field

E. R. Stettinius, of the J. P. Morgan banking firm and a director of General Motors, together with several associates has become interested in platinum properties in the Transvaal. The syndicate has purchased extensive property in South African platinum fields, which includes

[163] *Who Was Who, 1951–1960, loc. cit.*
[164] RS 405, ERS to Thompson, May 12, 1924.
[165] RS 656, memorandum, ERS to Cochran, Dec. 30, 1924.
[166] RS 656, memorandum, ERS to Lamont, Dec. 31, 1924.
[167] RS 656, memorandum, Lamont to ERS, Dec. 30, 1924.

diamond and gold mines. This is of particular interest to the automobile industry because of the general use of platinum in automobile manufacture.

It is significant, however, that no South African securities are listed in Stettinius's estate after his death.[168]

Stettinius's Lieutenants

In looking at the remarkable amount of work Stettinius was able to accomplish in the short period of his active career as a Morgan partner, we must not fail to give credit to his lieutenants in the Morgan office, the men in the next echelon down, who served him so well. Particularly important in this group were Martin Egan, Raleigh Hansl, and F. Carrington Weems, to whom we owe so much for his history of the Export Department and his biographical notes on his chief's wartime activities.

Stettinius was also helped greatly by his secretaries, Miss Mary Winter at the Diamond Match Company and, later, John J. Bennett at J. P. Morgan & Co., and by H. C. Cranz of the Diamond Match Company, who kept his personal books and securities records even after Stettinius had left Diamond.

[168] PS 31, Estate of E. R. Stettinius, Statement of Securities, Sept. 5, 1925.

XIV. *Locust Valley (1922–1925)*

EDWARD STETTINIUS went into the Morgan office as a result of the war and its demands, and his duties within the firm and his activities after the United States entered the war continued to be primarily related to the war and its immediate aftermath. By 1920, with the return to more stable conditions, Stettinius entered into the normal business and social life of a partner in J. P .Morgan & Co.

The family was based in New York City, but they found it desirable to have a country house as well as a town house. There was no thought of returning to Staten Island. The house at Dongan Hills had been turned over to the Red Cross during the war and then sold at a loss for a girls' school in 1919.[1]

It was logical to begin country living again on Long Island. A number of Morgan partners and their friends had estates on Long Island, and the Stettiniuses now had more in common with the Long Islanders than with the Staten Islanders. Long Island was already familiar to them as a place to live. They had spent a month at Southampton in the summer of 1915, when Stettinius took out a one-month summer membership in the Shinnecock Hills Golf Club.[2] It was to Southampton, again, that Mrs. Stettinius and the children were spirited away for their own safety in the spring of 1916, and later that year they had rented the Weir house at Locust Valley.[3] Stettinius had even considered building on Long Island as early as January 1917, but nothing came of it.[4]

In 1920 Stettinius was invited to participate in the Cravath Syndicate. A group of neighbors of the lawyer Paul D. Cravath formed a syndicate to buy for $1,200,000 his estate at Locust Valley just east of Glen Cove on the north shore of Long Island. The original members were George F. Baker, Jr., Henry P. Davison, George Galt Bourne, and Harvey D. Gibson. Stettinius took over a third of

[1] RS 734, Staten Island file, ERS to Red Cross War Council, May 29, 1918; C. J. Fay to ERS, Feb. 13, 1919.
[2] PM 5, miscellaneous, S-Z, Frederick A. Snow to ERS, July 19, 1915.
[3] RS 676, ERS to ERS, Jr., Jan. 19, 1922.
[4] RS 333, ERS to Wendell P. Blagden, Jan. 24, 1917.

Davison's interest and a third of Gibson's.[5] The Cravath property extended inland from Long Island Sound along a creek that flowed due north into the Sound halfway between Peacock and Fox Points. Part of it was to be developed for building lots by Olmsted Brothers, the well-known landscape architects of Brookline, Massachusetts, successors to Frederick Law Olmsted, who was responsible for the laying out of Central Park in New York and other major projects. The remainder was subsequently acquired for a new golf club, The Creek.[6] Stettinius, though not a founder, became one of the early members of The Creek. He already belonged to the nearby Piping Rock Club.

When E. H. Wells of Babcock & Wilcox wanted to join the Piping Rock Club, Stettinius supported his application and then wrote a typical dryly humorous note to Wells about it: "I have written the Board of Governors of the Piping Rock Club although, as you anticipated, it has strained my conscience to say what I did say in your behalf." [7]

Stettinius started a serious search for a house on Long Island in 1920. In March of that year he found the George C. Smith house at Brookville and might have bought it, but Mrs. Stettinius did not like it, and that was that.[8] During the next two years real-estate agents showed him a great assortment of country houses and estates.

In the summer of 1921 he rented Winston Pierce's place "Dunstable," at Bayville, Oyster Bay.[9] At that time he received a letter from the agent Worthington Whitehouse giving a glowing description of a house which had come on the market at Locust Valley. This was The Hedges, the house of Viscountess H. Y. de Lendonck, widow of Levi C. Weir, the late head of Adams Express, a businessman who had sat on the boards of a dozen major United States companies.[10] Stettinius was interested, but not surprised; this was the house the family had rented in 1916. The Weir house was just across the road from the Cravath property, and the neighborhood was a familiar one. His friend and partner Henry Davison lived down the road on Peacock Point, and J. P. Morgan lived on East Island, later Morgan Island, just to the west of Davison.

[5] PS 33, Cravath Property file, Davison to ERS, Jan. 24, 1920; deeds, July 7, 1922, and July 13, 1922.
[6] PS 33, Cravath Property file, brochure, "The New Golf Club at Locust Valley, Long Island," n.d.
[7] RS 219, ERS to Wells, April 7, 1920.
[8] RS 734, Wheatley Hills Real Estate Corp. file, ERS to Henry A. Rogers, April 7, 1921.
[9] RS 734, Bayville, N.Y., file, lease agreement, May 9, 1921. The rental was $3,000 a month.
[10] RS 734, "Loose Items" file, Whitehouse to ERS, June 13, 1921.

Negotiations with Emma de Lendonck progressed slowly, with discussions of price and of the disposition of various items of furniture. Stettinius finally bought the property. An agreement was signed on January 30, 1922. The purchase price was $200,000, of which $5,000 was paid at the time of the agreement and $95,000 at the closing. A mortgage was given for the balance, payable in four installments of $25,000 each.[11] The *New York Herald* announced the purchase on February 10, 1922, and gave a description of the property: "The Weir estate is one of the best landscaped and most elaborate properties of its kind in a district noted for its beautiful country homes. It has three water views, a house of stone and shingle and a cottage and garage. It is known as 'The Hedges' and was left by the late Mr. Weir to his widow, now the Viscountess de Lendonck." The Stettiniuses renamed The Hedges; they called it The Shelter.

The *New York Times* reported the sale on February 11, 1922, and in the same issue announced that Stettinius would sail that day on the Munson Line for Nassau with his wife and daughter Betty. This trip was a vacation to help Stettinius recover from his illness of the end of 1921. This was the first of a series of illnesses culminating in his death in 1925.

The terrain of Locust Valley is uneven and heavily wooded. The Hedges was a roughly pentagonal parcel of land of about thirty-four acres comprising the only real hill in the region. The original architect made the most effective use of the site and gave the house a fine view northward across the Cravath lands in the foreground to the Sound and across the Sound to the distant Connecticut shore.

The house, three stories high, was finished on the exterior with rough-textured walls of fieldstone and shingles. One entering through the front door on the south or landward side found himself in a vast entrance hall leading into an even larger central hall. To the left lay the living room, measuring twenty-five by thirty-five feet, with a bay window overlooking the Sound. To the right was the dining room, slightly larger and also having a bay window with a view. On the second floor were seven master bedrooms and four baths and eight staff bedrooms with one bath. The third floor contained two master bedrooms and a bath, two staff bedrooms, and a large attic.[12]

Upon buying The Hedges, Stettinius hired the architectural firm of Peabody, Wilson & Brown of New York to redesign a con-

---

[11] RS 734, Locust Valley file, ERS to Thomas Cochran and George Whitney, Feb. 7, 1922.
[12] RS 734, "Loose Items" file, Whitehouse to ERS, June 13, 1921.

siderable part of the main house.[13] In the course of the reconstruction, some special refinements were added, such as the installation of a safe-deposit vault door with combination lock for the wine cellar,[14] and the renovation involved extensive interior decoration as well as structural changes.

Mr. and Mrs. Stettinius did not always see eye to eye in matters of decoration. Several years after they had bought the Locust Valley property they were in the Bahamas together and visited an artist's studio, where they saw some paintings of the local scene that they wanted to buy. The painter seems to have taken sides in the ensuing difference of opinion. Stettinius wrote to him after the pictures arrived:

The paintings of East Nassau were apparently selected in order to satisfy Mrs. Stettinius. They did not appeal to me when I saw them in Nassau, nor do they appeal to me now. As long as Mrs. Stettinius is satisfied that is quite sufficient. I am, therefore, enclosing my check for $556. in payment of your bill.

When I was in Nassau you showed me two paintings which pleased me greatly but did not appeal to Mrs. Stettinius. They were marine views rather than views of the harbor. They made such an impression upon me that I thought it was understood they were to be sent to me.[15]

Stettinius carried out extensive improvements on the grounds and commissioned new landscape design and planting, especially of rhododendrons.

On May 23, 1923, Stettinius totted up the assorted items of expense involved in the buying and refurbishing of the Locust Valley house:

Purchase price		
Cash	$100,000	
Paid on Mortgage	25,000	
Mortgage	75,000	
		$200,000
Acquisition expenses		5,757.63
Furnishings		17,178.63
Improvements		172,679.46
Maintenance		11,473.46
Total		$407,089.18 [16]

[13] RS 734, Special Contracts file, bill from Peabody, Wilson & Brown, Dec. 18, 1922.

[14] RS 734, Buildings file, No. 2, Rogers & Blydenburgh to John J. Bennett, Feb. 1, 1923.

[15] RS 163, ERS to Hart L. Woodcock, June 27, 1924.

[16] RS 734, Accounts–Cost Statements file, May 23, 1923.

The Locust Valley establishment was run on a generous scale consistent with the style of the community. By 1925 there were nine full-time gardeners working on the place, and Stettinius directed his head groundsman to try to reduce this number.[17] But all did not run smoothly in this suburban Eden. There were labor problems on the large places. The estate superintendents in the neighborhood met at Oyster Bay early in 1923 and on the motion of J. P. Morgan's head gardener Kelly resolved that gardeners should be paid $4.75 a day.[18]

Distances are great at Locust Valley and common carriers virtually nonexistent, except for the Long Island Railroad. This made it necessary to have more automobiles in the Stettinius garage. That garage contained in December 1923 a total of six cars: two Cadillacs, a Buick sports roadster, and three Fords—a runabout, a station wagon, and a dump truck for use on the grounds.[19] The following month a new Pierce-Arrow limousine replaced the older Cadillac.[20] Later in the spring a second Pierce-Arrow limousine took the place of the other Cadillac.[21] A Buick roadster for Elizabeth Stettinius replaced the older Buick in 1925.[22]

Domestic Finances

Edward Stettinius brought his businesslike approach and systematic bookkeeping to the family's personal expenses and the running of the household. It is of enormous value to the student of economic and social history to have reliable itemized figures on family expenditures. It is particularly interesting to have those statistics for one of the outstanding financiers of the postwar era. We have a picture of how a family in the upper income bracket—though not in the Morgan or Rockefeller category—lived in the year 1924.

It cost about a quarter of a million dollars to run the entire Stettinius establishment in 1924. The chief items of expense in round numbers were family maintenance (food, clothing, servants' wages, medical expenses, Mrs. Stettinius's allowance, etc.), $82,000; charity, $50,000; Locust Valley property maintenance, $36,000;

[17] RS 734, Personnel file, ERS quoted, [J. J. Bennett] to Charles S. Plumb, April 28, 1925.
[18] RS 734, Personnel file, R. Hughes to John J. Bennett, April 4, 1923.
[19] PS 26, Account No. 1, Trial Balance, Dec. 1923.
[20] RS 451, Automobiles file, A. B. Ashforth, Inc. to ERS, Jan. 28, 1924.
[21] PS 26, Account No. 1, Trial Balance, June 1924; Sept. 1924.
[22] RS 451, Automobiles file, A. B. Ashforth, Inc. to ERS, April 29, 1925.

general expenses, including pocket money, $32,000; travel, $30,000; automobile maintenance, $10,000. Lesser items included club dues with expenses, $6,000, and the remarkably low figure of $3,000 for maintenance of 1021 Park Avenue.[23]

Postwar Philanthropies

Edward Stettinius was a generous man. Year after year he received countless requests for money. He gave gladly. As we have just seen, in 1924 his listed contributions to organized charities and welfare organizations totalled over $50,000.[24] Other of Stettinius's benefactions were anonymous, and we shall never know how many causes he supported or how many individuals he quietly helped.

Certain of his philanthropies deserve special attention because of the size of the contributions or the nature of the causes and what they tell us about the man himself and the things that aroused his interest or compassion.

The French Officers' Orphans Scholarships

Early in December 1919 Stettinius discussed with Nelson Dean Jay of Morgan, Harjes an idea he had in his mind for helping the families of French soldiers killed or disabled in the war. He wanted Jay to take full charge of the program and make all the decisions. He proposed to make an initial contribution of one million French francs. At the current rate of exchange of almost twelve francs to the dollar, this came to approximately $85,000.[25] Stettinius confirmed this in a letter to Jay on December 12, 1919:

Referring to my conversation with you a week or ten days ago, I beg to advise that I am arranging to make available to you in Paris Fcs. 1,000,000. which I understand you are willing to handle for me in consultation with Commandant Varaigne in assisting families of French officers and soldiers who lost their lives or who were disabled in the late war.

I do not wish to hamper you by designating any particular organization, or by defining too exactly the classes of people to whom assistance should be extended. However, as I told you, I would be particularly

[23] See Appendix F, Domestic Finances, 1924.
[24] See Appendix G, Charitable Contributions, 1924.
[25] The French franc was quoted in the *New York Times* on December 12, 1919, at 11.72 to the dollar. The franc had lost half of its value since March. See Chapter VIII, note 18.

glad if I could do something to aid widows and orphans who, in consequence of the death or disability of the head of the family, are now deprived of the comforts and educational advantages to which they were accustomed in the past. As to the utilization of the fund, I wish you to be free to distribute either the principal in its entirety, whenever it may appear to you desirable to do so, or the income thereof. In other words, I want you to have the greatest possible latitude of action and to be limited only to the extent of extending aid solely to the dependents of men who lost their lives or who were disabled in the late war.[26]

Jay inquired into existing welfare organizations through which these funds could most effectively be used and decided on the Association d'aide aux veuves de militaires de la Grande Guerre.[27] A plan was worked out with la Baronne Edgar Lejeune (née Princesse Murat), president of the association, and Mme. la Générale Lavisse, whose special interest was the care of the children of officers' widows. The money was used to provide educational scholarships for these children to enable them to become self-supporting. In cases where there were several children in a family, the scholarship was given to the eldest so that this one could in turn help with the education of the younger brothers and sisters. It seemed wise to use the capital rather than dole out the interest. After all, the war orphans were not going to remain children indefinitely.

A total of 235 young people were helped by the Stettinius fund. The results were very gratifying. The largest group of recipients, 58, followed their fathers' military careers: 33 graduated from Saint-Cyr, 12 graduated from the Naval Academy, and 13 became officers through promotion from the ranks. The next largest group, 32, became teachers. Thirty-one graduated from engineering schools. Thirty went into business. Others went into various professions including law, medicine, architecture, the priesthood, and scientific agriculture.[28]

The gifts were anonymous, listed only as from "un ami de la France," but Mme. la Générale Lavisse apparently felt so keenly that credit should be given where it was due that she told the beneficiaries who the donor was.[29]

The final payment was made in 1924. It brought the total of the gift to 1,650,000 francs.[30]

[26] RS 210, ERS to Jay, Dec. 12, 1919.
[27] RS 210, Jay to ERS, July 8, 1920.
[28] Scrapbook II, M. Pesson-Didion to ERS, Jr., May 30, 1933.
[29] RS 210, Jay to ERS, Aug. 28, 1922.
[30] RS 210, ERS to Jay, March 7, 1924.
Stettinius might have been pleased to know that even now, fifty years after

The Pershing Scholarships at the Académie Française

In July 1920, at about the time the machinery was set up for disbursing the funds to the orphans of French officers, Stettinius provided funds to endow an Académie Française scholarship with a gift of 120,000 francs and asked that it be named in honor of General John J. Pershing.[31] At the same time that Stettinius established his fund, J. P. Morgan gave money for a scholarship at the Arts Décoratifs in memory of his father, John Pierpont Morgan (1837–1914), and Henry Davison contributed a scholarship to the Académie Française in memory of Jane R. Delano, head of the America Red Cross Nurses, who died in the service.[32]

The idea of giving these scholarships or prizes to promising young French writers and artists originated with Mrs. George Blumenthal of New York. She acted as intermediary between the donors and the French government and handled the financial arrangements.[33] The organization that was set up to receive and administer these gifts was called the Fondation américaine pour la pensée et l'art français, and winners were named by the Académie Française or the Arts Décoratifs. Within the organization the identities of the individual donations were preserved. There were fourteen scholarships, given by such well-known figures as George F. Baker, Thomas Fortune Ryan, Miss Helen Clay Frick and her mother, and George and Florence Blumenthal. Outside the foundation, however, one did not hear of the individual contributors. The contributions were in effect pooled, and the winners were called simply "lauréats" of the foundation.[34]

the establishment of his fund, families of recipients of these scholarships are deeply appreciative, as I learned from the French military family Broyelle. When research into Stettinius's years in France took me to Paris in December 1970, by chance one of the students I engaged to speak French with was Jean-Yves Broyelle, whose aunt was the recipient of a Stettinius scholarship. Her father had been killed on the Western Front in the summer of 1918. His father, also an officer, had been killed in 1870. The scholarship helped to make it possible for Jean-Yves's own father, brother of the beneficiary, to attend Saint-Cyr. He subsequently resigned his commission to protest de Gaulle's abandoning of the French North African possessions and now lies buried in the Invalides.

[31] RS 210, Jay to ERS, March 13, 1920; RS 489, ERS to Jay, July 26, 1920.
[32] RS 489, ERS to Pershing, July 14, 1920.
[33] RS 489, cablegram, Florence Blumenthal to ERS, July 8, 1920; Morgan, Harjes & Co. to ERS, Sept. 23, 1920.
[34] Memorandum to the author from M. Georges Hilbert, sculptor, scholarship winner (1948), secretary, Association Florence Blumenthal, 30 rue Bonnefous, Sèvres 92, with covering letter dated August 1, 1971; *Association*

The very first winner of a scholarship under this program in 1920 was the writer Jacques Rivière (1886–1925), who was voted the first recipient of the General Pershing Scholarship given by Stettinius.[35] It is surprising, then, to discover in the biography of Rivière by Bradford Cook that he won the "Blumenthal Prize";[36] not a word about Stettinius or Pershing. In writing to Stettinius to thank him for the scholarship, Rivière expressed his appreciation to both Stettinius and Mrs. Blumenthal.[37] Ultimately Mrs. Blumenthal received all the credit; the organization became known as the Fondation Blumenthal and the association of former scholarship winners —the alumni—officially changed its name from Lauréats de la fondation américaine pour la pensée et l'art français to Association Florence Blumenthal.[38] Scholarships were awarded in alternate even-numbered years from 1920 through 1940, then sporadically through 1956, when the money finally ran out.[39]

Florence Blumenthal; Anciens lauréats de la fondation américaine pour la pensée et l'art français, membership booklet (1955).

[35] Extract from the 1922 annual report of the Fondation américaine pour la pensée et l'art français, kindness of M. Hilbert. At the time Rivière received the scholarship he was still suffering from the effects of four years as a German prisoner of war. Before the war he had written a book of essays on Baudelaire, Claudel, Gide, and others titled *Etudes*, and in 1918 he published *L'Allemand*, his reflections as a prisoner. He sent a copy of *L'Allemand* with his handwritten letter of thanks to Stettinius.

After winning the award Rivière wrote his novel *Aimée* (1922), the essays *A la trace de Dieu* (1925), and the posthumously published *Rimbaud* (1930) and *Felonce* (1935). His correspondence with Paul Claudel was published in 1926 and that with his brother-in-law Alain-Fournier in 1926–28. (See *Grand Larousse Encyclopédique*, 10 vols. [Paris, 1960–1964], IX, 298.) Bradford Cook, in his *Jacques Rivière: A Life of the Spirit* (Oxford, 1958), summarizes Rivière's position in French literature and thought as follows:
"In France, Rivière ranks with Charles Du Bos, Gide, Proust, Claudel and Valéry as one of the best of twentieth-century French critics. From 1919 to 1925 he directed *La Nouvelle Revue Française*, perhaps the foremost French review of the century. Throughout his life he wrote penetratingly, and often prophetically, on literature, painting, music, ballet and politics. It is probable that in the coming years his name will be synonymous with fine criticism; and it is to be hoped that the English and American publics will soon become more familiar with that criticism. But Rivière was more than a critic. I have written this book in the belief that he was also one of the most interesting, moving and at time, profound of French religious thinkers" (p. ix).

[36] *Ibid.*, p. xv.   [37] RS 489, Rivière to ERS, Oct. 11, 1920.

[38] French Ministry of Cultural Affairs, "Note sur la Fondation Américaine pour la Pensée et l'Art Français," prepared for the French Embassy in Washington in response to the author's inquiry to the French Ambassador and forwarded by the embassy Sept. 22, 1971; *Association Florence Blumenthal*, membership booklet.

[39] French Ministry of Cultural Affairs, "Note."

Children's Relief—Czechoslovakia

Shortly after Stettinius's death, Henry Noble MacCracken, the president of Vassar College, wrote a letter to the *New York Times* telling of Stettinius's gift of $25,000 to the crippled children in Prague, gathered homeless immediately after the war around their teacher, a Dr. M. Bakule. The letter said that the singing tour of Czech children to the United States in 1923 was an expression of their thanks.[40]

This story is confirmed and details added in a letter Stettinius received in March 1921 from Livingston Farrand, Chairman of the Executive Committee of the American Red Cross:

About a year ago you very generously contributed the sum of $25,000.00 for child welfare work in Europe. As we reported to you shortly after the receipt of your gift, this sum was used for the purchase of a school home and for the maintenance and vocational education of a group of crippled boys rescued from the slums of Prague. The education of this group of boys is now far enough along that they are able to act as assistants to Dr. Bakule, the Director of the Institute, in the vocational education of other crippled children who come in for the day classes only.

We are enclosing herewith an album giving photographs and descriptive sketches of the original group of crippled children. These boys, upon their own initiative, drew up and engrossed a very beautiful memorial in token of their gratitude to their unknown benefactor. A photograph of this memorial is included in the album. In accordance with your wishes, no announcement was made as to the name of the giver. The boys also made the frame and have now asked that we see to it that their unknown friend receives this testimonial of their gratitude. We hold this testimonial (size 27½ in. x 38 in.) now ready to send to whatever address you may name. We join heartily with the boys in this expression of gratitude for your generosity.[41]

St. Louis University

Stettinius retained a lifelong interest in his college, St. Louis University. He corresponded at some length with President Robison— Father W. F. Robison, S.J. But the true test of his devotion was the Centennial Endowment Fund drive planned for 1920. To encourage

[40] *New York Times*, Sept. 18, 1925.
[41] RS 279, Farrand to ERS, March 1, 1921.

the drive, he sent in his contribution on December 23, 1919. It was a cheque for $50,000. Father Bernard J. Otting, who was then president, wrote a letter of thanks in which he said, "Your princely gift of $50,000 . . . was a great surprise." [42]

Recipients frequently professed themselves nonplussed by Stettinius's generosity. We don't know how he reacted to this recurring astonishment.

The University of Virginia

Stettinius had a long association with the University of Virginia. Both of his sons attended the university and the university seized upon this fact to solicit money from him or to induce him, as a figure in the financial world, to solicit money from others.

In 1919 Professor Albert G. A. Balz of the Philosophy Department, chairman of a committee to choose a graduation speaker, invited him to give the commencement address. William Carrington Stettinius, newly returned from the wars, was a student at the university at the time, a fact which gave point to the invitation. Stettinius declined, pleading his planned stay in France.[43] The following year he was asked to be on the national committee of the Centennial Endowment Fund. He replied that he would, but would only solicit money from alumni of the university.[44] The Committee was pleased to accept him as a member on those terms.[45] President Alderman thought it would be nice if Stettinius would contribute to the Centennial Endowment himself. His letter suggesting an early declaration of the amount of the intended gift is a masterpiece of fundraising unction:

We are coming down the home stretch to our Centennial Celebration. I recall with great appreciation and gratitude your expression of a purpose to contribute towards the fund we hope to announce on that day. We have raised to date $810,000, which is not so bad for six or seven weeks' work, in view of the situation in the world today. We are striving toward the announcement of at least the *first* million on June 3rd. I hope you will make known your subscription, for its moral and substantial influence would be very great at this moment. I do not mean

---

[42] RS 409, Otting to ERS, Dec. 28, 1919.

[43] RS 263, Balz to ERS, Feb. 12, 1919; ERS to Edwin A. Alderman, Feb. 13, 1919.

[44] RS 263, John S. Bryan and Frederic W. Scott to ERS, Oct. 19, 1920; ERS to Bryan and Scott, Oct. 21, 1920.

[45] RS 263, Armistead M. Dobie to ERS, Oct. 22, 1920.

to be importunate. I was genuinely touched by your friendly and intelligent interest in and knowledge of the University of Virginia, and my affection for your boys is based upon a knowledge of their fineness and high character.

Stettinius replied two weeks later that he would give $10,000.[46] Mrs. Stettinius attended the centennial graduation exercises, and Alderman sent Stettinius one of the one hundred and fifty medals struck to commemorate the university's foundation.[47] An attempt was made later in the year to interest Mrs. Stettinius in raising money to move the medical school from Charlottesville to Richmond. Stettinius wrote back that his wife was ill in hospital and he did not want her involved in a controversy anyway.[48]

One of Alderman's pet projects was the establishment of the *Virginia Quarterly Review*. Would Stettinius subscribe $100 a year for five years to get this publication started and on its feet? Stettinius wrote back that he would send the money as requested.[49]

The last recorded plea for money from Charlottesville came not from the University of Virginia but from the Episcopal church that was being built across the street from the university grounds. S. Buford Scott wrote a letter thanking Stettinius for his "generous contribution to the building fund of St. Paul's Church at the University of Virginia. Knowing what wonderful work Ed did while he was there, I feel almost as if you were making this contribution in his name."[50]

General E. Harmonius

We have mentioned the private, unobtrusive giving that was such an important, though invisible, part of Stettinius's way of life. We can document one example in the period following the war.

The Russians were a source of exasperation and irritation to everyone who tried to help them in their struggle against the German and Austrian forces in the war. Their representatives, when not incompetent, were simply uncooperative or offensive. An exception to this was General E. Harmonius, of whom Stettinius became very fond when the work of the Export Department of

[46] RS 263, Alderman to ERS, May 6, 1921; ERS to Alderman, May 25, 1921.
[47] RS 263, Alderman to ERS, June 15, 1921; Alderman to ERS, June 16, 1921.
[48] RS 263, George G. Battle to Mrs. ERS, Nov. 23, 1921; ERS to Battle, Nov. 25, 1921.
[49] RS 263, Alderman to ERS, July 19, 1924; ERS to Alderman, July 24, 1924.
[50] RS 263, Scott to ERS, April 29, 1925.

J. P. Morgan & Co. brought them together. The Russian Revolution left Harmonius and his wife in Paris along with hundreds of other upper-class White Russian refugees, desperately poor and ill-equipped to make new lives for themselves at their age. Harmonius tried to find a job without success and finally decided to set up in his Paris apartment a small business for the manufacture of knitted woollen and silk clothes, using knitting machines. He asked Stettinius to lend him $5,000 to start this venture.[51] Stettinius did lend him the money. The debt appears as an asset in the inventory of Stettinius's estate.[52]

More important than the "investment" in this harebrained knitting scheme was the request Stettinius made to Nelson Dean Jay of Morgan, Harjes to take care of the old general. He wrote: "There is something very pitiful about the old man's letter and I am afraid that he is in pretty bad shape. If he calls on you, please give him the benefit of any advice that you think may be helpful. Incidentally, do not hesitate to give him for my account any reasonable amount you may find he requires. I should doubt the wisdom of giving him any large amounts, say up to $1,000., and imagine it would be better to dole out say up to this amount in small sums of $100. or $200. a month." [53]

The New York Association for Improving the Condition of the Poor

The principal established charity with which Stettinius was associated was the New York Association for Improving the Condition of the Poor. This was one of the oldest and best-known social-service agencies in the country. It is still an outstanding agency under the shorter, less patronizing, and less Victorian name of Community Service Society of New York. Stettinius was elected to the board of managers of the association in 1923. He was undoubtedly led to accept this job by his friends at J. P. Morgan & Co. His first assignment, logically enough, was to the finance committee, of which his partner Dwight Morrow was chairman. He was also appointed to the trade membership committee under Henry Davison's son-in-law Artemus L. Gates. His own contribution for the fiscal year ending September 30, 1923, was $2,500.[54]

[51] RS 182, Harmonius to ERS, Feb. 17, 1922.
[52] RS 182, ERS to Harmonius, April 10, 1922; P.S. 31, Estate of ERS file.
[53] RS 182, ERS to Jay, Jan. 18, 1923.
[54] *Eightieth Annual Report* (1922–23), New York Association for Improving the Condition of the Poor.

He continued his position on the board and his committee assignments in 1924. Mr. and Mrs. Stettinius are listed together as life members of the association, and Stettinius gave $4,000 in that year. As a partner in the firm, he was also in part responsible for J. P. Morgan & Co.'s contribution of $10,000.[55] He was a member of the board and of the two committees at the time of his death in September 1925.[56] The Board of Managers passed a memorial resolution at their regular meeting on December 2, 1925.[57]

Crippled Children's Hospital, Richmond

Mrs. Stettinius's family, the Carringtons, lived in Richmond, Virginia. Among the interests of the Carringtons was the Crippled Children's Hospital. Mrs. Henry Carrington was a member of the board of trustees. So it was very logical for Mr. and Mrs. Stettinius to establish a fund at the hospital in memory of Mrs. Stettinius's mother.

On December 29, 1923, Stettinius wrote to Mrs. Henry Carrington enclosing a cheque for $12,000 to endow a bed at the hospital.[58] The president of the hospital acknowledged the contribution with thanks, but asked if the money might not be used to maintain a playroom for the young patients instead of a bed. Stettinius replied that unless they heard to the contrary within two days, the hospital authorities were to assume that the fund in memory of Mrs. Carrington was to be used for the playroom as suggested.[59]

American Relief Committee for German Intellectuals and Artists

Having devoted himself for so long to the destruction of German military power, Stettinius was just as interested in alleviating the plight of the victims of that power. We saw his efforts to help the French.

Former Ambassador James W. Gerard and Professor Ludwig Stein, foreign editor of the Berlin *Vossische Zeitung*, formed a committee in New York for the relief of German intellectuals, who

[55] *Eighty-first Annual Report* (1923–24).
[56] *Eighty-second Annual Report* (1924–25).
[57] "A Resolution of the Board of Managers of the New York Association for Improving the Condition of the Poor," December 2, 1925.
[58] RS 367, ERS to Hazel Carrington, Dec. 29, 1923.
[59] RS 367, H. W. Ellerson to ERS, Jan. 4, 1924; ERS to Ellerson, Jan. 9, 1924.

were among the greatest sufferers in the postwar economic collapse and runaway inflation in Germany. Stettinius became treasurer of that committee and served through its critical period.[60]

The Locust Valley Cemetery

With his overabundance of vigor, Edward Stettinius was temperamentally incapable of leaving alone something that he thought needed improving. We saw that when he moved to Staten Island he took the golf club in hand and completely reorganized it. At Locust Valley he took over the cemetery.

There was a modest country burying ground next door to the Reformed Church in the village. Stettinius looked it over and found it inadequate. But he saw that there was a vacant area adjacent to the cemetery, behind the church, so he bought it in the spring of 1922, shortly after buying the Weir place. Briefly, what he did was to buy the land and then pressure the cemetery association into accepting it as a gift. He supervised the landscaping of the addition and the sale of lots and put his friends on the board of the cemetery association. What resulted was a double cemetery; the older, open section of small plots continued very much as it had been, while the new section of woods and spacious glades became a Valhalla for Morgan partners and their friends.

After the land for the cemetery extension was bought, it remained to join it to the original burying ground. The first obstacle was a New York State law that prohibited the expansion of existing cemeteries.[61] To get around this there had to be a special act of the legislature. This was pushed through on April 24, 1923.[62] Stettinius engaged Olmsted Brothers, whose work he had seen at the Cravath development, to lay out the addition and determine the planting, the course of roads and paths, and the location of the lots. Walker and Gillette, architects of 128 East 37th Street, New York, were given the responsibility for designing the architectural features— the entrance with wrought-iron gates and the stone walls.[63] The landscaping work went forward through most of 1924.

In July Stettinius suggested to B. W. Downing, the agent of the old Locust Valley Cemetery Association, that the size of the board

[60] *New York Times*, Editor's note, Letters to the Editor, Feb. 9, 1924; RS 838.
[61] RS 450, Title file, F. M. Sullivan to ERS, June 24, 1922; ERS to F. T. Davison, Dec. 7, 1922.
[62] RS 450, Title file, State of New York, No. 2286, Int. 1902, April 24, 1923.
[63] RS 450, Improvements file, Olmsted Brothers to ERS, Dec. 11, 1923.

of trustees be doubled to twelve members and that it include representatives of the purchasers of lots in the extension. In the same letter he explained that he had set up a perpetual care endowment fund
of $99,776.96.[64] The final takeover of the Locust Valley Cemetery
occurred at the annual meeting of the directors on June 1, 1925.[65]
At that meeting the extension was formally accepted, the sale of
lots approved, and the number of board members increased from
six to twelve. The six new directors were Paul G. Pennoyer, son-in-
law of J. P. Morgan; F. Trubee Davison, son of Henry Davison;
Artemus L. Gates, son-in-law of Henry Davison; Robert A. Lovett,
son of Robert S. Lovett, the financier; Lyman N. Hine; and Edward
R. Stettinius. Downing continued in his role as nominal head of
the cemetery. He shared his position on the executive committee
with Artemus Gates. Stettinius reported on the condition of the
cemetery addition. Lots had sold briskly and fetched a total of
$179,181.92 to date. Charter Members—original buyers of lots—of
the extension were Mrs. Henry Davison (Lot No. 4), J. P. Morgan
(No. 20), Francis L. Hine (No. 13), Robert S. Lovett (No. 16),
Charles A. Coffin (No. 11), Paul D. Cravath and Anton G.
Hodenpyl (No. 8), and Edward R. Stettinius (No. 9, exchanged
immediately after his death for the smaller No. 7 in which he was
buried). Stettinius himself was out of pocket for expenses in the
amount of $109,779.87. He proposed to accept $53,279.87 in cash
from the association and $56,500 in 5 percent twenty-year certifi-
cates of indebtedness. It was voted to accept this proposal.

The entire enterprise was a triumph of Stettinius's will and force
of character. It also produced a very handsome cemetery.

Worsening Health

In the fall of 1922 Stettinius became ill and went to recuperate at
the Greenbrier in White Sulphur Springs, but he was taken ill again
in November.[66]

In January 1923 he wrote Miss Lucy Lee Brownlee: "I am back
again at the office but expect to take things very easily for the next
week or so and am planning to go South for the greater part of

[64] RS 450, Improvements file, ERS to Downing, July 28, 1924.
[65] RS 450, Legal Box No. 5, minutes, annual meeting of directors, Locust
Valley Cemetery Association, June 1, 1925.
[66] RS 679, White Sulphur 1922 file, telegram, ERS to Frank Ryall, Sept. 28,
1922.

the months of February and March. Judith and Betty will, of course, accompany me."[67]

The trip was interrupted by an even more serious illness. Bennett, his secretary, wrote:

Mr. Stettinius left New York on January 25th for a vacation in the South, and, after spending some time in Florida and southern Georgia, located for a somewhat extended stay at Augusta, Georgia, where he was later joined by his family. He seemed to be obtaining substantial benefit until, in the week beginning March 11th, he had a recurrence of his old digestive trouble, accompanied this time by severe pains in the abdomen. Later in the week his condition grew more serious, and on Saturday the 17th, Mrs. Stettinius telephoned Dr. W. W. Herrick to come from New York. The doctor arrived at Augusta on Sunday afternoon, March 18th, and he diagnosed the case as an intestinal obstruction. That evening Mr. Stettinius left for New York on a special train, arriving here Monday evening, the 19th. He was met by Drs. Peck, Russell and Cave, who rushed him to the hospital and decided on an immediate operation. The trouble was found to be due to a deep-seated abdominal abscess, and before the operation was concluded Dr. Herrick emerged from the operating room with the good news that the patient would come through successfully.

Since the operation Mr. Stettinius has been improving slowly and his complete recovery is assured. He is now at home and has asked me to tell you that he is getting along very nicely; the doctors expect that he will be able to sit up in the course of two or three days, and he is looking forward to going down to his country place on Long Island about the middle of May.[68]

Stettinius had no sooner recovered from his illness when Mrs. Stettinius was stricken too and was sent to the Johns Hopkins Hospital in Baltimore. The young William Carrington Stettinius family lived in Baltimore and assumed some of the responsibility during her stay. In discussing his wife's hospital bill with his daughter-in-law Achsah Stettinius, Stettinius wrote whimsically on May 3, 1923, "The bill seems to be all right except that covering '1 pair of mules.' I cannot conceive what Mother would want with '1 pair of mules.' "[69]

Stettinius was slow to mend. In mid-July he wrote to John F. Bowie, his son-in-law's law partner and the counsel to the board of directors of the Western Pacific Railroad: "Mrs. Stettinius is immensely better, however, and her improvement during the past two

---

[67] RS 274, ERS to Brownlee, Jan. 3, 1923.
[68] RS 679, Inquiry file, Bennett to Rev. W. F. Robison, April 11, 1923.
[69] RS 677, ERS to Achsah Stettinius, May 3, 1923.

or three weeks has been really amazing. I am just where you left me; no better, no worse. The doctors this morning definitely decided to abandon, for the time being, all idea of a secondary operation. A change, however, will be made in my regime in that I will begin at once to exercise moderately in the hope that, as I put myself in good shape physically, my wound will close naturally and without it being necessary to adopt any heroic measures. I am sick and tired of myself and any change, whatever it might be, would be welcome." [70]

J. P. Morgan, the senior partner of the firm, had just the solution. He offered Stettinius the use of his magnificent steam yacht *Corsair* for a cruise in New England waters. Mr. and Mrs. Stettinius embarked on July 29, 1923, at the foot of 23rd Street, Brooklyn. [71] Morgan sent them a bon voyage radiogram from the *Homeric*, on which he was crossing the Atlantic: "Hope you will have perfect weather and get health and amusement out of your short cruise. Affectionate Regards. Jack." [72]

Stettinius felt greatly refreshed by the cruise. He later cabled his host in London:

Improvement which set in on Corsair has continued so satisfactorily I am now out of hands of surgeons and nurses Stop Am leaving for short fishing trip and on my return will spend rest of month hardening up so as to return to office in October Stop The Corsair was a very real factor in my recovery and I thank you again for your kindness Stop Affectionate regards

Edward R. Stettinius

Morgan replied:

From Jack
For E. R. Stettinius.
Very glad to receive Egan's letter August 21st and to know you are getting on so well. I had hoped Corsair would be effectual. Affectionate greetings and congratulations. [73]

Mr. Morgan followed up his cablegram a few days later with another warm and solicitous message to his associate: "Be sure not to overdo or start work before you are really ready for it." [74]

J. P. Morgan and Stettinius were very good friends with a strong liking and mutual respect, although both men tended to be reserved.

[70] RS 165, ERS to Bowie, July 19, 1923.
[71] RS 679, *Corsair* file, ERS to Capt. W. B. Porter, Aug. 25, 1923.
[72] RS 248, Morgan to ERS, July 29, 1923.
[73] RS 248, ERS to Morgan, Aug. 31, 1923; Morgan to ERS, Aug. 31, 1923.
[74] RS 248, cablegram, Morgan to ERS, Sept. 3, 1923.

This is not to say that Stettinius was not aware of Morgan's temperament and its effect on the morale at 23 Wall Street. This last is subtly expressed in a letter written to Henry Davison at his winter home in Georgia, during Davison's long final illness: "I want to tell you how happy I have been since you had a visit from Jack. When I heard that he was going down to see you, I was a little apprehensive, not because I feared that anything unpleasant would develop, but only because I feared that you might be apprehensive yourself. I am delighted that the visit was a source of pleasure to you both. He is, as you yourself saw, in the finest possible form, and when I say that he is and has been himself, I am saying everything that I can say by way of making clear that everything and everybody here has been, and is, happy and contented." [75]

By September, Stettinius was feeling much better. He ventured on a fishing trip to Alexandria Bay in the Thousand Islands of the St. Lawrence River.[76] In November Stettinius was strong enough to go to Europe for five weeks.[77] While in London he had the pleasure of being elected an honorary member of the Windham Club on St. James Square on the nomination of Colonel F. Byrne.[78] Stettinius belonged to a number of clubs. He does not appear to have made much use of them, but a successful businessman and public figure tends to be invited to join. Sometimes he conferred the honor in joining; sometimes, particularly at the beginning of his rise to prominence in New York, membership marked an advance in status, social or other.[79]

Stettinius was taken ill once more in February 1924.[80] He rested up in Nassau and then at White Sulphur Springs.[81] At the end of April he returned to New York in the private railroad car "Peacock Point," which was owned by J. P. Morgan & Co.[82] The firm had bought it from Henry Davison, who had used it during his wartime tour of duty as head of the Red Cross. It will be recalled that "Peacock Point" was the name of Davison's place at Locust Valley.

[75] RS 154, ERS to Davison, March 26, 1921.
[76] RS 679, Alexandria Bay file, telegram, ERS to J. F. Bowie, Sept. 24, 1923.
[77] RS 679, Europe—1923 file, cablegram, ERS to Bennett, Nov. 10, 1913; Meurice bills; Claridge's bill.
[78] RS 312, notice of election to membership, Windham Club, Dec. 5, 1923.
[79] See Appendix H, Memberships: Clubs and Civic Organizations, Jan. 18, 1922.
[80] RS 274, ERS to Brownlee, March 6, 1924.
[81] RS 679, Nassau March 1924 file, memorandum, Bennett to ERS, April 7, 1924.
[82] RS 679, Nassau March 1924 file, telegram, Bennett to ERS, April 19, 1924.

In the summer of 1924 Stettinius became ill again.[83] But he rallied and was able to go to Hot Springs, Virginia, in August.[84] In the fall he vacationed in the south of France.[85] The return of a Morgan partner from Europe was always news. The *Wall Street Journal* reported on November 26, 1924:

Stettinius Returns

E. R. Stettinius of J. P. Morgan & Company returned on the White Star Liner Majestic from a pleasure trip. He appeared the picture of health. He was met at the pier by William H. Woodin, president of the American Car & Foundry. Mr. Stettinius said: "I have only been working for the past three weeks and am more or less out of touch with things."

The paper exaggerated. He was not "the picture of health" by any means. Within a month of his return from Europe, a day or so after Christmas 1924, he became seriously ill again. Bennett wrote:

In the latter part of December, Mr. Stettinius had a very serious breakdown, accompanied by cerebral congestion and acute neuritis and up to the end of January he went through a critical period of suffering and anxiety. He went South in early March in the hope of regaining his strength but returned to New York a week ago with some bladder and intestinal complications which apparently have a direct relation to his intestinal operation of two years ago. Mr. Stettinius called in Doctor Tom Brown, of Baltimore, last week, to take charge of the case and we are now very hopeful that, under his direction, Mr. Stettinius will recover his health. He is not a well man by any means and, for some months at least, will have to give himself over completely to the care of the doctors and nurses.[86]

The southern vacation in February and March of 1925 followed the familiar pattern, and Stettinius went to White Sulphur Springs for the month of April.[87]

In the middle of July Mr. and Mrs. Stettinius and Betty went on a cruise in J. P. Morgan's *Corsair* up to Penobscot Bay. On Saturday the 25th they put in at Rockland, Maine, for the homely purpose of picking up the family laundry which John Bennett was instructed to have sent down by special delivery from Locust Valley.[88] It was

[83] RS 200, ERS to Thomas Lamont, Aug. 15, 1924.
[84] RS 29, ERS to ERS, Jr., Aug. 22, 1924.
[85] RS 679, Europe—September 1924 file, memorandum, Bennett to ERS, Aug. 28, 1924; radiogram, ERS to Martin Egan, Sept. 14, 1924.
[86] RS 274, Bennett to Brownlee, May 15, 1925.
[87] RS 679, Augusta 1925 file, telegram, Bennett to ERS, April 3, 1925.
[88] RS 679, Illness file, telegram, ERS to Bennett, July 22, 1925.

arranged for Edward Stettinius, Jr., to join the yachting party at New Bedford on August 7.[89] The cruise of the *Corsair* was Stettinius's last sojourn of any consequence outside of Locust Valley.

On September 2 the *Wall Street Journal* reported that he was at home ill and confined to his bed, though it noted hopefully that his condition was "not regarded as serious."

On September 3, 1925, Edward Stettinius died.

John Bennett described the circumstances in a letter: "He had been ill for many months and had steadily grown worse until around the 1st of August when his heart became seriously affected. From then on, his condition grew worse each day finally culminating in his heart giving out on the 3rd of September and causing death."[90]

The following day this obituary appeared in the *Journal of Commerce:*

E. R. Stettinius Dies After Long Illness

J. P. Morgan & Co. Office Closed as a Tribute to Oldest Partner.

Edward R. Stettinius, the oldest partner of J. P. Morgan & Co., died at his home in Locust Valley yesterday morning, after a long period of illness following an operation performed in March, 1923. Death was caused by cerebral embolism.

The office of J. P. Morgan & Co. was closed all day yesterday except for necessary routine business, but several well known financial and industrial leaders called to express their grief. Through his service as former Second Assistant Secretary of War and later as adviser to General Pershing in France, as well as his numerous financial connections, Mr. Stettinius had made a host of friends who were shocked yesterday at the announcement of his death.

Not having enjoyed robust health since he was stricken with an intestinal disorder in Augusta, Ga., two years ago, Mr. Stettinius had not been at his desk in recent months. His advice, however, was continually sought by his associates and until the last month he was frequently consulted on important issues of the firm.

Besides his partnership with Morgan's, which he had held since 1916, he was a director of the General Electric Company, Guaranty Trust Company, International Agricultural Corporation, Babcock & Wilcox, Atlantic Coast Lumber Company and the General Motors Corporation.[91] During the war he was appointed surveyor general of supplies

---

[89] RS 679, Illness file, telegram, ERS to Bennett, Aug. 3, 1925.

[90] RS 439, Bennett to H. B. Slaughter, Sept. 30, 1925.

[91] Stettinius's corporate directorships at the date of his death were: Atlantic Coast Lumber Corporation; Babcock & Wilcox Company; Essex Cotton Mills, Inc.; Foreign Finance Corporation; General Electric Company; General Motors Corporation; Guaranty Trust Company of New York; International Agri-

for the War Department and served as a member of the War Council from March, 1918, to April 6 when he was made Second Assistant Secretary of War. He represented the United States on the Interallied Munitions Council in Paris in July, 1918.

General Pershing was one of the first to express his sorrow yesterday, when he telegraphed the widow on the death of his friend who had served so well. Jackson E. Reynolds, president of the First National Bank, said the "Street" had lost one of the finest, squarest and ablest financiers, and one of the finest characters.

William C. Potter, president of the Guaranty Trust Company, said: "The Guaranty Trust Company has suffered a great loss in the death of Mr. Stettinius. Those of us who have had the privilege of knowing him realize only too keenly that we have lost a friend who possessed the rare qualities of unusual ability and sound judgment, combined with sincerity, loyalty and great human sympathy."

Albert H. Wiggin, president of the Chase National Bank, said, "The term of service of E. R. Stettinius in the banking business was comparatively short, but the results were tremendous. He was a man of the highest character, courageous and resourceful, and his death is a great loss."

His wife, two daughters and two sons were at his bedside when he died. It was later announced that funeral services will be held this afternoon from his home, and that there will be no church services. Burial at Locust Valley will be private.

Perhaps the most graceful comment on Stettinius appears in the resolution passed on his death by the board of managers of the New York Association for Improving the Condition of the Poor at their meeting of December 2, 1925. Embedded in the usual eulogistic prose is the characterization of Stettinius as "a man of great personal charm." [92]

---

cultural Corporation; International General Electric Company (RS 679, Miscellaneous (directorships), [Bennett] to A. Ensign, Directory of Directors Company, July 31, 1925).

[92] Copy of resolution provided kindness of Miss Anna Fazakerley, Community Service Society of New York.

XV. *The Work Ethic*

Wᴴᴬᵀ kind of man was Stettinius, and what motivated him in his career?

This whole study, of course, has been an attempt to answer these questions, but it is time to take stock of our findings and add to them the evidence of Stettinius's own statements. One comes out of this examination of Stettinius's life with a great liking, even affection, for the man, but wishing that more of his personality would emerge from the papers and the reminiscences of his family and associates.

At home Stettinius was an Edwardian blend of sternness and tenderness. His daughters say that his children adored him but stood in awe of his rare expressions of cold disapproval. For his part, he loved them dearly, even though he failed to understand his younger son. We saw him horseback riding with the children at Staten Island and following their activities at school and on vacations with their contemporaries with enormous interest, concern, and paternal pride. He was generous to them in the conventional ways—allowances, trips, cars, and gifts of securities.

To Mrs. Stettinius he was a devoted husband. He wrote her voluminous and affectionate letters when they were apart and was deeply concerned about her recurring illnesses, which he frequently mentioned in correspondence. He was faithful to her as a matter of course; witness the letter in which he expressed the wish that he were as blameless in his tendency to gamble in the stock market as he was in his private life.[1] He was also generous to her in financial matters, as we see from the inventories of investments.

Stettinius's sense of humor has appeared time and again throughout this study. He had a Mark Twain-like enjoyment of incongruity and the absurd and a lively gift of expression. He had a vigorous vocabulary and a gift for strong language that was an extension of this robust sense of humor.

In politics, Stettinius was a conservative. Until the second World War, the Catholic vote in the United States was predominantly Democratic, and we saw Stettinius referring to that party as "the

---

[1] See Chapter I, note 21.

faith of my fathers" when deploring the candidacy of Charles Dawes for the vice-presidency of the United States in 1924. But by this time Stettinius had come to vote Republican while preserving a detached outlook on the parties and their candidates.

What were Stettinius's religious views? He was baptized and brought up a Roman Catholic, but as an adult he was an irregular participant in organized religion. He was a spiritual man, but not a church-oriented one. George E. Foley, one of his assistants at the Export Department of J. P. Morgan, recalls incidents that show he had not entirely forsaken his childhood training: "I think it was on the first trip, before our country entered the war, we were at the Ritz Hotel in Paris and had a suite of rooms together. I awakened about four o'clock one morning and, glancing through into your father's room I saw him at his bedside, on his knees, praying. We went to Mass several times at the Madelaine [*sic*] in Paris and to Brompton Oratory, and to another lovely Roman Catholic church in London, the name of which I have forgotten. I think your father had been there before, for he seemed to be familiar with the surroundings." [2]

More revealing is this account from C. J. Fay: "He also spoke of his early religious training and connections and what later happened. He concluded with a characteristic remark as to a person's religious affiliations. — 'I do not give a d — — what a man's religion is. What I look for are the results.' " [3]

Judith Carrington Stettinius was an Episcopalian, and the Stettinius family tended generally toward that church for weddings and funerals. They rented pew No. 15 at St. James's Episcopal Church on Madison Avenue in New York.[4] On the strength of this association and his prominence, Stettinius was elected to the vestry. But he was not happy about it. At the end of 1921 he resigned from that body. He had clearly given the matter a great deal of thought.

You will recall that, about a year and a half ago, you were kind enough to invite me to join the Vestry of St. James' Church. I had some doubt as to the propriety of my taking the step and I pointed out, as you may remember, that, although I occasionally attended services at St. James, I was not a communicant and was not at all sure that I ever would be. You informed me, however, that this would not affect my eligibility and accordingly, and because of my very earnest desire to support you in every possible way in your work, I accepted the invitation and in due course was elected a member of your Vestry.

[2] Scrapbook I, Foley to ERS, Jr., Sept. 18, 1933.
[3] Scrapbook II, Fay, "Recollections," Dec. 22, 1936.
[4] RS 547, St. James Church file. The annual rent for pew No. 15 was $150.

During the last year and a half, I have been giving much more attention than formerly to spiritual and religious matters and I have come to feel strongly that a Vestryman should not only be a regular attendant at your services, but also a communicant and an ardent and consistent supporter of the Episcopal faith. Unfortunately, however, I find myself steadily drawing away from, rather than toward, the Episcopal Church.

Under these circumstances, it seems to me improper and also unfair to you and my associates on the Vestry, as well as to myself, to continue a member of that body. Deeply, therefore, as I regret to do so, I feel compelled to tender my resignation as a member of your Vestry.

In presenting this matter to the members of the Vestry, I beg you to assure them of my appreciation of their uniform courtesy and kindliness and, as for yourself, please be assured that I am sincerely grateful to you for the help you have so freely given me and the inspiration I have always derived from you.[5]

Generosity toward the less fortunate was a major element in Stettinius's character, as we have seen.

In his career and anything remotely related to it, Edward Reilly Stettinius was a driven man. He was passionately ambitious, but not in the usual sense. Certainly he was motivated in his impecunious youth by the need for financial security. But his life was not dominated by a desire for wealth and fame. The wealth and fame that he did achieve were by-products of an undefined urge to triumph over obstacles. And the first obstacle was a compulsive urge to speculate. The longer-range objectives were never clearly stated. Stettinius saw an immediate job to do and promptly threw himself with incredible energy into doing it as effectively and rapidly as possible. This quality was apparent early in his life. Dr. Louis C. Boislinière of St. Louis, a schoolmate, describes "the intensity amounting almost to feverishness, which he brought to bear upon every situation with which he was confronted, the never-failing faculty of intense concentration on the matter at hand, to the exclusion of everything else, I believe to be his most dominating characteristic."[6] An extension of this quality was a prodigious capacity for sustained effort and an urge to shoulder additional jobs and duties. Stettinius always carried an enormous load of work without ever appearing to spread himself too thinly. He had enough energy to take care of all his commitments. Ultimately this driving force, which was largely responsible for his success, was to

[5] RS 547, ERS to Rev. Frank Warfield Crowder, Dec. 13, 1921.
[6] Ridings, "Missourians Abroad, No. 5—Edward R. Stettinius, Assistant Secretary of War," p. 38.

break his health and cause his early death, but it explains a great deal about the course of his career.

Throughout Stettinius's most productive period, his years as an active business partner in J. P. Morgan & Co., he worked against a background of progressively worsening health. The year 1921 saw Stettinius at the very height of his powers, but it was a gruelling time. As we have seen from a close examination of his principal undertakings of that year, he was engaged in winding up the business of the Foreign Commerce Corporation, in keeping a restraining hand on the finances of General Motors, and in rescuing the Guaranty Trust Company from threatened failure. That summer the affairs of the Guaranty Trust Company were in their most critical phase. On October 5, 1921, Stettinius was elected to the board of the Guaranty. His old friend Walker Hill of the First National Bank in St. Louis wrote him the following day with the candor of long acquaintanceship:

Dear Ed.: —
The Associated Press tells me you have gone into the Guaranty. I am glad to see this because I believe you would not go in unless the institution was not only good but had a great future. Your old friends have great confidence in your judgment of the future.
One thing I want to say to you and I do not want you to forget it. New York has a reputation for putting loads on hard working, energetic working men which sometimes kills them. The last time I saw you your head was very, very white, your eyes showed crow's-feet down to your chin and your skin looked as though if pinched it would crack. Let the fellows who love $2.00 more than $1.00 do the work. You cannot take any of it with you as no money will stand the heat of the hereafter.[7]

Hill's letter is revealing in what it has to say about the ravages of overwork, but Stettinius's reply gives the real key to his character and purpose: "In growing older I like to think that I am also growing in wisdom and that if at times I may have to work under high pressure, I have sufficient good sense to relax frequently, and recognize that I cannot work as hard or continually as I did in days gone by. So, please don't waste your sympathy on me; and remember another thing, and that is, that men sometimes work not for the sake of money, but in order to discharge what seems to them to be their duty."[8]

Stettinius set forth this idea of the work ethic in a statement titled

---

[7] RS 313, Hill to ERS, Oct. 6, 1921.
[8] RS 313, ERS to Hill, Nov. 14, 1921.

"Getting On," which appeared in the January 1922 issue of *Business Philosopher*. Stettinius, who usually expressed himself in a forthright style, tended to become stuffy and cliché-ridden when writing or speaking for publication, but his moral is clear, and he believed it:

The law governing what is called "getting on" is just as sure and inevitable in its operation as the law of gravity. Any healthy young man of average intelligence and education who sticks courageously, persistently and perseveringly to his job, who refuses to be overcome by obstacles but fights on until he has overcome them, who exercises all the industry and all the commonsense at his command—any man of right principles who puts forth sustained effort and application is bound to win recognition. He will get the reward he has thus won. It is inevitable. The rolling stone gathers no moss. The youth or man who is constantly shifting from one place to another is less apt to win out than the one who conquers the difficulties of whatever job he has and proves master of it. If the man has the right qualities and is doing notably effective work, either his employer or someone else will sooner or later note the fact and recognition and reward will be forthcoming.[9]

This habit of hard work became so ingrained that Stettinius was restless and uncomfortable when not working. This comes out in a paradoxical paragraph he wrote to thank an old friend for a present: "Let me thank you sincerely for the books which you sent me. I know I will enjoy them if I ever have time to read them. Unfortunately, however, I am so situated that my days, as well as many nights, are completely filled by ever recurring problems and by persistent pressure which leaves little time for relaxation. For I am now back in harness again and my vacation, which I frankly admit became quite irksome towards the last, is now over."[10]

Stettinius was the kindest and most considerate of men when he thought about it, but he was unable to comprehend the need to conserve one's strength to survive. He overworked the willing "Slaves of Stettinius" in the Morgan Export Department during the war, working harder himself than any of them. So he overworked his secretary John Bennett. James Mimnaugh says, "He drove Bennett into the ground," to the point where his resistance was so weakened that Bennett developed a tubercular spot on his lung.[11]

So Stettinius was spurred on by a sense of duty. But one is tempted to ask what he would have done if he had not kept oc-

[9] *Business Philosopher*, XIX, 1 (Jan. 1922), 33.
[10] RS 640, ERS to Griff G. Glover, Dec. 11, 1920.
[11] Author's interview with James F. Mimnaugh, New York, April 22, 1968.

cupied with business and business-related activities. He had no intellectual interests. He read little. While he had a box at the opera at least one season, he was not a music enthusiast. Many of his colleagues were avid sportsmen, with yachts and shooting preserves and other accoutrements of wealth. This sort of thing did not interest Stettinius. He fished infrequently, golfed only seldom (and badly), played poker occasionally (very expertly).

Part of Stettinius's drive would seem to have been the need for an outlet for tremendous energy, but to point this out is in no way to detract from the important part played by his sense of duty and his meticulous conscientiousness.

Great stress has been laid on Stettinius's sense of responsibility. He did not take on assignments casually. When he was made director of a company or undertook to do a job he felt bound to protect the interests of everyone concerned. He was profoundly interested in the well-being of the match company workers. He did not drive a harsh bargain with the munitions suppliers. He was interested in the general health of General Motors, not merely the stockholders' short-run dividends and stock prices. This outlook makes Stettinius particularly important in the evolution of the genus business man in the United States. One of the first of a new breed, he was publicly so recognized. The *New York Times* ran an editorial on September 23, 1925, barely three weeks after Stettinius's death:

The New Business Type.

The business world of New York has been left poorer by the death within a short period of Mr. Henry Davison, Mr. Stettinius and now Mr. A. C. Bedford. All of them men comparatively young, as age is now reckoned, all of them men of large affairs, they had strikingly illustrated the possibility of adjusting a high and flexible talent for business to changed modern conditions. They belonged to a new type of business man of which there are happily multiplying examples. Their distinctive characteristic is that they unite great ability with a sense of great responsibility. They feel themselves responsible, first of all, to the interests represented in the large enterprises over which they preside. These they labor to make as efficient and successful as possible. But they also feel their responsibility to the public. This they show in seeking to do away with as many as may be of the old features of corporation management which became both offensive and dangerous in the popular mind. The main thing has been the aim to establish franker relations. Open books and fully published accounts of financial transactions are now the rule. Complaints are not contemptuously ignored in the ancient fashion, but are actually welcomed for the sake of looking into them to discover if there is anything in the conduct of the business which ought to be corrected. The lines of an altered corporation policy are slowly being framed, and the men mentioned above, with many others, have been doing their best to complete the work.

Stettinius was a businessman with a sense of responsibility that went beyond any compulsion to maximize profits.

Appendixes
Bibliographical Note
Index

Appendix A

Resolution of the Board of Directors of the Diamond Match Company, August 2, 1910, for the Licensing of the Nonpoisonous Sévène-Cahen Process

Resolved that the President be and he is hereby authorized and directed to submit in behalf of the company to the match manufacturers of the United States a proposal to grant each manufacturer a license to manufacture in his present factory and to sell in the United States friction matches employing in the composition of the head Sesquisulphide of Phosphorus under, and to the end of the term of, our Letters Patent of the United States No. 614,350, dated November 15, 1898, subject nevertheless to the following conditions:

(a) That each licensee shall pay to the Company a percentage of $100,000 equal to the percentage that his production of matches during the twelve months ending June 30, 1910, bears to the total production in this country of "strike anywhere" matches during such period of all match manufacturers accepting licenses under the said Sesqui patent, such amount to be paid to the company at the option of the licensee either in cash upon the execution of the license or in four (4) equal annual payments, bearing interest at 6% payable semi-annually;

(b) That for such consideration the licensee shall be entitled in each year to produce and sell the same percentage of the country's gross sales of matches containing the patented composition as is represented in his percentage of the total output during the year ending June 30, 1910, of all match manufacturers accepting licenses under the said Sesqui patent, but if he shall produce in one year a larger quantity of matches (in the manufacture of which Sesquisulphide of Phosphorus is used) than his pro rata share of the country's business as just specified, he shall in respect to such excess quantity pay this Company a royalty of four (4) mills ($.004) for each one thousand (1,000) matches;

(c) That no manufacturer accepting such license shall be required to use Sesquisulphide of Phosphorus exclusively but shall be at liberty to use any other substitute for White Phosphorus that may be available and satisfactory to him.

Further Resolved that the president be and he hereby is authorized in behalf of the Company to execute the proposed license under Let-

ters Patent No. 614,350 to each of the match manufacturers execu-
ting the proposed agreement.

Further Resolved that the proposed license shall be in such form and
contain such reasonable and proper conditions as may be imposed
by the Counsel of the Company.

Source: Minutes, board of directors' meetings, Diamond Match Company,
Legal Department, Diamond International Corporation, New York.

Appendix B

Editorial, *Scientific American*, CIV (February 11, 1911), 143

The Dedication of the Diamond Match Patent to the Public

On January 28th, 1911, there was recorded in the United States Patent Office a remarkable instrument. This was the formal, legal relinquishment by the Diamond Match Company of its rights under Letters Patent No. 614,350, granted November 15th, 1898, to Henri Sévène and Emile David Cahen, of Paris, France, for an "Improvement in Match Compositions."

This action by the Diamond Match Company was the outcome of a series of events which were of international importance. The deleterious effects of the use of white phosphorus in the manufacture of matches has long been the subject of serious investigation, with the result that in European countries the use of this poisonous substance, except in combination with counteracting agents, is regulated by law. It is well known that white phosphorus causes necrosis of the jawbone and teeth, and the principal sufferers therefrom have been those employed in the manufacture of the common parlor match.

The Bureau of Labor at Washington, Charles P. Neill, Director, has conducted a series of experiments, covering an investigation of match factories in the United States, and the conclusions reached were so overwhelmingly against the existing process of match manufacture, through the use of white phosphorus that it led to a recommendation by the President in a message to Congress, looking to the attaching of a heavy tax on those factories using the phosphorus in this form.

The result of such legislation would, of course, compel the manufacturers to devise a suitable substitute for white phosphorus, with the possibility of being charged high royalties for the use of processes already controlled. The suggestion for legislation was looked upon with disfavor among some members of Congress, who considered it an abuse of the tax privilege, and also saw in its operation the possible building up of a huge monopoly on the part of those who controlled patented processes of substitutes for white phosphorus.

The Sevene-Cahen patent covered a non-poisonous sesqui-sulphide of phosphorus, one of the few known adequate substitutes for white phosphorus. The Diamond Match Company was the sole owner of this patent, and the company was thus in a position, if prohibitive legislation were enacted against white phosphorus, of controlling the match output of the country, or else of being able to collect large royalties for the use of the Sevene-Cahen process.

Rather than be placed in the position of being a beneficiary under legislation that was needed for humanitarian reasons, the Diamond Match Company has abandoned its right to the sesqui-sulphide process and has dedicated the invention described in the patent to the people of the United States forever. The instrument abandoning its rights to the Sevene-Cahen patent was accordingly prepared, and was recorded in the Patent Office, Commissioner of Labor Neill, Edwin R. A. Seligman and Jackson H. Ralston acting as trustees. The relinquishment is also signed by Edward R. Stettinius, president of the Diamond Match Company.

The effect that this will have on the match industry of the United States is far-reaching. It will enable every match manufacturer in the country to operate without endangering the health of his employees or putting upon the market a substance well known to be poisonous and disease-spreading.

The Sevene-Cahen substitute for white phosphorus, while being harmless to the health of the workmen, possesses a definite chemical composition and is easily inflammable. This sesqui-sulphide of phosphorus is obtained in a state of purity by distillation. The formula described in the patent is as follows: Sesqui sulphide of phosphorus, 90 grams; chlorate of potash, 800 grams; peroxide of iron, 110 grams; zinc-white, 770 grams; powdered glass, 140 grams; glue, 100 grams; water, 290 grams. The advantage of this formula as claimed over the various preparations of mixed pastes for matches, such as a mixture of amorphous phosphorus and sulphur either in powder or the state of fusion, is due to the fact that the sesqui-sulphide of phosphorus is very stable, resists moisture, and can easily be utilized and manipulated industrially.

It is not known whether the action of the Diamond Match Company in thus freely giving to the people of the United States the use of this valuable formula will have the effect of rendering unnecessary the proposed legislation against the use of white phosphorus, but as the Sevene-Cahen process has been used with great success by the Diamond Match Company and it is the only non-deleterious substitute that is commercially practical, there appears to be no good reason why the other manufacturers of matches in the United States shall not now use the harmless process, thus doing away altogether with the use of white phosphorus.

The legality of the document signed by the Trustees and the Diamond Match Company will hardly be questioned. While the patent has about five years to run, it is assumed that the contract between the Diamond Match Company and the inventors has been fulfilled, or will continue to be fulfilled. Since the inventors are not recited in the instrument lately recorded in the Patent Office as being parties at interest, it can be reasonably deduced that their claims under the patent have already been satisfied.

There is apparently no "string" tied to this free will offering to the American public, and the Diamond Match Company by this act places itself in the position of a public benefactor. In these days of monopolies and trusts it is an unusual spectacle to find a large corporation relinquishing for the benefit of the public interests which if taken advantage of can be made to yield hundreds of thousands of dollars.

Appendix C

Chief Categories of Matériel Purchased by the Export Department of J. P. Morgan & Co. for Britain and France, 1915–1917

1. Explosives, including propellants and chemicals.
   Smokeless powder (nitrocellulose powder) was the most important item in this group and was second only to steel in total value purchased. The other principal products were picric acid, trinitrotoluene (TNT), cotton linters (nitrated gun cotton), cordite, and acetone.[1]
2. Shells, both complete rounds and components.
   Artillery shells, particularly in the form of complete, ready-to-shoot rounds, comprised the larger part of this category. Of lesser importance were such components as empty shell casings, fuses, etc.[2]
3. Shell steel, forgings, miscellaneous metals.
   In a separate group from projectiles were raw (bars and billets) and semifinished shell materials. Copper, spelter, zinc, and aluminum were placed under this same head.[3]
4. Rifles, machine guns, and ammunition.
   Infantry arms comprised a vast subdivision of their own.[4]

Less susceptible of being isolated in large groupings were a number of other purchases:

chemicals: phenol and alcohol, etc.
artillery: field guns and howitzers and their components
motor transport: automobiles, trucks, and tractors
railway material: rails, locomotives, cars
machine tools: lathes
foodstuffs: grain, cattle, corned beef, "fat backs" (hog products)
wire
aircraft
miscellaneous: small tools, hardware, clothing, rubber boots, textiles.[5]

[1] Weems, *America and Munitions*, pp. 99–118.   [2] *Ibid.*, pp. 119–48.
[3] *Ibid.*, pp. 149–76.   [4] *Ibid.*, pp. 177–220.   [5] *Ibid.*, pp. 225–38.

Appendix D

Guaranty Trust Company, Financing Plan of May 31, 1921: Original Syndicate Members, Exclusive of the Guaranty Trust Company

Participant	Original participation
American Exchange National Bank	$ 474,000.00
Bankers Trust Company	1,188,250.00
Bank of Manhattan Company	237,000.00
Central Union Trust Company	474,000.00
Chase National Bank	474,000.00
Corn Exchange Bank	713,750.00
Chemical National Bank	713,750.00
Equitable Trust Company	713,750.00
First National Bank of New York	592,750.00
Hanover National Bank	474,000.00
Irving National Bank	713,750.00
Mechanics & Metals National Bank	713,750.00
J. P. Morgan & Co.	1,665,750.00
National Bank of Commerce	1,188,250.00
National Park Bank	713,750.00
The New York Trust Company	713,750.00
National City Bank	1,188,250.00
	$12,359,750.00 [1]

Source: RS 820, "Memorandum for Mr. Stettinius," Dec. 20, 1924.

[1] This total is incorrect and should be $12,952,500.00. Subsequent calculations in the memorandum are based on the lower figure.

Appendix E

Imports Advancement Corporation: Guarantors of $8,000,000 One-Year 6 Percent Note Held by J. P. Morgan & Co., 1921

Class "A" Guarantors

J. P. Morgan & Co.	$1,000,000
Harry Payne Whitney	1,000,000
Payne Whitney	500,000
Thomas F. Ryan	1,500,000
Marshall Field	200,000
Daniel Guggenheim	75,000
Isaac Guggenheim	75,000
Murray Guggenheim	75,000
S. R. Guggenheim	75,000
Simon Guggenheim	75,000

Class "B" Guarantors

J. P. Morgan & Co.	$1,000,000
Harry Payne Whitney	1,000,000
Payne Whitney	500,000
John D. Ryan	250,000
Myron C. Taylor	100,000
Marshall Field	200,000
Daniel Guggenheim	75,000
Isaac Guggenheim	75,000
Murray Guggenheim	75,000
S. R. Guggenheim	75,000
Simon Guggenheim	75,000
	$8,000,000

Source: RS 236.

Appendix F

Domestic Finances, 1924

June 15, 1925

1924 Figures

Automobile Mtce.	$10,562.28
Charity	50,351.10
Club Dues & Expenses	5,876.82
Expense	32,264.06 *
Family Mtce.	82,038.23
Locust Valley Property Mtce.	36,425.74
Elizabeth Stettinius	6,000.00
Travel	30,576.00
1021 Park Ave. Mtce.	2,822.52
	$256,916.75
	J.B.

* Includes $5,000 to H. D. Gibson for Creek Club and $8,400 to Mr. Stettinius in currency.

June 9, 1925

Family Maintenance 1924

Clubs (JCS), Church & Theatre	$2,495.67
Fuel, Light, Gas, Telephone	3,245.80
Laundry	144.52
Papers, Books & Stationery	750.33
Flowers & Candy	3,087.44
Medical Supplies & Dental Service	1,451.93
Medical Service	6,422.
Jewelry & Repairs	2,623.48
Food	9,913.93
Clothing	13,944.59
Furniture & Furnishings	6,293.36
Miscellaneous	5,500.
Wages & Bonuses	10,814.
Mrs. Stettinius' Empire Account	15,000.
	$81,687.05
	J.B.

	Wages & Bonuses 1924	June 9, 1925
Peter O'Neill	$1,800	600
Eilen Holmgren	1,200	300
Lottie Simmons	1,200	300
Margaret O'Brien	780	10
Alma Magnussen	840	10
Anna Bohm	720	10
David McCoy	640	10
Margaret Pendergast	840	10
Joseph Pagnozzie	540	10
Carrie Bergstrom	984	10
	9,544	1,270
	1,270	
	$10,814	

Source: RS 724, Maintenance (Box 34).

Appendix G

Charitable Contributions during Year 1924

Young Men's Christian Association	$ 200.00
Navy Young Men's Christian Association	25.00
Young Men's Christian Association (Nassau & Suffolk Counties)	250.00
Young Women's Christian Association	1,000.00
Council on Immigrant Education	1,000.00
The Fifth Avenue Hospital	200.00
The Catholic Actors' Guild	50.00
Florence Baker House	210.00
Boy Scout Foundation	100.00
Boy Scouts of Nassau County	100.00
British Great War Veterans of America	25.00
Calvert Associates	1,500.00
Newspaper Women's Club	25.00
Military Order of the World War	50.00
Oratorio Society of New York	325.00
Englewood Hospital Building Fund	6,666.66
The Civic Forum	50.00
Medford Tuberculosis Sanitarium	25.00
N.Y. Association for the Blind	4.40
N.Y. Nursery & Child's Hospital	150.00
Welfare League Association	100.00
Country Lanes Committee	25.00
H. C. Van Wagner Post, American Legion	3.00
Madonna House	50.00
Crippled Children's Hospital, Richmond, Va.	158.00
American Relief Committee for German Intellectuals & Artists	500.00
Association for Improving the Condition of the Poor	2,200.00
Maternity Center Association	100.00
Little Sisters of the Poor, St. Louis	2,600.00
Holy Family Mission, Montana	350.00
National Committee for Prevention of Blindness	25.00
Federation des Veterans Francais de la Grande Guerre	10.00
The Lights	50.00

The Strangers' Welfare Fellowship	200.00
Convalescent Relief Fund, Bellevue Hospital	50.00
Stony Wold Sanitarium	50.00
St. Joseph's Summer Institute	100.00
The Actors' Fund of America	200.00
St. Ignatius Mission, Montana	300.00
Association d'Aide aux Veuves Militaires de la Grande Guerre	19,454.04
Society of the Lying-In Hospital	250.00
Societe Francaise de Bienfaisance	100.00
Society of St. Johnland	50.00
Soldiers & Sailors Club of New York	25.00
St. Labre's Mission, Ursuline Convent, Montana	100.00
Bowling Green Neighborhood Association	100.00
Carmelite Nuns, St. Louis	10,100.00
Fordham University Glee Club	10.00
Henry St. Settlement—Visiting Nurse Service	100.00
Church of the Nativity, New York	100.00
Emergency Tuberculosis Relief Committee	225.00
Florence Crittenton League	10.00
St. Francis Xavier's Church, New York	250.00
Little Sisters of the Poor, New York	100.00
Sisters of Mercy, St. Louis	100.00
State Charities Aid Association	250.00
Total	$50,351.10

Source: RS 366, Misc. Memos and Papers (1).

Appendix H

Memberships: Clubs and Civic Organizations, January 18, 1922

	Dues—including tax		
	Periodic payment	*Period covered*	*Yearly total*
Academy of Political Science	$ 5	Cal. yr.	$ 5
American Forestry Association	8	2 yrs. (pd. to 12/31/22)	4
American Museum of Natural History	10	Cal. yr.	10
American Numismatic Society	5	"	5
Automobile Club of America	27.50	6 mos. (Feb. 28 & Aug. 31)	55
Chamber of Commerce of the State of NY	100	Cal. yr.	100
Civic Forum (As guarantor deficit to $25)		Season	?
Economic Club of NY	20	Yr. end. Sept. 30	20
India House	96.25	6 mos. (Aug. 30 & Oct. 31)	192.50
Italy America Society	100	Life	—
The Links	110	6 mos. (Aug. 30 & Oct. 31)	220
Meadowbrook Hounds (Subscriptions)	150	Season	150
Merchants Association of NY	50	Yr. end. Feb. 1	50
Metropolitan Club (New York)	137.50	Cal. yr.	137.50
Metropolitan Club (Washington)	41.25	Cal. yr.	41.25
Metropolitan Opera Club	27.50	Season	27.50
Nassau Country Club	110	6 mos. (Apr. 1 & Oct. 1)	110
Nassau County Association	2	Yr. end. Sept. 1	2
National Golf Links of America	110	Cal. yr.	110
New York Botanical Garden	10	Cal. yr.	10
New York Electrical Society	3	Yr. end. Feb. 1	3
New York Yacht Club	110	Cal. yr.	110
Oakland Golf Club	82.50	6 mos. (Apr. 1 & Oct. 1)	165
Piping Rock Club	275	Cal. yr.	275
Racquet and Tennis Club	82.50	6 mos. (May 1 & Nov. 1)	165
The Recess	165	Yr. end. Sept. 1	165
Richmond County Country Club (Honorary)	—		—
Stony Wold Sanatorium (Donor)	50	Cal. yr.	50
Union League Club	165	Cal. yr.	165
National Economic League	5	Cal. yr.	5
Guaranty Club (Honorary)	—	—	None
The New York Club			
The Fifth Avenue Association, Inc.	100	year	100
Army Athletic Assn.	60	year	60

Note: two of Stettinius's clubs which do not appear on this list are the Colony [1] and The Creek, Locust Valley,[2] joined at a later date.

Source: RS 312.

[1] ERS obituary, *New York Evening Post*, Sept. 3, 1925.
[2] PS 33, Cravath Property file.

Appendix I

The Stettinius Estate

Edward R. Stettinius left an estate valued for federal inheritance tax purposes at slightly more than $5,000,000.[1] He had already established trust funds for his wife and four children totalling approximately $2,500,000.[2]

The bulk of the estate was an interest in J. P. Morgan and Company valued at $3,374,024.44. In accordance with the partnership agreement,[3] Stettinius's contribution to the capital was repaid to his executors and his interest in the firm distributed to them.[4] These payments were made in a few large blocks of bonds and several smaller blocks of stock. The executors received U.S. Liberty Bonds totalling about one million dollars, Argentine government bonds valued at $477,500, Australian government bonds valued at $288,000, Interborough Rapid Transit bonds valued at $545,000, and Japanese government bonds valued at $230,000. The larger blocks of stock were 500 shares of Guaranty Trust Company of New York, $175,000; 2,700 shares of Marland Oil Company common, $159,300; 1,000 shares of General Motors Corporation common, $117,000, and 500 preferred, $57,500. The executors promptly sold most of these securities and diversified the Stettinius family portfolio.

Stock holdings listed in the estate inventory consisted of one large block of 595 shares in the First National Bank-First Security Company valued at $1,660,000; 260 shares in the Guaranty Trust Company, $93,000; and various lesser items. Real estate was valued at $560,005 and mortgages at $93,271.72. From a grand total of $5,987,033.20 was deducted a miscellaneous figure composed of funeral expenses, executors' commissions, attorneys' fees, debts, etc., of $810,723.32, leaving a net estate for tax of $5,176,309.88.

Stettinius drew up the final version of his will on June 19, 1925.[5]

[1] PS 31, U.S. Treasury Department, return for federal estate tax, Sept. 17, 1925.
[2] PS 31, financial statements, Oct. 16, 1925.
[3] *Wall Street Journal*, June 3, 1933. Text of partnership agreement.
[4] PS 31, Estate of E. R. Stettinius, Statement of Securities, Dec. 20, 1926.
[5] RS 679, will of ERS.

He named George B. Case of White & Case and E. H. Wells of Babcock & Wilcox as his executors. That was the same E. H. Wells he had outsmarted years before in the sale of the Stirling Consolidated Boiler Company. He appointed his partner Russell C. Leffingwell and the Guaranty Trust Company of New York to be his trustees. To his wife he left all personal property together with a lump sum of half a million dollars. She also received a life interest in the real property. Assorted annuities were left to relatives. The greater part of the estate was left in trust, the income to go to Mrs. Stettinius during her lifetime and to be divided equally among the children upon her death, the principal to be divided among his grandchildren upon the death of his children, as such deaths occurred.

The important man in the managing of the Stettinius estate was Leffingwell. Russell Cornell Leffingwell, a graduate of Yale and the Columbia Law School, had spent most of his working life with the Cravath law office, beginning in 1902. In 1923 he changed careers and joined J. P. Morgan & Co. as a partner on July 1 of that year, at the age of 45.[6] With the Guaranty Trust Company, he shared the fiduciary responsibility for the Stettinius estate and related trusts after Stettinius's death. But he was more than simply a legal figure. When ill health compelled him to resign from his trusteeships in 1939, he wrote to Edward R. Stettinius, Jr.: "I have, as you know, always thought your father in designating me as a trustee in his will had in mind not merely the trusteeship of his estate, but the wish that I should so far as possible be a friend and counselor in his place to your mother and his four children. I shall continue to have the quasi-paternal feeling of pride and affection that I have always had for you three.[7] If you should all continue to look on me, as you always have, as a loving old friend of your father and yours, you will make me very happy."[8]

---

[6] Swaine, *The Cravath Firm*, II, 17, 18, 315.

[7] William Carrington Stettinius had died in 1937.

[8] Files of Joseph Stettinius, Richmond, Virginia, Russell Leffingwell to ERS, Jr., March 25, 1939.

Bibliographical Note

THE principal source of material for this study of Edward Reilly Stettinius, Sr., is the Stettinius Papers in the Alderman Library of the University of Virginia, Charlottesville. The Stettinius Papers, an extensive collection of letters, documents, and other memorabilia, was assembled by E. R. Stettinius, Jr., and relates largely to the life of the younger man. A relatively small part of the collection includes material on the father, particularly files of business correspondence. These last are of uneven importance and completeness and generally arranged in the order in which they were received, which was haphazard. In addition, there are assorted scrapbooks, of which the most useful are Volumes I and II. These contain newspaper clippings and miscellaneous materials, including the results of the inquiry made by E. R. Stettinius, Jr., in the early 1930's into his father's life and career. He engaged a graduate student at St. Louis University, Miss Nancy Ring, to look into the older man's childhood and early life in St. Louis. He also wrote to a number of his father's friends and associates and asked them for their reminiscences.

Two systematic studies have been written about Stettinius's part in the World War. F. Carrington Weems, an officer of J. P. Morgan & Co. and a relative of Mrs. Stettinius, was commissioned by that firm to write a history of the firm's part in buying munitions for the Allies prior to United States entry into the war. The result was the two-volume *America and Munitions*, privately printed in 1923. Only six copies were produced. Mr. Henry Sturgis Morgan made his own copy available to me at the Pierpont Morgan Library.

Weems also wrote a thirty-six-page account, untitled and undated, of Stettinius's part in the American phase of the war. This was used through the kindness of Mrs. Weems and Mr. Andrew Rogers of Davis Polk & Wardwell.

There is in addition an anonymous thirty-page "Memoir" on Stettinius in the Stettinius Papers. This has been only moderately useful.

Outside sources that have yielded some information include the library of the Service historique de l'armée, the archives of the

French Army at the Château de Vincennes in that Paris suburb, the Thomas W. Lamont Papers at the Harvard Business School, the Newton D. Baker Papers in the Library of Congress, the Baruch Papers at Princeton University, and the minute books of the Diamond Match Company at the offices of Diamond International Corporation.

Excerpts from the minute books of other companies—Babcock & Wilcox, General Motors, and General Electric—had been requested earlier from the executives of those corporations by E. R. Stettinius, Jr., and are assembled in the scrapbooks in the Stettinius Papers. In general they are not very revealing.

Published sources have been of uneven value. Most illuminating are the two biographies of Morgan partners, Thomas W. Lamont's *Henry P. Davison, The Record of a Useful Life* (New York and London, 1933) and Harold Nicolson's *Dwight Morrow* (New York, 1935). Unfortunately, Nicolson was hampered by the British public school distaste for "trade" and tended to skimp on Morrow's business life—producing a somewhat truncated biography of a partner in J. P. Morgan & Co.!

There is no definitive history of J. P. Morgan & Co., and Henry S. Morgan says that the destruction of the firm's records has made the writing of such a book virtually impossible. The incomplete accounts that have appeared have not pretended to be more than popular works.

Assorted magazine articles on Stettinius, written for the most part during the war, tend to be thin stuff laced with wartime fervor. An exception is B. C. Forbes's "The Biggest Buyer in the World," an interview with Stettinius which appeared in *American Magazine*, September 1917, pp. 15–82, and which gives an excellent insight into the day-to-day problems of starting a munitions-buying program from scratch.

Personal conversations with people who remembered Stettinius have contributed to the over-all picture of the man. I have talked with Stettinius's two daughters, Mrs. John B. Marsh and Mrs. Juan T. Trippe, with his former Paris partner, the late Nelson Dean Jay, and with his sometime assistant secretary James F. Mimnaugh.

Index